JEWISH LITERARY EROS

SEPHARDI AND MIZRAHI STUDIES

Harvey E. Goldberg and Matthias Lehmann, *editors*

JEWISH LITERARY EROS

Between Poetry and Prose in the Medieval Mediterranean

Isabelle Levy

INDIANA UNIVERSITY PRESS

This book is a publication of

Indiana University Press
Office of Scholarly Publishing
Herman B Wells Library 350
1320 East 10th Street
Bloomington, Indiana 47405 USA

iupress.org

 The paper used in this publication meets the minimum requirements of the American National Standard for Information Sciences—Permanence of Paper for Printed Library Materials, ANSI Z39.48-1992.

Manufactured in the United States of America

First printing 2022

Cataloging is available from the Library of Congress.

ISBN 978-0-253-06015-0 (hardcover)
ISBN 978-0-253-06016-7 (ebook)

Cover art: *Roman de la Rose*, by Guillaume de Lorris and Jean de Meung, Fourteenth century, Plimpton MS 284 f 4v, Rare Book & Manuscript Library, Columbia University Libraries.

CONTENTS

FOREWORD

Raymond P. Scheindlin

Jewish Literary Eros is a book about a theme, a form, and a culture. The theme is, of course, love—or rather, writing about love. The form is a mixed one, combining poetry and prose, known as prosimetrum. The culture is medieval Jewish literature; this is not a simple phenomenon, for it was thoroughly interpenetrated by the non-Jewish cultures within which it flourished. Accordingly, the book deals extensively with two non-Jewish literary cultures: Arabic, which by the twelfth century—the book's starting point—had long exerted a strong influence on Hebrew literature; and Romance literature (in Italian, French, Occitan, and Spanish), which was coming into being concurrently with the Hebrew literary works that are the book's focus.

This study of the relationship between love and poetry in medieval Jewish prosimetra from the twelfth century on provides insights into attitudes toward poetry and fiction, as well as toward such varied subjects as ethics, autobiography, allegory, courting rituals, promiscuity, interreligious personal relationships, cross-dressing, and even blasphemy. By studying the literary forms and the varieties of love depicted in these works, we learn much more about social conditions and cultural values than might be expected from works that at first seem intended as pure entertainment.

This book is the first monographic study of medieval Jewish literature that weaves together all three cultural strands—Hebrew, Arabic, and Romance—on a basis of equality and kinship, treating Hebrew literature not merely as a product of the impact of a foreign literature on Jewish culture but as part of the same phenomenon that produced the non-Jewish literatures themselves. This is possible because the Jewish writings treated here, dating from the twelfth century and later, arose in a world in which a new literature was being born: the erotic writing in the vernaculars descended from Latin. This situation was quite different from the medieval Hebrew golden age, which emerged in Islamic Spain, where Arabic literature had long been well established, providing a model for imitation and adaptation.

Until now, the focus of most scholarship and literary history of medieval Jewry has been the Hebrew golden age, the period from the mid-tenth to the mid-twelfth centuries in which Jewish writers of Muslim Spain produced a great outpouring of superb Hebrew poetry consciously grounded in Arabic literary traditions. The Hebrew golden age has stood at the center of scholarly attention since the beginning of the academic study of medieval Jewish literature in the early nineteenth century; its poets set a literary standard that could not be matched by poets of the thirteenth century and later.

Of course, we have long been aware that after the golden age, when Hebrew poetry lapsed into epigonism, literary prose, especially rhymed prose, became the more prominent form. But we followed the medievals in thinking of these works simply as prose, giving no weight to the poetry that they invariably include; nor did we consider the particular literary style that emerges from combining the two forms. We missed the whole point of prosimetric composition.

Furthermore, the prose literature produced in the cultural sphere of later medieval Spain, including Provence and Italy, was generally studied in light of medieval Arabic literary prose. Here and there, scholars pointed tentatively to elements in medieval Hebrew literary prose that might be explained by Romance models. But though most students of medieval Hebrew literature had intensive training in Arabic, and though most had some knowledge of Romance literature, hardly any were trained as scholars of Romance philology.

Coming to medieval Hebrew prose from just this perspective, Isabelle Levy takes an entirely new approach to the subject. Hebrew erotic narrative now appears not as a secondary phenomenon in a world that, for the most part, valued poetry more than prose but as a mainstream phenomenon as to subject matter and literary form.

This brings us to the prosimetrum, a new concept in medieval Hebrew literary studies. Since literary texts of the kind studied here have, like the poetry, been evaluated against the background of Arabic literature, their outstanding formal feature has appeared to be their being written in rhymed prose. Accordingly, they have been seen as a continuation of the rhymed prose narrative type called the *maqama*, which was consciously adopted from Arabic by such Hebrew authors as Judah al-Ḥarizi. This judgment has not worked very well for most other writers of rhymed prose narrative. By shifting attention from the fact that medieval Hebrew narratives rhyme to the fact that medieval Hebrew narratives mix prose and verse, Levy has enabled us to place these narratives in a broader generic field, thus broadening the scope for comparative study. Within Arabic literature, her point of reference is not only the *maqama*, as it has been for most studies of medieval Hebrew prose narrative, but other Arabic works that can be viewed as prosimetra, such as ibn Dāwūd's *Kitāb al-zahra* (*The Book of the Flower*), al-Washshā''s *Kitāb al-muwashshā* (The book of ornamentation), and ibn Ḥazm's *Ṭawq al-ḥamāma* (*The Ring of the Dove*).

This shift of focus turns out to be instructive not only for the study of Hebrew but for the study of Arabic as well, for studies of these works have never engaged with the ways in which they manipulate the relationship between prose and verse. Thus, studies of *The Ring of the Dove* understand the verse quotations to be merely illustrations of the points made in the prose text, seen as primary; studies of *The Book of Ornamentation* understand the book as an anthology of verse, with the prose content being a mere framework. Levy shows us that prose and verse interact, in both works, to make a point about the nature of love and love poetry and that they are integral to each other as well as to their theme. Applying this method to the erotic stories of the Hebrew writers Solomon ibn Ṣaqbel and Jacob ben El'azar, Levy is able to elevate these works from the status of mere curiosities of Hebrew letters to works that are deeply engaged in the thematics of medieval literature in general. Further enlightenment on the use of metaphor in the context of love poetry and literary prose comes from a consideration of Jacob ben El'azar's prosimetric stories in relation to such Arabic works as the *maqāmāt* of al-Hamadhānī and Romance works such as *The Romance of the Pear*, *Aucassin and Nicolette*, and the poetry of the troubadours. Along the way, we are treated to extensive interpretation of two of Jacob ben El'azar's stories.

Thus, we come to eros, the main theme of medieval Romance narrative prose and prosimetrum. Levy's extensive study of the *Maḥbarot* of Immanuel of Rome, one of the most popular Hebrew literary works of the Middle Ages, includes a thorough discussion of that work in light of Dante's contemporaneous *Vita nuova*. Links between these works have been pointed out by earlier scholars, but Levy's comparative study permits us to explore the new vision of love underlying the work of both, thereby showing the shifts in sensibility of Hebrew writers between the erotic ideals of the

Arabic poets, the Romance poets of courtly love, and the new spiritual love poets of Dante's ilk. For the first time in Jewish literary history, Immanuel's Italian poetry is also brought to bear on the discussion.

For the book is not limited to Hebrew literature. It concludes with a consideration of Jewish Romance poetry from the period just after the expulsion from Spain, showing the continuity between the erotic imagination of the medieval writers and the anonymous folk poets of the Judeo-Spanish tradition. This integration of Hebrew and non-Hebrew writing is a welcome innovation in the writing of Jewish literary history.

This is a work of dazzling virtuosity and erudition, treating sources in many languages and grounded in mastery of academic scholarship in many fields not ordinarily treated together. Thanks to this breadth, the book illuminates important aspects of the medieval Jewish literary imagination while shedding not a little light on the literatures of the Jews' neighbors East and West.

ACKNOWLEDGMENTS

I BEGAN TO THINK OF THIS BOOK IN my first spring as a doctoral student. As I worked my way through a rigorous reading and translating curriculum of medieval Hebrew literature with Raymond Scheindlin, I began to envision how to reshape my practice of comparing literatures. I hoped, in the process, to enrich my philological, linguistic, theoretical, and historical horizons. I am most grateful to him for introducing me to the intricacies of medieval Hebrew literature during his semester at Harvard and for subsequently sitting through many hours of reading, translating, and discussing elaborate patterns across medieval literary traditions.

To be able to spend my years as a graduate student in comparative literature delving into philology and poetics was the ultimate gift, and for this I am tremendously grateful to Luis Girón-Negrón, whose impeccable scholarship, indispensable advice, and enthusiasm have served as ongoing inspiration; Jan Ziolkowski, who, significantly, introduced me to the world of the prosimetrum and who continually models scholarly generosity and conscientious attention both to the smallest details and to the overall view; and Mary Gaylord, whose sensitivity to what poems actually mean has deeply informed my own approach to poetic analysis. Though this book began as a dissertation that gave equal attention to prosimetra from the various literary traditions of the medieval Mediterranean and now strives to pinpoint innovations among texts by Jewish authors, its focus on secular love across shifting and developing literary forms remains central—a comparative gaze from a different angle.

My interests in poetics and philology have their roots in my undergraduate years, shaped by the singular experience of studying Dante and the *Duecento* poets with Teodolinda Barolini, whose continued encouragement of my work on Immanuel of Rome has been invaluable and meaningful. Soon after becoming entranced by Italian medieval lyric, I was truly fortunate to study the Occitan poets with Joan Ferrante and medieval Iberian literature with Patricia Grieve, both of whom imparted the wonder of literary possibilities inherent in vernacular Romance.

This book took shape during my year as postdoctoral fellow at the Institute for Israel and Jewish Studies at Columbia University, which supported my hope of bridging the not-so-distinct worlds of comparative literature, medieval studies, Romance studies, Mediterranean studies, and Jewish studies. I am profoundly grateful to Elisheva Carlebach for continuously supporting my research, to Rebecca Kobrin for regularly sharing words of wisdom with me, and to Jeremy Dauber, who provided thoughtful comments on an early outline.

My writing has benefited in myriad ways from insightful feedback from colleagues across an array of academic disciplines. I am grateful to the Italian Academy for Advanced Studies at Columbia, where I spent a rewarding semester exploring the poetic identity of Immanuel of Rome, furnished with thoughtful advice from David Freedberg and my inspiring cohort of fellows; to Dana Fishkin and Jonathan Decter, who arranged an innovative Shalom Spiegel session at the Jewish Theological Seminary devoted to Immanuel; to Francesca Bregoli for inviting me to the Center for Jewish Studies at the CUNY Graduate Center; to Akash Kumar and Elizabeth Hebbard, who included me in an interdisciplinary symposium on medieval lyric landscapes at Indiana University; to Natalia Indrimi for including me in the Centro Primo Levi's Rome Lab at the Center for Jewish History; to Thomas O'Donnell and Fordham Medieval Studies for convening a dynamic conference on medieval French without borders; and to Dana Fishkin, who masterminded an AJS panel on Immanuel. In each of these instances, I gathered important feedback from colleagues who work on an exciting and inspiring range of subjects.

Many other mentors, colleagues, and friends made this book possible and provided indispensable advice. I am particularly grateful to the late Samuel Armistead, who inspired me to think about Judeo-Spanish lyric in new ways: he enthusiastically discussed Judeo-Spanish balladry over the phone with me and most generously lent me cassette tapes of ballads he had recorded in the 1950s. In 2009, he made a joyful, unforgettable presentation to a seminar on Jewish languages and literatures that I organized with brilliant and spirited Debra Caplan under the expert guidance of Marc Shell, who has broadened my view of comparing literatures and shared invaluable advice about the writing process. I am thankful to Susan Boynton, who, during one of our energizing walk-and-talks in Riverside Park, encouraged me to reach out to Indiana University Press, beginning what has been a fruitful experience; to James Loeffler, who offered vital comments on an early draft; to Gregory Nagy, who enthusiastically introduced me to the study of oral tradition; to Vera Basch Moreen for sharing enduring words of wisdom; and to Fabian Alfie, who has encouraged my bridging the worlds of Italian and Jewish studies.

I am truly grateful to Miriam Meir for our ongoing conversations on all matters, from poetic meaning to the complexities of transliterating and the wonders of grammar; to Jeannie Miller, with whom I spent countless hours in Butler Library in writing solidarity, for continual generosity; to my fellow Immanuel of Rome enthusiast Dana Fishkin for being ever ready to discuss anything and everything Immanuel related; to Andrew McLaren, who with perpetual good humor discussed ethics, historiography, and transliteration with me; to Tamar Menashe for conscientiously reading particular sections with the crucial gaze of a historian; to David Torollo for our ongoing discussions about Jacob Ben Elʿazar; to Adriana Valencia for her joyful wisdom; to Lital Levy, who inspired me to persevere through my initial efforts at reading and translating; to Judith Cohen for her meaningful singing and our inspiring talks; to Michelle Margolis Chesner for talking about—and examining! —manuscript and print stichometry with me; to Emily Runde for facilitating the ideal book cover; and to Meredith Levin for our lively discussions of all things Romance. I thank Dana Kresel, Betty Beecham, and Dina Mann for their ever-ready superpowers and my immensely talented students for never ceasing to amaze me with their innovative ways of reading.

The entire team at Indiana University Press has made this process wonderfully seamless and rewarding. I am very grateful to Brian Carroll, Gary Dunham, David Hulsey, Nancy Lila Lightfoot, Dee Mortensen, Brent Starr, Ashante Thomas, Stephen Matthew Williams, and Megan Schindele for graciously guiding me throughout and to series editors Matthias Lehmann and Harvey Goldberg, who supported my work on literary form. I am truly indebted to Jonathan Ray and the anonymous readers who took tremendous care to provide invaluable and rigorously detailed comments that helped me improve this book in ways granular and broad.

I am thankful to my parents for endless enthusiasm and encouragement; to my sister and brother-in-law for continuous moral and tech support; and to my wonderful husband and delightful children, whose love of literature has given my work deeper meaning.

Finally, I thank my cousin Stella for impressing on me the importance of treating these interdisciplinary worlds and poetic universes in the most conscientious and humane way possible, and that truly—as she continuously shows many of us—*los corassones avlan*.

This publication was supported in part by a research grant from the Institute for Israel and Jewish Studies at Columbia University and was subsidized in part by Harvard Studies in Comparative Literature.

December 31, 2020
New York City

NOTE ON TRANSLATION AND TRANSLITERATION

TRANSLATIONS ARE MY OWN UNLESS OTHERWISE INDICATED. I have translated key primary texts in as literal a manner as possible to allow for the greatest ease of comparing texts across literary traditions. I draw on others' translations for some texts that provide supporting evidence, such as Maimonides's *Guide of the Perplexed* and al-Ḥarīrī's *Maqāmāt*. I have primarily opted for translations that are similarly literal.

My transliterations of Hebrew and Arabic follow Library of Congress romanization guidelines. I have adjusted my Hebrew scheme in the following ways: instead of *ts*, ṣ; I use s rather than ś; when a *he* is quiescent, it is not transcribed (e.g., *tevuna* and not *tevunah*). Any vocal *sheva* is transliterated as *e*; an originally vocal *sheva* that follows a small vowel and closes a syllable (*sheva meraḥef*) is treated as quiescent (e.g., *bi-lshon ha-qodesh* and not *bi-leshon ha-qodesh*). I have opted for long-standing Anglicized forms of commonly used words (e.g., Moses instead of Moshe). For words that have slight variants in their Hebrew and Arabic transliterations, I have chosen to leave out diacritics for ease of reading and comparing (e.g., rather than maqāma pl. maqāmāt in Arabic and maqama pl. maqamot in Hebrew, I write maqama pl. maqamas).

JEWISH LITERARY EROS

INTRODUCTION

I've searched the world—long and wide, by land and by sea—with little reward.
I saw Syria all the way to Armenia and Romania, a large part of it, it seems to me.
I saw the Sultanate, from the mountains to the valleys, and
I can tell you about the Great Khan:
of all I heard and saw and understood, I am now inflamed,
desiring to recount.[1]

AND RECOUNT HE DOES. IN A FEAT OF unprecedented onomatopoeia and in a new form of prosaic poetry, Immanuel of Rome figures himself as a court poet to none less than Dante's patron. He embodies a persona inspired by Love and by Lady Philosophy, who basks in the fictional, secular escape of vernacular Italian lyric. Composing in a language devoid of the same hermeneutic implications and amalgam of literary precedents that he confronted when writing in Hebrew, he is momentarily detached—or is he?—from his monumental efforts as a biblical commentator and Hebrew *maqama* author. Yet is this freedom that Immanuel carves out via Italian language and flexible compositional form truly freeing? If it were, then the melancholy of his outsider pessimism—the emptiness that remains at the end of the poem, after he has given his voice to a lyric piteously destined for an outrageously aspirational patron—would perhaps not be as pronounced, and his reliance on a robust battery of onomatopoeia (boorish in the Latin West but praiseworthy in the Arabo-Andalusian sphere) would be less striking. And if he truly sought freedom in lyric form and content, why would he write a poem in a new form, in a language whose audience undoubtedly regarded him as alien? I think he did so because of the exquisite promise of a momentary love that hovers somewhere between the limits of prose and verse: "For Love is in the hall of Cangrande della Scala: here without wings, seemingly I fly."[2]

Profane love is the common driving force, the one theme that medieval prosimetra across Arabic, Hebrew, French, and Italian consistently share. Though the mixed form enjoyed broad appeal in Hebrew and Arabic—providing the structure for an array of literary, scientific, and historical exploration—the nascent and inherently profane Romance languages produced prosimetra predominantly related to love. At the crossroads of these literary cultures, Jews of the medieval Mediterranean composed creative texts that combined dominant cultures' literary stylings with Biblical Hebrew and with a particularly perceptive diasporic gaze. Building on recent investigations into the literary hybridity of the Jews of medieval Iberia, I trace Jewish authors' treatments of love in the prosimetric context and find them creative and complex, not mere fusions of their Arabo-Andalusian predecessors and Romance-language counterparts.[3] Indeed, scholars across disciplines have dedicated significant studies toward defining the medieval Mediterranean with precision: it is notably a site of exchange and synthesis amid a world defined by various geographical, linguistic, religious, and chronological parameters. My contribution is a pause amid definitions; in slowing down to look at the intricacies of literary form and genre across traditions, I find particular moments of innovation among textual practices by Jewish authors.

Partially freed from the consistent restraints of both meter and rhyme built into fixed poetic forms, some Jewish authors of prosimetric or polymetric texts found new ways to foster inquiries into secular love. Though the most conspicuous examples come from certain Hebrew maqamas, I also consider other works, including Immanuel of Rome's Italian lyrics, polymetric Judeo-Spanish oral poems, and experimental poetic and prose compositions from the fifteenth through seventeenth centuries. I situate these examples with respect to classical Arabic, Castilian, French, Galician-Portuguese, Italian, and Occitan counterparts. When viewed in the comparative context of the medieval Mediterranean, the evolving relationship between the mixed form and the theme of love in secular Jewish compositions refines our understanding of the ways in which the Jewish literature of the period negotiates the hermeneutic and theological underpinnings of Islamicate and Christian literary worlds.

My principal examples, which are drawn from the twelfth through fourteenth centuries, might seem to cover an unwieldy chronological span, but it is a necessary one to grasp Jewish authorial innovations amid continuities and across what might otherwise be viewed as cultural, political, and theological divides. To avoid the pitfalls of thinking in terms of the struggles of a minority or minor literature (though I do draw on Deleuze and Guattari's powerfully instructive paradigm at times), I rely on the breadth that the region provides to pinpoint the difference between influence and innovation.[4] Accordingly, to appreciate the generic and formal novelties of particular Hispano- and Italo-Hebraic authors' amalgams of poetry and prose, I look to ninth-century Arabic compositions—and even farther back to the Bible and ancient Greek—for a thorough understanding of rhetorical conventions. Likewise, to get the full effect of interactions with Romance, I turn toward the nascence of Romance-language compositions in the twelfth century. The medieval Mediterranean encompasses this range, within which the golden age of Hebrew letters (c. 950–c. 1150) and the births of Romance vernaculars exist in continuity and deserve a chance to display their formal particularities, side by side. Finally, to grasp the staggering ramifications of Jewish textual innovations borne of these hybrid environs, I fast-forward to Jewish and converso compositions dating from the fifteenth century and onward that embrace generic and formal variation to wildly diverse ends, serving divergent cultural needs.

While the study of medieval prosimetra is not a new area of literary inquiry—the term itself was already in use in the beginning of the twelfth century—scholarly efforts at a systematic treatment of the mixed form are recent, and of these studies, very few aim at elucidating the complex role of their verse passages.[5] In a pioneering contribution, Wolfhart Heinrichs formulated an outline of the functions of poetry in three types of rhymed prose narratives composed in classical Arabic.[6] Toward the end of the essay, he notes that the most interesting poems are, naturally, those that do not fit these schemes, but because it is a first attempt in Arabic studies, "we have to indulge in taxonomy and classification."[7] Peter Dronke takes a different, non-classificatory approach: not an "exhaustive history or an all-encompassing theory" of prosimetrum but rather "an enquiry into poetics."[8] His investigation spans thirteen centuries and eight linguistic traditions—hence the futility of designing a comprehensive system of classification. To highlight the particular beauty in each tradition, Dronke avoids generalizations while still presenting some tantalizing suggestions: in some vernacular texts, for instance, form variations frequently mark an author's effort to differentiate the empirical self from the poetic *I*, a tactic Dante certainly employs in his prosimetric *Vita nuova*.[9] I owe to these form-conscious and rigorously philological studies a sustained conviction that mixed-form texts are poised to gauge medieval Jewish authorial postures toward the poetics of profane love in ways that poetry or prose unalloyed cannot as fluidly articulate.

Despite these foundational inquiries, the prosimetrum is generally not positioned among the most desirable literary forms, perhaps because its formal variations require both attention and flexibility on the part of the reader. Accordingly, when readers encounter a prosimetrum, they often skip (or are tempted to skip) over the poetry—hence the enjambed first sentence of this book: an invitation to (re)read the opening verses. Perhaps readers see interspersed poems as a break from the narrative flow, a chance to gaze at or to listen passively to the composition without putting too much effort into understanding its meaning, let alone its function in the context of the prosimetrum. This attitude unfortunately echoes conventional scholarly opinion of poetic passages contained in prosimetra across a variety of literary traditions: seen as artistic interludes or as exemplars of particular theoretical points articulated in prose, they do not contribute or add to the plot or conceptual development of the composition. Scholars have arrived at this conclusion honestly, given that many prosimetra do indeed relegate poetry to this position; for Judah al-Ḥarizi, rhymed, metered poems in the *Taḥkemoni* truly are artistic interludes that corroborate the author's brilliance and simultaneously provide variety.[10]

But when it comes to medieval treatments of a "courtly" tinged love—a problematic term that I will thoroughly unpack—the dismissal of poetry's import has limited the comprehension not only of the role of the lyric but also of the intricate interactions among prose, poetry, and erotic love in mixed-form texts. This lacuna makes sense: since love lyric frequently favors emotion over action, poetic passages in prosimetra centered on the theme of love are not necessarily action packed enough to garner close attention as arbiters of the storyline, unless one treats the philosophy of eros as an active pursuit, as do some of these authors. For some—but certainly not all—Jewish authors of the medieval Mediterranean, prosimetra on profane love provided a space to carve out new formal possibilities for prose and poetry; in turn, these compositions elucidate the shifting status accorded to prose and poetry amid fluctuating formulations of love.

Across the literary cultures of the medieval Mediterranean, comparable precepts of ethical import regulated both loving and composing, so that these two actions became nearly synonymous and the lover as poet one entity.[11] From the outbursts of lovestruck poets enamored with language to their more reflective musings, the poetic personae of Jacob ben Elʿazar's *Sefer ha-meshalim* (The book of stories), Solomon ibn Ṣaqbel's *Ne'um Asher ben Yehuda* (The words of Asher, son of Judah), and Immanuel of Rome's

Maḥberot Immanuel (The maqamas of Immanuel) attempted to use the mixed form to chart elaborate courses for becoming both better lovers and better poets—and perhaps better people as a result. The exact formulation of love and the ensuing textual implications across these texts vary. Together, and alongside Arabic and Romance counterparts, they help articulate the complex and shifting interplay between the erotic and the poetic in mixed-form aesthetics.

What poetry was to the golden age of Andalusi Hebrew letters, the mixed form is to the authors whose works are discussed here; it is an ideal gauge of Jewish authors' cultural orientations. I pair the mixed form and the theme of love because of the way in which shifting attitudes toward compositional styles—concurrent with shifting political and social underpinnings—influenced the kinds of texts authors composed: written as prose began to garner attention in literary cultures that had initially privileged poetic composition, prosimetra offer a unique perspective on what Jewish authors in the twelfth-, thirteenth-, and fourteenth-century Mediterranean singled out as the special capabilities of poetry and prose. In an effort to examine shifting attitudes toward the poetics of profane love, the second, third, and fourth chapters piece apart the relationship between love and poetry in mixed-form compositions by Jewish authors of this period. The first chapter, which dissects the views of poetry and prose in medieval literary criticism, provides the necessary critical gaze with which to view these texts.

Framed by an analysis of Jacob ben Elʿazar's second maqama, a debate between the personified Man of Prose and Man of Poetry, the first chapter situates Jewish authors' experiments with the mixed form with respect to medieval literary criticism in classical Arabic, medieval Hebrew, Latin, and nascent Romance sources. I weigh the meaning of ben Elʿazar's debate within the divergent constructs of classical Arabic, on the one hand, and Romance languages, on the other: while interspersed poetry is a convention in all classical Arabic and medieval Hebrew treatises regardless of subject matter, it is less common in Romance literature, whose prosimetra present poetry as the centerpiece.

After parsing the controversial term *courtly love*, the second chapter traces the evolution of this phenomenon in Romance languages alongside postures toward love in Arabo-Andalusian literary culture in the preceding centuries. I draw on ibn Dāwūd's *Kitāb al-zahra* (*The Book of the Flower*), al-Washshāʾ's *Kitāb al-muwashshā* (The book of ornamentation), and ibn

Ḥazm's Andalusian *Ṭawq al-hamāma* (*The Ring of the Dove*)—all classical Arabic prosimetric treatises on profane love—to weigh the validity of applying the term *courtly love* to the Arabic tradition. Then, after reviewing positions of Moses ibn Ezra, Moses Maimonides, and Shem Tov ibn Falaquera, among others, with respect to profane lyric, I map the development and treatments of love in the Occitan and Galician-Portuguese troubadour traditions with respect to the geographic and lyric orientations of Jewish maqama authors. With these varied notions of courtliness and varieties of love poetry in mind, I turn to treatments of love poetics in Hebrew maqamas: diverging from fellow Hebrew maqama author al-Ḥarizi, ibn Ṣaqbel and ben Elʿazar manipulate both the prose and verse of their prosimetra to experiment with the Romance vision of profane love as ennobling.

In the third chapter, I draw on attitudes toward and treatments of metaphor in mixed-form texts to more deeply examine the interplay between poetry and prose. As authors begin to tinker with conventional uses of metaphor, they adapt the prosification of verse (originally a didactic practice) to this literary context, resulting in an unexpected and wondrous array of metaphors that challenge both the formal and fictional boundaries of these prosimetra. I first focus on the phenomenon of poetry as a physical object that stands in for the beloved, comparing this to kindred instances in Biblical Hebrew, classical Arabic, ancient Greek, Latin, Italian, French, and Spanish, to position the Jewish authorial approach to this literary practice. Next, I address instances in which authors move metaphors from poetry into extended prose passages, creating what I term concrete metaphors. These profoundly imaginative moments of formal maneuvering add additional layers to our understanding of these mixed-form compositions: ibn Ṣaqbel and ben Elʿazar developed visions of worldly love steeped in poetics even when articulated in prose.

In keeping with the decadence and decline of courtly love, the fourth chapter moves to Italy to examine Immanuel of Rome's Hebrew and Italian compositions, both of which combine elements from his post–courtly love late thirteenth-century Italy and his keen familiarity with Hispano-Jewish literary precedents. I demonstrate how the prosimetric structure of his Hebrew maqama collection, the *Maḥberot Immanuel*, is indebted formally not only to al-Ḥarizi's *Taḥkemoni* but also to Dante's *Vita nuova*—Dante's early-career manifesto on the new poetics that replaced the waning trend of courtly love. I then look closely at one of Immanuel's Italian love sonnets and identify his Italian composition *Bisbidis* as a maqama-esque prose-poem because of its dramatic variation from the strict formal, lexical, and thematic regulations of the sonnets and *canzoni* of late thirteenth- and early fourteenth-century Italian lyric.[12] Immanuel's literary bilingualism is itself, I argue, an experimentation in form. Finally, I pause to explore the unusually powerful poetic voices of the female protagonists in these prosimetra by Jewish authors as keys to the texts' discourses on metaphor, poetics, and love; in granting the female unusually vocal and didactic powers, these authors—not exactly proto-feminists—allude to themselves: outsiders with creative potential.

My examinations of poetry and prose grapple with the extent to which Jewish authors embraced the dominant cultures' literary traditions or formulated their own authorial paths. As in the case of the brilliant literary outpouring of the Hispano-Hebraic golden age beginning in tenth-century al-Andalus, innovation among Jewish authors in the centuries that followed more often than not corresponds to times of political and social strife for Jewish communities. Jacob ben El'azar and Immanuel of Rome, for instance, composed intricate masterpieces in Toledo and Italy, respectively, amid fraught historical realities: ben El'azar likely had to contend with increasingly stringent papal and monarchical controls on Jewish businesses and religious practice, and although compositions by Immanuel "the Jew" appear alongside poems by the most famous Italian Christian poets of the period, it is useful to remember that Immanuel and his fellow Jews were decidedly outsiders, perhaps expelled from Rome by a purported 1321 papal order from Avignon.

Although Jewish authors of medieval prosimetra borrowed compositional trends from the dominant cultures' literary traditions, they remained not only profoundly ensconced in Jewish culture but also deeply indebted to Biblical Hebrew—even, I argue, in some vernacular Romance compositions that seem to slip between language boundaries. Authors of these formally and thematically specific compositions demanded a readership fluent in languages, theology, and literary criticism across cultures. I ask to what extent these were reasonable expectations and to what extent authors intended various levels of meaning. The ultimate arbiter is duration and survival: manuscripts of these formally innovative visions of eros remain today, attesting to their enduring worth and meaning.

I consider the cultural ramifications of this literary landscape—one that over time coalesced into the essential medial place between poetry and prose that Giorgio Agamben so profoundly defined: "enjambment thus brings to light the original stride, neither poetic nor prosaic, but, in a manner of speaking, the bustrophedon of poetry, the essential prosimetry of every human discourse."[13] Accordingly, I propose Judeo-Spanish oral composition not as a rejection of the intellectualism inherent in literary environs that cultivated complex poetic practices and prose theories of this poetry, but rather as a refocusing of secular expression; while this new mode certainly rehearsed Romance composition, it simultaneously met the artistic needs of generations that navigated perilous surroundings in new ways. At the same time, in Italy, generically experimental texts in poetry and prose by Jewish authors tested the limits of love amid an ever-changing landscape rife with newness, instability, and creative promise.

Notes

1. Del mondo ho cercato per lungo et per lato con un caro mercato per terra et per mare
Vedut'ho Soria infin Herminia, et di Romania gran parte mi pare,
Vedut'ho 'l soldano per monte et per piano et si del gran Cano poria novellare,
Di quel c'haggio inteso veduto et compreso mi sono hora acceso a volerlo contare,
Che pur la corona ne porta Verona per quel che si suona del dire et del fare.
In Cipolla and Pellegrini, "Poesie minori riguardanti gli Scaligeri," 51.

My translation of Immanuel's poem, known in the manuscript tradition as *Bisbidis* or *Bisbio*, first appeared in *Digital Dante*, "Immanuel of Rome and Dante." Many thanks to Teodolinda Barolini for her thoughtful translation advice. For the complete text and translation of *Bisbidis*, see the appendix.

2. "Ch'Amor e'n la sala del Sir de la scala / Quivi senza ala mi parea volare" In Cipolla and Pellegrini, "Poesie minori riguardanti gli Scaligeri," 52.

3. In the past two decades, scholars have delved into the multiplicity of literary traditions of medieval Iberia, devoting studies to Hebrew and Sephardic literature within the Iberian setting. See, for instance, Decter, *Iberian Jewish Literature*; Hamilton, *Representing Others in Medieval Iberian Literature*; Pearce, *Andalusi Literary & Intellectual Tradition*; Wacks, *Framing Iberia*; and Wacks, *Double Diaspora in Sephardic Literature*. These studies complement research that confronts the multiplicities of medieval Iberia, such as Menocal, Sells, and Scheindlin, *Literature of Al-Andalus*; Akbari and Mallette, *Sea of Languages*; and Robinson and Rouhi, *Under the Influence*.

4. Deleuze and Guattari, *Kafka*.

5. Hugh of Bologna (early twelfth century) is the first person known to have used the term *prosimetrum* for mixed-form compositions. Dronke, *Verse with Prose from Petronius to Dante*, 2. The following are among the very few who focus systematically on this topic: Dronke, *Verse with Prose from Petronius to Dante*; Pabst, *Prosimetrum*; the scholars whose essays appear in *Prosimetrum: Crosscultural Perspectives*; Eckhardt, "Medieval Prosimetrum Genre." For overviews of the history of *prosimetrum*, see Ziolkowski, "Prosimetrum in the Classical Tradition"; and Brogan, "Prosimetrum." In addition, Boase proposes literary form

as one of five modes through which to compare Romance and Arabic literatures: "Arab Influences on European Love-Poetry," 461.

6. Heinrichs, "Prosimetrical Genres in Classical Arabic Literature," 249–75.

7. Heinrichs, 267.

8. Dronke, *Verse with Prose from Petronius to Dante*, 2.

9. Dronke, 114.

10. *Taḥkemoni* is a proper noun: the name of one of David's warriors in 2 Samuel 23.8. In addition, it contains the root *ḥ-k-m*, thus implying that the book contains wisdom. For further context, see Mirsky et al., "al-Ḥarizi, Judah ben Solomon."

11. A frequently cited example on the European side is the early fourteenth-century poetic treatise *Leys d'amors*, attributed to Guillem Molinier. See Zeeman, "The Lover-Poet and Love as the Most Pleasing 'Matere' in Medieval French Love Poetry," 821, and Anglade's 1919 edition of the treatise. Arabic love poetry provides another example: love is one of the most common themes of pre-Islamic poetry, but with the spread of Islam, love became increasingly disesteemed, leading in the ʿAbbāsid period (from the ninth century onward) to the "spiritualization of love . . . understood by its practitioners as the ennobling service of beauty itself." Scheindlin, *Wine, Women, and Death*, 89. Some of the most celebrated love poets in classical Arabic belong to this period, including Abū Nuwās and al-Mutanabbi, intermittent champions of "l'esprit courtois." Vadet, *L'Esprit courtois en Orient dans le cinq premiers siècles de l'Hégire*. The concept of courtly love is addressed in detail in the second chapter.

12. See Levy, "Immanuel of Rome's *Bisbidis*."

13. "L'*enjambement* porta così alla luce l'originaria andatura, né poetica né prosastica, ma, per così dire, bustrofedica della poesia, l'esenziale prosimetricità di ogni discorso umano." Agamben, *La idea della prosa*, 20.

1

THE RELATIVE MERITS OF POETRY AND PROSE

"Young man, thou hast manifested thy diction; how does thy poetry compare with thy prose?" He replied: "There is no comparison between my prose and verse." Then he summoned aid from his natural ability, raised his voice to such a pitch that it filled the valley, and recited.

—al-Hamadhānī, *The Maqāmāt of Badiʿ al-Zamān al Hamadhānī*

To understand the secret of wisdom and knowledge,
do not look to words of poetry;
To become wise and to know, direct your path to holy knowledge.

—Ibn Falaquera, *Sefer ha-mevaqesh*

What is set out in poetry serves as a model for those who write prose,
and not the other way about.

—Dante, *De Vulgari Eloquentia*

THE SECOND MAQAMA OF JACOB BEN ELʿAZAR'S *SEFER ha-meshalim* comprises a debate of the relative merits of prose and poetry, at the end of which the explicitly deceitful Man of Poetry is crowned winner. The prosimetrum—for the reader must keep in mind the occasionally ironic detail that the text contains both rhymed prose and poetry—begins with the narrator's description of a place of study (*bet midrash*) in which the following question is posed: "What kind of speech is it that when a person speaks it he will be considered praiseworthy?"[1] The first one to respond asserts that pithiness is the most important quality in speech. The second begins by praising the speech of wise men and scorning that of fools but turns his response toward an endorsement of poetry: his definition of praiseworthy is "a learned person who sings his words in meter."[2] This initiates the debate between personified Poetry and Prose, who submit standard arguments according to classical Arabic poetics for and against poetry—arguments that will soon become clear. The Man of Poetry argues that prose, unlike poetry, is scattered and that poetry delights all people and delights the soul; the Man of Prose, conversely, claims that poetry consists of lies and that the ancients relied on prose, not on poetry.[3] The judges declare Poetry the victor of the debate. In a surprise ending, however, the defenders of Prose accuse the judges of rigging Poetry's win, and in a further twist, the Man of Poetry gloats that he has won under false pretenses. At the end of the story, the Man of Poetry recites a poem in which he praises wisdom as that which validates poetry.

Jacob ben Elᶜazar and the Prosimetric Maqama

Ben Elᶜazar, a Jewish philosopher, poet, translator, and grammarian, composed *Sefer ha-meshalim* in Hebrew in early thirteenth-century Toledo.[4] Often regarded as a maqama collection, his ten prosimetric stories and debates on a variety of topics seem to draw more or less freely from both Arabic and Romance literary models, which corroborates the author's historical circumstance: though ben Elᶜazar lived in Toledo roughly a century to a century and a half after Christian powers gained control (1085), the city had maintained much of its Arabic character.[5] *Mozarabs*, Arabic-speaking Christians who had lived among Muslims for centuries, continued to populate Toledo, though they had been forced to Romanize many of their practices. Ben Elᶜazar seems to have composed *Sefer ha-meshalim* in the decades before Alfonso X of Castile (king from 1252 to 1284) took power and began a campaign to bolster the language and culture of Christian Iberia, in part through translations of scientific and literary works from Arabic to Romance.[6] Thus, although most of ben Elᶜazar's writings might appear to draw primarily on spheres of Hebrew and Arabic learning, his cultural environs suggest that he could also navigate Romance-speaking settings.

Sefer ha-meshalim has been termed a Hebrew maqama, a form of fictional Arabic rhymed prose narrative with interspersed metered poems.[7] In a model Arabic maqama, a storyteller recounts his encounters with an eloquent trickster protagonist who is usually in disguise until a moment of recognition at the story's end.[8] The first collection of maqamas, composed in the tenth century by Badīᶜ al-Zamān al-Hamadhānī (968–1008) in Nishapur (in northeastern Iran), is considered a parody of *adab* (learned secular) materials.[9] Although al-Hamadhānī is the genre's inventor, the fifty maqamas of al-Ḥarīrī of Baṣra (1054–1122) became the "symbol of Arabic eloquence and stylistic dexterity" that intentionally showcased the author's compositional and linguistic prowess via his didactic and entertaining stories.[10] In an attempt to compete with al-Ḥarīrī, al-Saraqustī (d. 1143), a native of al-Andalus, invented a complex two-consonant rhyme scheme for his own maqama collection.[11] Other Andalusian maqamas differed from the classic scheme, fulfilling a courtly rather than didactic function.[12]

In the early twelfth century, Jewish writers in al-Andalus and farther east soon embraced the maqama as they had Arabic poetic styles in earlier centuries and began to experiment with Hebrew renditions. Ibn Ṣaqbel, the first author with a partially extant Hebrew maqama, might have been living under Islamic rule, though his fellow maqama authors had their origins in Christian Spain.[13] Some of these authors followed the canonical scheme of the Arabic maqama, such as Judah al-Ḥarizi (1165–1225), in whose *Taḥkemoni* the fictional narrator Heman ha-Ezraḥi relates his encounters with the antiheroic Ḥever ha-Qeni.[14] Al-Ḥarizi's reliance on al-Ḥarīrī is understandable: he was familiar with the classic scheme, having translated the Arabic maqamas of al-Ḥarīrī into Hebrew sometime before 1218, at least two years before composing the *Taḥkemoni*.[15] Other prosimetric Hebrew texts that are often called maqamas, like *Sefer ha-meshalim*, opted for varied narratives that relied on fiction and allegory as guiding frameworks rather than on the narrator-hero model.[16] Despite their diverse forms, many Hebrew maqama-esque works, including the *Taḥkemoni* and *Sefer ha-meshalim*, share an urge to justify the composition of the work in Hebrew, as opposed to the purportedly more dexterous Arabic language.[17]

The Poetics of Deception

Poetry across traditions has long been associated with lying, a concept derived from its association with imitation (*mimesis*), as Plato (428/427 or 424/423–348/347) contends.[18] Still, even Plato allowed for poetry "which is imitative in the good sense," at least theoretically.[19] Others were more nuanced in their condemnations of poetry's imitative nature: indeed, as Kathy Eden explains, it is "Aristotle [384–322] who first formulates the logical and psychological arguments in poetry's defense, just as it is Aristotle who first defines fiction to include both the poetic and legal fiction."[20] This view had some precedent in Gorgias (483–375) who, in his "Encomium on

Helen," justifies Helen's actions because "poetry not only moves its audience to sympathize with the good and bad fortunes of another, it even persuades its listeners, through its deceptions (*doxēs apatēmata*), to pursue a particular course of action."[21] The notion of poetry as lying—nuanced or not—became a prevailing opinion across many literary traditions and with few detractors, notably Philip Sidney, whose *Defense of Poesy* was published posthumously in 1595. Of course, poets were eager to flout such theoretical considerations, and poetic composition continued to develop and flourish across literary worlds.

Classical Arabic poetics had an even more challenging task of justifying poetry, given specific Quranic injunctions, shortly discussed in further detail.[22] To leave theological objections to the side for a moment, one finds that verses of ancient love poems "were supposed to pretend to account for real life events, and at the same time to be accepted as disclaiming any commitment to reality"—an attitude that meant that "the world represented in the love poems is thus a fiction that explicitly proclaims itself to be such."[23]

Overt fictionality mitigates the factor of deception in classical Arabic (and by extension Hebrew) poems and maqamas, as Rina Drory further explains: "This open declaration of fictional status was, then, the common denominator of the love poetry and the *maqāmāt*. It was this common denominator that was called upon to legitimize the *maqāmāt's* new poetics. If we were now to reexamine our traditional definitions of poetry and prose, we would be unable to avoid the conclusion that the fundamental distinction between these two major modes of expression in classical Arabic literature lies mainly in the conveying of reality in a fictional or a non-fictional way, rather than in formal constraints of meter and rhyme."[24]

In the hands of ben Elʿazar, however, the two major modes of poetry and prose both rely on the all-consuming fictionality long associated with poetry. Further, in the second maqama of *Sefer ha-meshalim*, the characterization of poetry (whether in verse or prose) does not merely assert fictionality; it flouts lying. The evil-minded Poetry is poised to inform the reader's perspective on poetry in ben Elʿazar's collection and, more broadly, in medieval Hebrew prosimetra.

This represents quite a shift from the first maqama of the collection, in which ben Elʿazar designates poetry as the mode for relating the most crucial portion of the story—a Neoplatonic explanation of the origins of the soul. In that first story, prose and poetry work equally to convey the events of the allegory, and the text features frequent poetic passages.[25]

In the second story, however, the Man of Poetry turns to verse only twice to support his argument, and of these two poems, the first is not only an anomaly in *Sefer ha-meshalim* but is also out of place in the broader corpus of medieval Hebrew poetry from al-Andalus and Christian Spain: in all other poems in *Sefer ha-meshalim*—and in the majority of secular medieval Hebrew poetry since its tenth-century adoption of Arabic quantitative meter—the verses are broken into hemistichs with a uniform metrical pattern of long and short vowels throughout and a constant end rhyme. Though some medieval Jewish poets experimented with syllabic meter, primarily in liturgical poetry, and though some poets in Christian Spain deliberately toyed with Romance metrics, ben Elʿazar's poem is still unusual, particularly given its placement amid a discussion of poetics: in this poem the first and third verses consist of eleven long vowels and the second and fourth of eight.[26] To further complicate the pattern, the first and second verses rhyme and the third and fourth rhyme, but the verses that rhyme are not equal in length, as is strikingly visible here, even in transliteration:

ve-asir mimeni khol devar shamir ve-shayit
leḥazeq et bedeq ha-bayit
ve-khol devarai be-mozne ṣedeq ve-efa shelema
ve-itkhem efat razon zeʿuma[27]

I remove from myself everything with thorns and thistles
to strengthen the crack in the house.
And all of my words are balanced correctly and measured perfectly.
Your measure is a measure of emptiness.

Why would ben Elʿazar choose to present such an unusual poem in this context? The Man of Poetry has just finished claiming in prose that "to all who hear them, my poems are sweet, and as for me, my flock is whole and complete, each one perfect."[28] The very poem he recites does not conform to this standard of wholeness, and the second verse of the poem hints at this deficiency. The word *bayit* (house) is also the technical term for a verse of poetry; the crack in the house thus clearly refers to the poem's imperfections. Still, the third verse of the poem, in which the Man of Poetry asserts the perfection of his craft, denies any defects and embodies the irony of the poem and of the story as a whole. Ben Elʿazar might have included this unusual metrical form as a nod to Romance verse patterns: it was not uncommon to have verses of mixed lengths in medieval Latin and Romance compositions.[29] Further, it is reasonable that ben Elʿazar would address the topic of Romance prosody, given his seeming familiarity with and incorporation of Romance notions of love and love poetry into the love stories of *Sefer ha-meshalim*, but it is curious that this is the only instance of metrical aberration in the text. Perhaps ben El'azar purposely complicated the accepted pattern to further problematize the status of poetry, for these lines are indeed intended to be a poem, as they are prefaced by the standard opening *va-yisa meshalo va-yomar* (and he began his speech, saying). In the only surviving manuscript of *Sefer ha-meshalim*, the copyist correctly interpreted these unusual lines as poetry, setting the rhymed and metered verses apart slightly from the rhymed prose, and even if the stichometry is not as pronounced as it is in manuscript and print editions of other Hebrew maqamas, it is consistent with the appearance of other poems in this manuscript.[30] This metrical deviation complicates ben El'azar's idea of poetry, and the strikingly ironic third verse ("all of my words are balanced correctly and measured perfectly") corroborates the story's complex and ambivalent portrayal of Poetry—one that veers far from the overwhelmingly favorable depiction of poetry in the other stories of the collection, in which poetry not only serves its standard formal function but also takes on roles of narrative control and didactic counsel.

Before contemplating the connections among prose, poetry, and love, as do the other chapters of this book, the reader must first consider the use of literary form—apart from love, if possible—since this choice figures into the author's illustrations of love. Where does Jacob ben El'azar fit with respect to his Arabic and Romance-language counterparts when it comes to the relative merits of prose and poetry? And what do various opinions on the worth of prose and poetry tell us about Jewish literary culture of thirteenth-century Christian Spain? To answer these questions, the modern reader of literary criticism must recalibrate not only what precisely constitutes poetry (rhymed prose was decidedly prose) but also what defines literary creation and criticism: in contrast with the modern distinction between theory and practice, the very authors to inaugurate new literary forms in classical Arabic, and subsequently in medieval Hebrew, were also the literary theorists, many of whom contributed to a range of other secular disciplines in addition to fulfilling roles as religious leaders and exegetes.

Poetry versus Prose in Classical Arabic

Given that Arabic poetry and prose fulfilled varying purposes and carried particular cultural and theological connotations, their sometimes tense or sometimes harmonious coexistence in Arabic mixed-form texts created a complex hermeneutic experience that has generated very little notice, as Heinrichs notes.[31] Despite Heinrichs's innovative conviction that this oversight in scholarship on prosimetra in medieval Arabic texts "is strange to see and embarrassing to admit," the dominant view among scholars has been that interspersed verse citations were merely a convention of prose compositions and deserve no further attention as noteworthy components of the text.[32] Under this assumption, adab texts with an abundance of verse citations become problematic, since they more closely resemble compilations of poetry than prose treatises and their authors, accordingly, might be described more accurately as compilers than composers.[33]

Yet it would be counterproductive to undermine the authority of compilers, whose very selection and ordering of verse created narrative meaning. Poetry—especially that of the pre-Islamic era (roughly 500–622)—was long considered by intellectuals to be the greatest human achievement to showcase the Arabic language.[34] The poet, likewise, was regarded as "the creative artist par excellence of his civilization."[35] Following the advent of Islam, these characterizations of poetry existed more specifically with regard to the Quran, whose inimitability (a concept termed *iʿjāz al-qurʾān*) cannot be surpassed by human compositions.[36] Further, the Quran, which contains no poetry, tells that the Prophet Muhammad was expressly not instructed in poetic composition (sūra 36) so that his prophetic pronouncements could not be confused with the proclamations of poets, whom the Quran characterizes as lying (sūra 26).[37]

These deprecations of poetry, which pious poets consistently managed to rationalize, served to limit Arabic poetry more distinctly and crucially to the realm of human accomplishment and usually to the secular sphere, though poets peppered their secular lyrics with religious references.[38] Accordingly, not only was poetry considered an essential component of formal secular education that any male of means would pursue, but it was also discussed in rigorous scholarly terms: renowned Muslim polymaths whose work was not limited to the field of literary criticism—such as al-Jāḥiẓ (c. 776–868/69), ibn Qutayba (828–89), ibn al-Muʿtazz (861–908), and ibn Rashīq (1000–1063/64 or 1070/1071)—devoted treatises to various aspects of poetics.

Although less explicitly theologically controversial than poetry, Arabic rhymed prose possessed its own set of precarious connotations. While to the modern reader rhymed prose might seem to fall somewhere between the categories of poetry and prose, writers of Arabic, and subsequently those of Hebrew, considered it a variety of prose generally reserved for writing that required eloquence, such as formal epistles and treatises.[39] Originally used to describe "oracular pronouncements" of the pre-Islamic period, *sajʿ* (Arabic rhymed prose) seems to predate both prose and metrical poetry.[40] Though potential association with paganism perhaps discouraged rhymed prose compositions at the advent of Islam, the opposite—association with the Quran—also dissuaded authors: a number of Quranic passages are expressed in sajʿ, and authors were wary of writing in a manner that might be perceived as challenging the inimitability of the Quran.[41] Despite these concerns, rhymed prose regained popularity starting in the late seventh century as the preferred form for official court writings, and it became increasingly replete with rhetorical flourishes. A notable use of sajʿ, of course, is in the maqama, alternating with rhymed, metered poetry.

Once poetry and prose had been established as worthy (though potentially problematic) conveyers of secular knowledge—but well before the invention of the maqama—Arabic literary critics began to compare the two compositional modes.[42] There were two diverging methods of comparison: one technique was an inquiry known as either *ḥall al-naẓm* (or *ḥall*, "prosification" of verse) or as *naẓm al-ḥall* (or *ʿaqd*, "versification" of prose); the other entailed theorizing the relative merits of prose and poetry as an aesthetic measure.[43] *Naẓm*, which literally means "ordered" or "stringing"—as in the stringing of pearls—is the term for verse, as opposed to *nathr* (literally "scattered"), which is the term for prose.[44] Accordingly, *ḥall al-naẓm* has the literal sense of "stringing up," "tying," or "binding," and *naẓm al-ḥall* "untying" or "unstringing." Although the theorizing of ḥall and ʿaqd became a popular topic in literary criticism beginning in the eighth century, prosification and versification were principally didactic methods. Much like educators in first-century Christian schools of rhetoric, instructors in the world of Arabic letters routinely asked students to turn prose passages into verse, and vice versa, to train them in the arts of prose and poetry.[45] The latter method—that of theorizing the relative merits of the two forms—informs readers about the views of literary critics on prose and poetry: when ʿAbbasid-era literary critics considered the significance of poems within the context of prose treatises, they did so to analyze the theoretical qualities of verse rather than to contemplate the prosimetric compositional structure.[46] This theoretical treatment corroborates the perceived role of poetry in a prosimetrum: authors of classical Arabic and, in turn, medieval Hebrew treatises deemed poetry a necessary stylistic flourish and accordingly sprinkled poems throughout rhymed prose narratives on subjects ranging from medicine to history and from love to biography.

Of the classical Arabic literary critics who discussed the relative merits of prose and poetry, earlier scholars tend to favor poetry, and later thinkers showed a preference for prose, with the exception of ibn Rashīq (c. 1000–1070/71), a later theorist who favored poetry.[47] These nathr and naẓm arguments, briefly summarized in the pages that follow, range from those based on formal elements of composition to those grounded in historical or social realities and to those with theological underpinnings.

In his *Bayān wa-l-tabyīn* (Treatise on clarity and clarification), Abū ʿUthmān ʿAmr ibn Baḥr al-Fuqaymī al-Baṣrī, known as al-Jāḥiẓ (c. 776–868/69), does not directly address the relative merits of prose and poetry, but he does include the following quotation of the rhetorician Sahl ibn Hārūn (d. 859) at the end of his discussion of the eloquence (*balāgha*) of prose and poetry: "Balāgha of speech and good poetry are rarely united in one person. It is even more difficult to excel in the balāgha of poetry and the balāgha of pen (prose)."[48] Far from singling out either writing style as superior to the other, this stance treats prose and poetry as comparable endeavors. Al-Jāḥiẓ also justifies poetic composition in his *Risālat al-qiyān* (*The Epistle on Singing-Girls*): "There is hence no reason for regarding it [verse] as prohibited, nor is there any basis for such a view in Qur'an or Sunnah."[49] These two remarks capture what appears to be the author's stance on the matter: prose and poetry are equally virtuous.

The philologist Abū al-ʿAbbās Muḥammad b. Yazīd b. ʿAbd al-Akbar al-Thumālī al-Azdī al-Mubarrad (826–899/900), a native of Baṣra, is best known for his *Kitāb al-kāmil fī al-adab* (The complete book of adab), a prosimetric text that addresses a variety of topics of adab, but he also authored a lesser-known epistle on the merits of prose and poetry, which seems to be the first of its kind.[50] Framing his argument as a response to the question of whether prose and rhymed prose are more eloquent than poetry, al-Mubarrad writes that eloquence (*balāgha*) consists of "comprehensive rendering of the idea, (careful) selection of the verbal expression, and beauty of composition."[51] He adds that if two compositions—prose and verse—successfully incorporate these three qualities, the poem is more praiseworthy than the prose equivalent because it must also incorporate meter and rhyme (*wazn wa-qāfīya*).[52]

The most systematic and thorough discourse on the nathr and naẓm debate up to this point is *Kitāb al-ṣināʿatayn, al-kitāba waʾl-shiʿr* (Book of the two crafts: Prose and poetry), in which Abū Hilāl al-Ḥasan ibn ʿAbd Allāh al-ʿAskarī (828/29–c. 1010) offers thirteen points to validate his preference for poetry: Unlike prose, poetry has meter, which orders its words and makes the composition beautiful. In all languages and among all peoples, poetry outlasts other written media because of the connection between the parts of the composition. Like proverbs, poetry enjoys broad popularity. Poetry, unlike epistles and speeches, can have an effect on a person's character and honor.[53] Courtly gatherings must include poetic recitation because only poetry can move and relax kings and men of power; recitations of poetry add elegance and pleasantness to literary gatherings; and poetry is a nice complement to music. The next set of statements more directly addresses the connection between poetry and Arabs: the virtue of poetry is its words—eloquent, excellent, and rare—such that one who does not recite the poetry of the Arabs is lacking in skill. Poetry provides much of the *shawāhid* ("probative quotations"), thus helping to explain words from the Quran and ḥadīth.[54] It preserves the genealogy and history of Arabs and thus is essential to secretaries, preachers, and all educated people. Directly addressing others' observations with regard to the Quran's disapproval of poetry, al-ʿAskarī remarks that it is not necessary to renounce all poetry, since God finds only those poets who act unjustly to be blameworthy. To conclude, he offers two comments on the idea of poets as artists: poets, unlike other types of writers, may praise themselves without seeming shameful; and people of power can discuss their love and passion for their beloveds in poetry.[55]

Hilāl b. al-Muḥassin b. Ibrāhīm al-Ṣābī (969–1056) seems to have written his epistle in favor of prose before his contemporary al-Marzūqī composed his own comments on the matter, and it has been argued that al-Ṣābī influenced al-Marzūqī's (and others') thinking.[56] Al-Ṣābī argues that prose, which is the exact opposite of poetry, is easier to understand than poetry and has broad parameters that facilitate writing for a variety of contexts. He believes that poetry, which is confined to particular topics (*al-aghrāḍ*), meters, and rhymes, and which must express thoughts in distinct verses, lacks cohesion and purpose and can therefore cause confusion. Unlike his contemporaries' arguments on this matter, his is based primarily on his analyses of the forms of both writing styles.[57] He also considers the practical uses of each and praises prose for its utility to society.[58]

In his *Sharḥ dīwān al-ḥamāsa* (Commentary on the *dīwān al-ḥamāsa*; a commentary on the poetry of Abū Tammām), the philologist Aḥmad ibn

Muḥammad al-Marzūqī (d. 1030) favors prose for the following reasons: poetry is historically inferior to prose, since leaders before and after the rise of Islam delighted in hearing the artistic speeches of the orators; poets write poetry to earn a profit, which leads them to commune not only with the nobility but also with the lowly; and since the status of poetry is lower than that of prose, the poet must also be less eloquent than the prose writer.[59] Quoting sūra 36, he adds that the Quran contains no poetry and that the Prophet was not instructed in poetic composition. Finally, he notes that prose enables the writer to broach a larger range of subjects than poetry because of poetry's limiting system of specific topics.[60]

Perhaps no one promotes the superiority of poetry over prose more overtly than the poet and literary critic Abū ʿAlī Ḥasan b. Rashīq al-Qayrawānī (1000–1063/64 or 1070/71). Ibn Rashīq opens his famous book on poetics *al-ʿUmda fī maḥāsin al-shʿir wa-ādābihi* (The pillar on the good qualities of poetry, and its customs) with a discussion titled "Chapter on the excellence of poetry" (*bāb fī faḍl al-shiʿr*). Like al-Mubarrad, he writes that poetry and prose come in three categories—good, fair, and poor (*jayyida wa-mutawassiṭa wa-radīʾa*)—and that if neither is more graceful than the other, poetry is preferred because "all that which is rhymed is better than all that which is prose of the same kind, according to the recognized custom."[61] He further insists on the preeminence of poetry by noting that before the rise of writing, elders created poetry to carry on the memories of their past.[62] Then, citing sūra 36, he explains that those who criticize poetry note that according to the Quran the Prophet was not a poet. Like al-Jāḥiẓ, al-ʿAskarī, and ibn Ḥazm, ibn Rashīq manages to use the Quran's disparaging posture as a defense of poetry: he reasons that if the Prophet had studied poetry, others would have too, and if they had been successful as poets, they might have claimed prophethood. He adds that the language of the Quran must be inimitable, rather than poetic, to avoid having people think themselves capable of rivaling it.[63]

Ibn Rashīq also addresses the ability of poetry to express varying meanings to different recipients: a panegyric addressed to a king, for example, might attract the reader to the cleverness of the poem rather than to the greatness of the poem's subject.[64] The poem, in other words, reflects the prowess of the poet. Then he comments on the importance of poetry in Greek society in order to draw a comparison to Arab society: like the Greeks (*al-yūnānīyīn*), who used poetry to preserve information they feared they might otherwise lose over time, Arabs regard poetry as a point of pride for its ability to preserve history.[65] Next, he places poetry in context with music: musicians claim that the tune is the element of a song that produces sweetness; meter is the foundation of tune, and poetry is the foundation of meter, so poetry generates the sweetness found in music.[66]

With this theoretical background on Arabic composition in place, we can now turn toward Hebrew.

Compositional Propriety: Poetry versus Prose in Hebrew

Medieval Jewish literary critics (who also doubled as poets) adapted this theoretical paradigm to fit Hebrew writing, just as Jewish poets in tenth-century al-Andalus adopted the meters, forms, and tropes of Arabic poetry for use in secular Hebrew poetry. While at first some Jews worried that the use of Arabic quantitative meter and secular subjects in Hebrew poetry debased the biblical tongue, others reasoned that writing poetry in Hebrew—far from honoring the Arabic language—asserted the legitimacy of the biblical language.[67] The latter view prevailed, and soon quantitative meter constituted the standard mode of poetic composition. Poetry quickly became a prestigious endeavor, capturing the talents of the most educated and esteemed members of society. For instance, besides being the vizier of Granada, an unprecedented post for a Jew in al-Andalus, Samuel ha-Nagid (993–1055/56) was also one of the most celebrated poets of the period.[68] Jewish poets of al-Andalus and Christian Spain were exceedingly well versed in the Bible and philology, and all poets from al-Andalus and likely many from Christian Iberia were also educated in Arabic science and poetics.[69] It follows that these poets addressed the same set of topics (wine, love, etc.) as their Muslim counterparts, and many also composed devotional lyrics using the same techniques. During the twelfth century, some Jewish poets in Christian Iberia began to experiment with different subject matters and forms, perhaps because of their exposure to Romance-language poetic practices, a subject addressed in greater detail in the chapters that follow.[70]

Although poets and poetry were generally venerated in this period, some intellectuals began to question the status of secular poetry.[71] Moses ibn Ezra (c. 1055–after 1135) is an unlikely critic. In his Judeo-Arabic treatise on poetics, *Kitāb al-muḥāḍara wa-l-mudhākara* (The book of discussion and conversation), he proposes a number of negative points about poetry after reviewing the prevailing Arabic opinion on the matter: poetry—being more elegant, powerful, and fit to utilize rhetorical devices—is preferable to prose.[72] Ibn Ezra's misgivings about poetry are complicated: in the second chapter of his treatise, he defines poets as prophets and notes the poet's ability to improvise, but in the sixth chapter he turns this seemingly positive characterization (which is a profound negative in the Quran) into an unfavorable one when he portrays the poet as one who uses imagination to compose lies.[73] His comparison of poetry to prose is similarly ambivalent. He cycles through the frequent arguments for poetry's superiority: it is more elegant than prose and is "connected," unlike prose.[74] Ibn Ezra adds that while poetry more successfully preserves the feats of humans than prose because it is more easily memorized, it became less admirable when poets began to compose for a profit.[75] Prose was likewise composed for a profit, but perhaps its utility beyond entertainment justified compensation and further discredited the professional poet, who, given the notion of poetry as lying, would in essence be remunerated for spreading lies. Ross Brann explains this fraught connection among poetry, profit, and lying: "Despite their interconnection, prose and poetry were critically distinct categories. If this supposition is correct, it is further evidence that the poets' deceit was primarily at issue in their professional, rather than occasional verse."[76]

Still, ibn Ezra does take pride in the achievements of his fellow Jewish poets, even if he seems to object to their creations, a discrepancy that leads Raymond Scheindlin to remark on his "disparagement of poetry and admiration for the poets themselves and their poems."[77] Further, ibn Ezra does not entirely denounce poetic composition; as Scheindlin further notes, he dedicates the lengthy final chapter to poetic instruction and therefore "seems to be encouraging the practice of poetry," somewhat ironically, given his earlier claim.[78] In an additional twist, ibn Ezra justifies love poetry by noting that a poet may compose such poetry without having experienced love.[79] Regarding such ambivalence, Dan Pagis reasons that ibn Ezra and his fellow literary critics were "aware of discrepancies between theory and practice."[80] Indeed, as a prolific poet who composed both sacred and profane lyrics, ibn Ezra was a paragon of the practice.

Maimonides (Moses ben Maimon; 1135–1204) took a seemingly nuanced approach to poetry in theory, even if his opinions did not as readily support poetic composition in practice.[81] Like Plato, Maimonides objected to the deceptiveness of poetic language.[82] He did not condemn the form of poetry itself as much as its potentially objectionable contents: "speech is not forbidden, permitted, recommended, or reproved, nor is its utterance commanded, on the basis of its language, but on the basis of its content."[83]

Accordingly, he especially disapproved of poetry that addressed wine or love—incidentally, themes found in most secular medieval Hebrew poems—for its potential to arouse unseemly behavior: "And whoever has applied his thought or his speech to some of the stories concerning that sense which is a disgrace to us, so that he thought more about drink or copulation than is needful or recited songs about these matters, has made use of the benefit granted to him, applying and utilizing it to commit an act of disobedience with regard to Him who has granted the benefit and to transgress His orders."[84]

Beyond his concern with poetry's potentially subversive contents, Maimonides objected to its inappropriate uses of Hebrew, which not only risked demeaning the language but also tempted blasphemy: "For it is inappropriate to employ [Hebrew] in what is not excellent, especially if to this is added the use of a verse of the Torah or of the Song of Songs on the same subject, for then [the poem] leaves the category of the reprehensible to enter that of the forbidden and the prohibited, since the Holy Law itself forbids prophetic discourse from being applied to types of songs about vices and unworthy acts."[85]

While his approach to poetry is seemingly nuanced, his particular objection to the use of biblical phrases in Hebrew poetry severely curtails what he would have classified as appropriate. Still, Maimonides was invariably familiar with such poetry, which was conventional during his lifetime; readers and listeners were accustomed to the clever and consistent intercalating of biblical phrases throughout both secular and devotional lyrics. Accordingly, in the same passage in his Avot commentary, Maimonides refers specifically to the *muwashshaḥ*, a strophic genre of lyric endemic to al-Andalus, to claim that a muwashshaḥ in Hebrew recited at a wine party or a wedding was no better—and potentially even more sacrilegious than—its counterparts in Arabic if its language and contents were improper.[86] It is clear that he encountered many poems and did not shy away from quoting appropriate passages by poets who also composed licentious lyrics; indeed, as Norman Roth notes, in a letter he wrote, Maimonides included an excerpt from a poem by Judah Halevi, many of whose compositions embraced ribaldry and enjoyed extensive circulation.[87]

Thinkers in the thirteenth century took up Maimonides's disparagement of poetry, including Shem Tov ben Joseph ibn Falaquera (1223/28–after 1290), who, in his *Sefer ha-mevaqesh* (*The Book of the Seeker*), criticizes poetry in a more comprehensive fashion than Maimonides does.[88] In the debate between the Seeker and the Poet, ibn Falaquera does not avoid mentioning the purported merits of poetry; in fact, he grants the Poet the opportunity to enumerate all of its virtues and, as a result, adds rationale and credibility to his exhaustive rejection of verse. The remarkable aspect of ibn Falaquera's critique is in its form: in brazen contradiction, he uses the form of poetry to denounce poetry, claiming that poetry is full of lies and empty of all virtue:[89]

> To understand the secret of wisdom and knowledge, do not look to words of poetry;
> To become wise and to know, direct your path to holy knowledge.[90]

Though this contradiction is a difficult one to justify, it is not without precedent: when one of the first Hebrew court poets, Dunash ben Labrat (mid-tenth century), introduced Hebrew poems written in Arabic quantitative meter, his opponents voiced their complaints about his unwelcome novelty via Hebrew poems written in quantitative meter. Perhaps ibn Falaquera hoped to win over those readers who held poetry in high regard with poems whose lyrics might convince them otherwise. Ibn Falaquera expresses this same sentiment on repeat in rhymed prose throughout the Seeker's encounter with the Poet, from denouncing the poet whose "way is one of foolishness, not wisdom, / his poems formed from vanity and lying words and deception" to criticizing the poet's use of "metaphors and figurative language which are far from signifying the truth, rather than the customary terms that are observed by wise men."[91] Perhaps ibn Falaquera chose the mixed form and repetition to assist comprehension; in the introduction to the book, he informs the reader that he has relied on the mixture of poetry and prose because he believes it facilitates memorization. The contradiction vanishes in the second part of the text, in which ibn Falaquera abandons prosimetra for unrhymed prose without interspersed verse, as he describes in the introduction to the treatise: I have "divided it into two parts, arranging the first section in the poetic language of versifiers and tellers of parables and composing the second part according to the words of the truly wise by supporting it on pillars of prose based upon the maxims and parables of the sages."[92] The narrative follows this dictate at the conclusion of the Seeker's meeting with the Poet, at which point ibn Falaquera writes the following: "This concludes the first section of this treatise; these are my final poems. From this day on I have no share in poetry and no part in songs. It is time to seek God, for He will kindly teach me the proper way and guard me against transgressing with my tongue."[93]

Brann reads this formal trajectory as deliberate: "the structure of the book implies that poetry and the social manners that accompany it are a stage through which one (or at least the author) must necessarily pass on the high road to philosophy."[94] This certainly reflects the historical reality: in the Hebrew writing of Christian Iberia, prose—even when interlaced with metered poems—became increasingly popular and praiseworthy as poetry lost favor.[95] The shift from prosimetrum to unrhymed prose also signals ibn Falaquera's seeming interpretation of rhymed prose as its own compositional category, given how the formal shift in *Sefer ha-mevaqesh* echoes the contents' disavowal of verse. If true, this altered view of rhymed prose would reflect a profound break with earlier categorizing of rhymed prose as a kind of prose—a break that moves away from a focus on various literary formulations as tools of virtuosity toward the goal of writing that conveys meaning but that shares neither rhyme nor meter with poetry and is thus unsullied by an aura of deception.

Qalonymos ben Qalonymos (ben Meir ha-Nasi; 1286–after 1328), who was likely born in Arles in Provence and moved among Salonica, Rome, Naples, and Catalonia followed suit: *Even boḥan* (Examination of stone)—a text that contains no rhymed, metered poems from the outset—switches from rhymed prose to unrhymed prose halfway through. Jonathan Decter equates the treatise's formal shift with its transition from upbeat to decidedly serious contents: "It is possible that the author intuited that rhymed prose carried a lighter tone inappropriate for the subject matter of the second part."[96] Further, Qalonymos, a prolific writer who has no extant poems to his name, claims in *Even boḥan* that poetry lacks wisdom. Though he comes in the generation following ben El'azar, his theoretical progression toward a rejection of poetry is important to note, as his opinions further attest to ben El'azar's writing in a time of formal unrest.

What ibn Falaquera and Qalonymos merely implied about the reconstrued categorizing of rhymed prose as its own category, separate from rhymed, metered verse and unrhymed prose, Yeda'ya ha-Penini (ben Abraham Bedersi; 1280s–1340) parses more overtly in his *Sefer ha-pardes* (Book of the orchard). Although ha-Penini is likewise out of the chronological range of ben El'azar (though he is perfectly aligned with Immanuel of Rome), his comments on form are nevertheless relevant here since they illustrate the progression toward reconsidering formal categories. In the last chapters of the treatise, ha-Penini distinguishes among poetry, rhymed prose, and unrhymed prose. In his scheme, the author of rhymed, metered verse is compared to "a horseman riding his horse on a high, tapered mountain" while the author of unmetered rhymes is described as navigating a "wider path" even if "he needs to be deliberate like the nimbly running deer."[97] Ha-Penini's reconceptualizing of compositional forms does not necessarily amount to a negative view of verse. According to his scheme, the author of rhymed, metered verse perhaps has a more arduous, but not necessarily less virtuous, task. Despite this careful attention paid to varieties of prose, ha-Penini also praises poetry in *Sefer ha-pardes*, even as he acknowledges that it is full of lies, a trope by this point, even if the author truly means it. Indeed, his theorizing of literary forms is seemingly more focused on identifying merits and utilities without submitting a definite hierarchical judgment. In this way, ha-Penini's framework mirrors Geoffrey of Vinsauf's early thirteenth-century *Poetria nova* (discussed later), which does not rank the forms but rather finds particular benefits in each.

As this survey suggests, the preference for prose over verse followed similarly complex paths in Arabic and Hebrew, creating an environment that spawned ben Elʿazar's prosimetric personification of the debate. Still, his debate only appears the second story of the collection. If, as some scholars surmise, the ten stories are allegories, perhaps one should approach them as a whole, in which case poetry—and more specifically and crucially love poetry—eventually wins out as both the narrative and didactic star.

Ideal Compositional Forms in Latin and Romance

To more fully comprehend ben Elʿazar's literary position with respect to prose and poetry, I now turn to Latin and Romance language opinions on the matter, keeping in mind that classical Arabic, and subsequently medieval Hebrew, experienced their literary golden ages when vernacular Romance languages were just nascent and had produced relatively little literature. Further, unlike classical Arabic literary theory, which was developed to explain (and then prescribe) classical Arabic literary practices, Romance language compositions developed within the culture of classical and medieval Latin literary theory. Yet the language boundaries—and the sacred and profane—were often blurred. In this period before the Council of Trent recognized the Vulgate as the church's official translation of the Bible, translations of the Vulgate into Romance vernaculars proliferated.[98]

At the same time, Latin arts of prose and poetry appeared alongside Romance vernacular renditions, some of which circulated widely and survive today in hundreds of manuscripts.[99]

The following classical and medieval Latin treatises that circulated widely in the Middle Ages weigh the merits of prose and poetry in the context of Latin composition: the pseudo-Ciceronian *Rhetorica ad Herennium* (c. 86–82 BCE), Cicero's *De Oratore* (55 BCE), Horace's *Ars Poetica* (18 BCE), Matthew of Vendôme's *Ars versificatoria* (c. 1170), Geoffrey of Vinsauf's *Poetria nova* (c. 1210), and John of Garland's *De arte prosayca, metrica, et rithmica* (after 1229).[100] The key Romance texts that consider formal qualities include Ramon Vidal de Besalú early thirteenth-century Occitan *Razos de trobar* (*Rational Principles of Poetic Composition*) and Dante Alighieri's Latin *De Vulgari Eloquentia* (*On Vernacular Eloquence*; 1302–5), both of which treat Romance vernacular composition.[101]

The author of *Rhetorica ad Herennium* does not specifically address the relative merits of prose and verse, though he implies that prose is more suited to simpler compositional style, which does not necessarily indicate the worth of prose with respect to poetry. The author defines "three kinds of style" that preside over discourse: "the Grand," "the Middle," and "the Simple."[102] These styles dictate word choice rather than choice of form, even if these two categories may overlap. For instance, the author notes that "our discourse will belong to the Middle type if, as I have said above, we have somewhat relaxed our style, and yet have not descended to the most ordinary prose."[103] In *De Oratore*, Cicero notes that poets are "the next of kin to orators" and that "although it is a fault of oratory if the connection of the words produces verse, nevertheless we at the same time desire the word-order to resemble verse in having a rhythmical cadence, and to fit in neatly and be rounded off."[104] In his *Ars Poetica*, Horace praises prose over a technically well-formed poem that lacks feeling, and while acknowledging the noble intentions of poets, he warns against long-windedness.[105] Rather than dwelling on the status of poetry with respect to prose, these comments communicate the importance of excellent compositions, appropriate to the given context.

The eleventh century's "new system of rhetoric" technically encompassed both prose and poetry, but because both syllabic and rhythmic poetic systems were at work, compositional categories were separated into "the metrical," "the rhythmical," and "the prosaic," with additional groups consisting of rhymed prose and mixed-form compositions.[106] While the comparatively more clear-cut divisions between poetry and prose in the ancient Greek and classical Arabic worlds facilitated frequent debates on the relative merits of the two forms, these abundant categories in the medieval Latin tradition made it difficult to distinguish clearly between poetry and prose, which in turn made it a challenge to debate their characteristics with great precision.[107]

Geoffrey of Vinsauf exhibits the complicated relationship between prose and verse toward the end of his early thirteenth-century *Poetria nova*: "Lo, I have given you a comb, with which, if they be combed, your poems may gleam—as well those in prose as the metrical." This ambiguous characterization of forms seems to undercut earlier distinctions that the author made: "meter is straitened by laws, but prose wanders in a freer road"; "the delightful comeliness of meter knows no equal for sequence of such sweetness to the ear"; "the prosaic line is a grosser thing." More than dwelling on superiority of form, however, he seems to encourage the aspiring poet to choose rhetorical colors to fit the context, as this is what will make the composition succeed: "in either case words should be ruled thus."[108]

In his *De arte prosayca, metrica, et rithmica*, John of Garland introduces the topic as follows: the usefulness of the text "is that it imparts a technique for treating any subject whatever in prose, quantitative verse, or rhymed syllabic verse." He adds that "there are some who might cut the art of prose out of the book for its own sake . . . and thus the poor book would be torn up into rags. As it is, you must take all or nothing."[109] He is more intent on defining all possible categories of composition than on judging their respective merits. For instance, he offers a straightforward definition of prose—"pithy and elegant discourse, not in meter but divided by regular rhythms of *clausulae*"—just as he does for the other compositional forms.[110] Unlike the other critics, Matthew of Vendôme does not address the status of poetry in his *Ars versificatoria* but instead focuses all of his attention on poetic composition.

The earliest vernacular prose treatises on the arts of poetry do not address the relative merits of prose and poetry at all; rather, these treatises outline ideal poetic composition and do not acknowledge the reality that they are unprecedented works of prose, as Elizabeth Wilson Poe explains: "the vidas, razos, and Old Provencal manuals of poetic composition . . . operate by extracting words from their original musical context and reassembling them into unsung, unmetered prose."[111] The prose is clearly a vessel for conveying aims of poetic composition rather than a competing mode of literary expression. In his early thirteenth-century *Razos de trobar*, Ramon Vidal de Besalú does not address the topic of prose, nor does he incorporate any principles pertaining to prose into his discussion of how one should compose "un cantar o un romans."[112] In his prose treatise, he demonstrates steadfast approval of Occitan lyric without any mention of prose: "And all the good and evil things of the world are made memorable by the troubadours. And you won't find a well-expressed or badly expressed idea that, once a troubadour has set it to rhyme, will not be remembered forever. For composition and song are what move all exceptional bravery."[113]

Further, the *Razos* acts as a benchmark for the many subsequent Occitan arts of poetry, all of which copy Vidal's method of quotation, which, as Sarah Kay describes, has far-reaching ramifications: "buoyed up by the prestige and unencumbered by political or ecclesiastical baggage, literary Occitan offers the dream of a genuinely new, secular and lay, poetic subjectivity. Quotations from its poetry are like seeds from which a new, secular and lay poetry can grow."[114] Far from furnishing foundering poets and tongue-tied lovers with apt sayings, as was customary in the Arabic tradition, such quotations inspired fellow poets to compose new poems.

While slightly out of the chronological range for a discussion of *Sefer ha-meshalim*, Dante Alighieri's *De Vulgari Eloquentia* adds an important perspective on the nature of Romance languages and their lyric potential, one that in turn sheds light on ben El'azar's own lyric position. Even though Dante was well aware of the Occitan prose treatises, he chose to theorize suitable uses for various styles of vernacular composition in Latin in this treatise. As with all of its fellow treatises, the text's insertions of vernacular poems as textual evidence render it prosimetric. Scholars presume that he composed the unfinished treatise sometime between 1302 and 1305, a decade after he composed/compiled his vernacular prosimetric *Vita nuova* (*The New Life*; 1292–95).

Dante begins the *De Vulgari Eloquentia* by defining vernacular as "natural" and "nobler" than the "artificial" grammatical language that one learns through formal instruction. Particular to the relationship between Latin and Romance vernaculars, this delineation affects the way theorists conceive of the languages of prose and poetry. Free from the potential blasphemy dangerously present in Arabic and Hebrew poetry, Romance vernacular is a kind of embodiment of humanness, entirely unholy but not precisely blasphemous since it exists apart from the sacred. Indeed, Dante brilliantly highlights the special potential of the vernacular by enlisting the

Hebrew of the Bible as a frame of reference: Dante's underlying argument that Biblical Hebrew was the original language, plucked away by the audacity of those in Babel (Gen. 11.1–9), figures into his notion of the language of poetry as a purely human accomplishment.

In the *De Vulgari Eloquentia*, Dante explains the implicit hierarchy that exists in the vernacular—that poetry came first and is thus superior to prose:

> Once more I call upon the resources of my swift-moving intellect, take up once more the pen used in my fruitful labors, and first of all declare that the illustrious Italian vernacular may as fittingly be used for writing prose as for writing poetry. But, because writers of prose most often learn the vernacular from poets, and because what is set out in poetry serves as a model for those who write prose, and not the other way about—which would seem to confer a certain primacy—I shall first expound the principles according to which the illustrious vernacular is used for writing poetry, following the order of treatment laid down at the end of the first book.[115]

In contrast to the lack of consensus among Arabic and Hebrew treatises, which slightly favor prose, in the Romance context the conviction of poetry's superiority to prose is a given that eclipses the need to assess the role poetry plays when surrounded by prose. For instance, though the prose of Dante's *Vita nuova* has other ends—though all in some way in the service of poesy—one of its main functions, as stated in the prose of the text, is to explicate the interspersed poems. Perhaps this seemingly hardwired high regard for poetry in Romance languages explains both the relative paucity of medieval Romance prosimetra—and the lack of attention paid to the role of poetry within medieval Romance prosimetra.

Dante continues to discuss formal merits: dissatisfied with a mere preference for poetry over prose, he argues that poetry can be technically sound but lacking brilliance unless in the service of the best language and the best poet: "And so the best language is not suitable for all versifiers, since most of them write their verses without knowledge or intelligence; and, as a consequence, the best type of vernacular is not appropriate for them either. On this account, if the illustrious vernacular is not appropriate for all, then not everyone should use it, since no one should do anything that is inappropriate."[116]

Dante goes on to write—within a century of ben Elʿazar's *Sefer hameshalim*, and in a manner akin to Maimonides's notion of the aptness of contents, combined with ibn Ezra's insistence on the esteem due to the poet—that the subject of a poem is as important as its form and language: "So these three things, well-being, love, and virtue, appear to be those most important subjects that are to be treated in the loftiest style; or at least this is true of the themes most closely associated with them, prowess in arms, ardor in love, and control of one's own will."[117]

Though Dante claims that these examples illustrate arms, love, and integrity, four of the five incipits that follow his pronouncement on the best subject matter are in some way connected to love and courtliness. In fact, Dante allows that no poet had yet addressed the topic of arms in vernacular Italian.[118] While arms perhaps suggest a more tangible subject, love reaches even greater heights and possesses a greater potential for engaging philosophical and theological inquiries.

The reader should not be surprised to learn that love is the prized theme of vernacular poetry, which, in turn, is superior to prose: love allows poetry to reach its full potential. This symbiotic relationship is not unique to Romance vernacular verse; to the contrary, love bolsters poetry in compositions by Jewish authors of the period as well, in both their Hebrew and vernacular writings, even if it is noticeably absent in the Man of Poetry versus Man of Prose debate in ben Elʿazar's second maqama. Accordingly, the reader will see Immanuel of Rome's clever collapsing of Dante's ideal categories in the fourth chapter. Perhaps the absence of love reflects the negative outcome for poetry in ben Elʿazar's second maqama; perhaps a formal debate that lacks the compelling thematic core of love has a greater likelihood of failure, despite its dazzlingly metatextual appeal.

It seems too straightforward to limit ben Elʿazar's opinion of poetry to his deprecating portrayal of the Man of Poetry in the second maqama.[119] The maqama was, after all, intended as a work of fiction.[120] It would be highly unproductive to draw from *Sefer ha-meshalim* the author's opinions on any topic; if he felt so strongly about poetry, he might have composed a work with a more sustained critique, as did ibn Falaquera in *Sefer ha-mevaqesh* and Qalonymos in *Even boḥan*. The bullying Man of Poetry in ben Elʿazar's second maqama serves as a striking foil to the ethical vision of poetry propounded at other points in the text, particularly in the love stories. Yet perhaps both of these seemingly distinct categories illustrate poetry's potency: both the Man of Poetry and the poet-lover enlist poetry to achieve their aims, a use encouraged by tenth-century authors al-Washshāʾ and ibn Dāwūd, whose adab treatises are discussed in the next chapter.[121]

Given that the Man of Prose accuses the Man of Poetry of lying, it is clear that ben Elʿazar was attuned enough to the adage that poetry consists of lies and to disparagements of poetry in Arabic and Hebrew literary criticism to devote a personified enactment to the subject. But the fact that his critique of poetry is not sustained beyond this story suggests that ben Elʿazar looks toward nascent Romance literature, which decisively favors poetry over prose.

In the next chapter, I offer documentation of the historical plausibility of ben Elʿazar's encounters with Occitan and Galician-Portuguese troubadours. In his hybrid world, love and poetry fluctuated between representing idealizations of the truth and outright lies—tricky extremes that he does not hide from the reader, who may readily observe both the artful side of poetry in the second story and its endearing sincerity in the love stories. Further, in the prologue of *Sefer ha-meshalim*, ben Elʿazar discloses the text's fictionality and distinguishes between himself as author and as fictional narrator, amounting to strikingly candid and self-aware compositional insights. Indeed, fiction served as theoretical underpinning of both Arabic and Hebrew maqamas, even if the goal was mimetic.[122] After situating ben Elʿazar with respect to the highly contested world of courtly love, the next chapter examines how his love poetry negotiates a path among prose, poetry, and the fictional underpinnings of the collection.

Notes

1. "Ei-ze mehadevarim yikhshar / she-yedaber bo ish ve-ushar." Ben Elʿazar, *Sipure ahava shel Yaʿakov ben Elʿazar*, ed. David, 23, line 6.

2. "Uve-yodeaʿ sefer u-devarav be-mishqal meshir." Ben Elʿazar, *Sipure ahava shel Yaʿakov ben Elʿazar*, ed. David, 23, lines 16–17. *Meshir*, a participle of *lehashir*, an infrequently used *hifʿil* form, stands out and further draws attention to the ill repute of Poetry in this story. Many thanks to Miriam Meir for pointing this out to me.

3. The notion of prose as scattered comes from Arabic, in which prose, *nathr*, literally means "scattering," as in the scattering of pearls; verse, *naẓm*, literally means "ordered," in the context of the ordering of pearls on a necklace. Hammond, *Dictionary of Arabic Literary Terms and Devices.*

4. David, "Jacob ben Eleazar." Not much about ben Elʿazar's life is known. His works include a translation into Hebrew of ibn al-Muqaffaʿ's eighth-century Arabic rendering of *Kalila wa-Dimna*; *Kitāb al-kāmil* (The complete book), a grammatical treatise on the Hebrew language in Judeo-Arabic; and the following works in Hebrew: *Sefer pardes rimone ha-ḥokhma va-ʿarugot bosem ha-mezima* (Book of the orchard of pomegranates of wisdom and the flowerbed of wisdom), a prosimetric philosophical text; *Sefer gan ha-teʿudot va-ʿarugot*

ḥuqot ḥamudot (Book of the garden of wisdom and the flowerbed of precious statutes), a philosophical work in rhymed prose; liturgical poems; a translation of *Kalila wa-Dimna* from Arabic into Hebrew rhymed prose; and *Sefer ha-meshalim*. Matti Huss has outlined scholarly dating of *Sefer ha-meshalim*, which ranges from the mid-1100s to the mid-1200s: "Clarifications Regarding the Time and Date of Composition of *Sefer HaMeshalim*." On the basis of my analyses in the next chapter, I contend that ben Elʿazar was active in the latter part of this range. For ben Elʿazar's version of *Kalila wa Dimna*, see ben Elʿazar and Jacob, *Deux versions hébraïques du livre de Kalīlah et Dimnāh*. See Allony's edition for the text of *Kitāb al-kāmil*. For excerpts of *Sefer pardes*, see Davidson, "Sarid mi-sefer filosofi li-mḥaber bilti nodʿa."

5. For scholarship on the Arabic and Romance elements in *Sefer ha-meshalim*, see Schirmann, "Les Contes rimés de Jacob ben Eléazar de Tolède"; Schirmann, *Toledot ha-shira ha-ʿivrit bi-Sfarad ha-noṣrit uvi-drom Ṣarefat*, 224–40; Scheindlin, "Sipure ha-ahava shel Yaʿaqov ben Elʿazar"; Decter, *Iberian Jewish Literature*; Wacks, *Double Diaspora in Sephardic Literature*; and Levy and Torollo, "Romance Literature in Hebrew Language with an Arabic Twist." The first story of the collection is a love-themed allegory of the self, the second a debate on the relative merits of prose and poetry, and the fifth, sixth, seventh, and ninth love stories.

6. Alfonso X called on Jews, among others, as translators from Arabic to Castilian, Catalan, or Latin since they were multilingual. See Gerber, *Jews of Spain*, 99–100; and Halkin and Sáenz-Badillos, "Translation and Translators." This program had a Latin counterpart: a century prior to this, Toledo's Archbishop Raimundo (1126–52) had likewise enlisted Jews as translators of texts from Arabic to Latin. Gerber, *Jews of Spain*, 99.

7. *Maqāma* (pl. *maqāmāt*) is an Arabic word meaning roughly "assembly" or "session." For further background on the maqama, see Drory, "Maqāma." Jewish authors refer to their works as either *maqama* (Hebrew pl. *maqamot*) or the Hebrew equivalent *maḥberet* (pl. *maḥbarot*). I have decided to write the word as *maqama* and the plural as *maqamas* rather than distinguishing between the respective Arabic and Hebrew plural forms with varying diacritics. Pagis refers to Hebrew maqamas as "rhymed narrative" and recommends that when it comes to genre, "most rhymed narratives should be examined individually" to represent the diversity of such texts rather than to limit them to one particular genre. "Variety in Medieval Rhymed Narratives," 81, 83. While I agree wholly that the term *maqama* is a restrictive one, I am hesitant to adopt Pagis's alternative "rhymed narrative," as this fails to recognize the interspersing of poetry in such texts.

8. Brockelmann and Pellat, "Makāma."

9. Drory, "Maqāma," 191. *Adab* is the general category for any learned secular pursuit in Arabo-Islamic literature. The term *adab* originally designated good comportment, later indicated humanistic achievement, and subsequently narrowed to refer more specifically to belles-lettres. Gabrieli, "Adab." For more on the origins of the term, see Gabrieli, "Adab"; Bonebakker, "*Adab* and the Concept of *belles-lettres*," 21, 27.

10. Drory, "Maqāma," 192.

11. Drory, 193.

12. Drory, 196.

13. Hamilton, *Representing Others in Medieval Iberian Literature*, 50. For a discussion of the development of Hebrew prose writing in Christian Iberia, see Decter, *Iberian Jewish Literature*, 99–101.

14. For the text of *Ne'um Asher*, see Schirmann, *Ha-shira ha-ʿivrit bi-Sfarad uvi-Provans*, book 1, 2:556–67. For a translation to English, see Scheindlin, "Asher in the Harem," 253–67.

For the *Taḥkemoni*, see the edition by Yahalom and Katsumata; for a translation to English, see Reichert's literal rendering.

15. Mirsky et al., "Al-Ḥarizi, Judah Ben Solomon."

16. Drory, "Maqāma," 202. For instance, ibn Sahula's *Meshal ha-qadmoni* (Story of the ancient one) consists of five parts—on wisdom (*tevuna*), penitence (*teshuva*), sound counsel (*ʿeṣa nekhona*), humility (*ʿanava*) and reverence (*yirʾa*)—that enlist animal fables to debate each topic. Ibn Sahula, *Meshal ha-qadmoni.* English translations of the Hebrew words for section headings from *Meshal ha-qadmoni* are from Loewe's edition and translation of the text.

17. For further study of the attitude toward Hebrew in Hebrew maqamas, see Sadan, "Identity and Inimitability."

18. Plato, *Republic*, X 596; Aristotle, *Poetics*, chaps. 1, 2. For background on poetry, fiction, and lying, see Hollander, "Shadow of a Lie."

19. Tate, "Plato and 'Imitation,'" 161.

20. Eden, *Poetic and Legal Fiction in the Aristotelian Tradition*, 5.

21. Eden, 26.

22. For a discussion and bibliography of poetry as lying in the context of classical Arabic, see Harb, *Arabic Poetics*, 35.

23. Drory, *Models and Contacts*, 23.

24. Drory, 23–24.

25. For more on the first story, see Rosen, *Unveiling Eve*; Levy and Torollo, "Romance Literature in Hebrew Language with an Arabic Twist."

26. For instances of syllabic meter, see Fleischer, *Shirat ha-qodesh ha-ʿivrit*, 340–68. For an overview of Hebrew prosody, see Hrushovski-Harshav, "Prosody, Hebrew." To determine a regular pattern, David has refrained from counting the *sheva naʿ*s in his edition.

27. Ben Elʿazar, *Sipure ahava shel Yaʿakov ben Elʿazar*, ed. David, 24, lines 31–34.

28. "Va-ani le-khol shomʿam shirotai ʿarevot / ke-ʿeder ha-qeṣuvot / ve-hema shelemot u-temimot." Ben Elʿazar, *Sipure ahava shel Yaʿakov ben Elʿazar*, ed. David, 23, lines 26–27.

29. Medieval Latin (for the most part) and Romance verses follow rhythmic, and not quantitative, meter. For examples of rhythmic verses of alternating lengths in medieval Latin, see Norberg, *An Introduction to the Study of Medieval Latin Versification.* Ben Elʿazar might have been exposed to troubadour lyrics—a topic discussed in the second chapter—so it is possible that he was familiar with rhythmic versification and was trying to represent it here. This might explain why the text's editor decided to force a quantitative pattern (one that discounts the *sheva naʿ*s and comprises only long vowels) onto the verses, but it does not account for the fact that this is the only such aberration, most ironically placed. While many scholars believe that early Romance vernacular poets based their compositions on medieval Latin models, some propose that they were influenced by Arabic prosody. For a discussion of Arabic influences, see Menéndez Pidal, *Poesía árabe y poesía europea.* Ben Elʿazar's implementation of a Romance model that had been influenced by Arabic meter would not necessarily represent a return to familiar ground; rather, it would make for an even more complex situation than if he had borrowed from a Romance-via-Latin model.

30. Bavarian State Library, Munich, Cod. Hebr. 207, fol. 32v.

31. Heinrichs, "Prosimetrical Genres in Classical Arabic Literature," 249–75.

32. Heinrichs, 249. Leder and Kilpatrick reason that since "juxtaposing prose and poetry is one of the characteristic features" of classical Arabic writing, mixed-form texts may be labeled justifiably as "classical Arabic prose literature." "Classical Arabic Prose Literature," 2.

33. Giffen, *Theory of Profane Love among the Arabs*, xvii, 27, 57; Goldziher, *Short History of Classical Arabic Literature*, 85; and Bonebakker "*Adab* and the Concept of Belles-lettres," 27. Poetic citations can be useful for reception history—for instance, for determining which cited poems were used frequently in subsequent texts. Giffen, *Theory of Profane Love among the Arabs*, 27. This practice is particularly useful in establishing common traits among a group of texts and in tracing the disseminations and receptions of individual poets' compositions but has very little to do with the lyric aspect of these writings.

34. Nicholson, *Literary History of the Arabs*, 285.

35. Grunebaum, "Arabic Poetics," 37. See Harb, *Arabic Poetics*, 203–51.

36. Goldziher, *Short History of Classical Arabic Literature*, 27.

37. Quran 36.69, trans. Abdel Haleem, 284: "We have not taught the Prophet poetry, nor could he ever have been a poet." Quran 26.224–26, trans. Abdel Haleem, 238: "Only those who are lost in error follow the poets / Do you not see how they rove aimlessly in every valley; / how they say what they do not do?" ("wal-shuʿarāʾ yattabiʿuhumu al-ghāwūn / a-lam tarā anna-hum fī kull wādin yahīmūn / wa-anna-hum yaqūlūn mā lā yafʿalūn").

38. Sells, "Love," 130.

39. Kanazi, *Studies in the Kitāb aṣ-Ṣināʿatayn*, 136. Grunebaum notes that fifteenth-century al-Marrākushī delineates "stages of the composition of discourse," from simple to complex, as follows: words, prose, rhythmically arranged prose, sajʿ, poetry. "Aesthetic Foundation of Arabic Literature," 327. Still, this fifteenth-century rubric does not hold for the rhymed prose of the medieval period.

40. Fahd, Heinrichs, and Ben Abdesselem, "Sadjʿ."

41. Fahd, Heinrichs, and Ben Abdesselem.

42. Kamal Abu Deeb notes that "it is not a coincidence that many of the leading [literary] critics were at the same time steeped in *kalām* ['the art of argumentation and polemics over religious issues,' 347], theology and religious studies in general; some of them were even professional judges." "Literary Criticism," 349. *Literary criticism* is an imperfect term here, as a present-day understanding of the term does not match the classical Arabic notion, which is an amalgamation of literary theory, criticism, and poetics. Likewise, the literary critic is one who both interprets and judges poetry and compiles anthologies. Wen-chin Ouyang explains that the notion of literary criticism arose in the ninth century and provides an outline of the figures and ideas associated with this field. *Literary Critic in Medieval Arab Society*, 277–330. To define the term, she mentions the following figures and key points: al-Jāḥiẓ excludes grammar, philology, and prosody from *ʿilm al-shiʿr* ("the science of poetry," 279); ibn al-Muʿtazz (d. 908) distinguished between the poets and critics, on the one hand, and "scholars of language and ancient poetry" ("al-ʿulamāʾ bi-l-lugha wa-l-shiʿr al-qadīm," 279), on the other hand; al-Ṣūlī (d. 947) defines the critic as learned in poetry, prose, and the history of poetic themes and ideas (288); ibn Ṭabāṭabā (d. 934) characterizes the critic as one who possesses both natural talent (*ṭabʿ*) and a rigorous education that includes language, grammar, adab, history, and poetic history (290); and Qudāma (d. 922) developed "specialized technical terms" to define literary criticism (*naqd al-shiʿr*, 306). Later critics al-Marzubānī (d. 994) and ibn Rashīq (d. 1063/64 or 1070/71) gathered these ideas and provided them with "a consistent theoretical framework" (310).

43. Goldziher, *Short History of Classical Arabic Literature*, 81; Nicholson, *Literary History of the Arabs*, 71; Grunebaum, "Arabic Poetics," 38; Abu Deeb, "Literary Criticism," 350.

44. Hammond, *Dictionary of Arabic Literary Terms and Devices*.

45. Sanni, *Arabic Theory of Prosification and Versification*, 1–4.

46. Abu Deeb, "Literary Criticism," 343–46, 350. Grunebaum notes that prose narrative, the "prosimetric" maqama, and the shadow play received "little attention from the theoreticians." "Arabic Poetics," 43. He does not include the relationship between prose and poetry in his outline of the five areas of literary observation.

47. Kanazi has pointed out that ibn Rashīq seems to be the only scholar to come after al-ʿAskarī who favors poetry over prose. *Studies in the Kitāb aṣ-Ṣināʿatayn*, 125. In addition to the featured critics, for comments on the superiority of poetry to prose, see ʿAbd al-Karīm al-Nashalī's (d. 1014) *Ikhtiyār min kitāb al-mumtiʿ fī ʿilm al-shiʿr wa-ʿamalih* and ibn Ṭabāṭabā's (d. 934) *ʿIyār al-shiʿr*. For the favoring of prose, see Khafājī's (d. 1031/32 or 1073/74) *Sirr al-faṣāḥa*. In addition, ʿAbbas comments that al-Maʿarrī (d. 1058) hints at praise of poetry over prose in his *Rasāʾil*: *Tāʾrīkh al-naqd al-adabī ʿinda al-ʿArab*, 387.

48. al-Jāḥiẓ, *al-Bayān*, 243. For a translation of the passage, see Omri, "'There is a Jāḥiẓ for Every Age,'" 37.

49. "Fa-lā wajh li-taḥrīmihi wa-lā aṣl li-dhālik fī kitāb allah taʿālā wa-lā sunnat nabīhi ʿalayhi al-salām." al-Jāḥiẓ, *The Epistle on Singing-Girls of Jāḥiẓ*, [in English] 24, [in Arabic] 12.

50. For a thorough account of al-Mubarrad's life and works, see Sellheim, "al-Mubarrad, Abu 'l-ʿAbbās Muḥammad b. Yazīd b. ʿAbd al-Akbar al-Thumālī al-Azdī."; Grunebaum, "Al-Mubarrad's Epistle on Poetry and Prose," 372. Grunebaum's article contains his opening comments, followed by the text of the epistle in Arabic. Al-Jāḥiẓ hints at the debate between prose and poetry either slightly prior to or contemporaneously with al-Mubarrad.

51. "Iḥāṭat al-qawl bi'l-maʿnā wa-ikhtiyār al-kalām wa-ḥusn." al-Mubarrad, trans. in Grunebaum, "Al-Mubarrad's Epistle on Poetry and Prose," 372; for full Arabic text, see 374.

52. After giving his answer, al-Mubarrad compares the Prophet's rendering of ideas to others' poetic executions of the same ideas, deeming the Prophet's formulations superior. Grunebaum, "Al-Mubarrad's Epistle on Poetry and Prose," 377–78. Grunebaum notes that this is a "remarkable discussion," given that in it al-Mubarrad presents a notion of *iʿjāz* (the inimitability of the Quran) slightly before the development of this concept, which would become a crucial addition to Arabic literary criticism (373). The hinting at iʿjāz is also particularly interesting given the context in which it appears: al-Mubarrad's discussion of the Prophet's superior stylistic talents within the context of his comments on the superiority of poetry over prose creates a parallel between the prestige of the Prophet's words and that of poetry. While later critics use iʿjāz as a reason to denounce poetry, al-Mubarrad seems to expand the hierarchy he establishes in the beginning of the letter: the Prophet's expressions are superior to poetry, which in turn is superior to prose.

53. al-ʿAskarī adds to this point that panegyrics can affect the reputations of the poet and the poet's subject. *Ṣināʿatayn*, 143.

54. See Gilliot, "Shawāhid."

55. al-ʿAskarī, *Ṣināʿatayn*, 143–45. Kanazi provides a more detailed summary of all thirteen points: *Studies in the Kitāb aṣ-Ṣināʿatayn*, 124–25.

56. Arazi comments that al-Ṣābī's text is "plagié en partie par al-Marzūqī et mal interprété par certains théoriciens les plus représentatifs de la poétique arabe": "Une Épître d'Ibrāhīm b. Hilāl al-Ṣābī sur les genres littéraires," 475.

57. Arazi, "Une Épître d'Ibrāhīm b. Hilāl al-Ṣābī sur les genres littéraires," 477.

58. For the text of the letter, see Arazi, "Une Épître d'Ibrāhīm b. Hilāl al-Ṣābī sur les genres littéraires," 498–503.

59. He adds that kings before and after the advent of Islam considered oratory skill an excellent attribute in a leader, while they scorned the achievement of fame through poetry.

60. al-Marzūqī, *Sharḥ dīwān al-ḥamāsa*, 16–18. For a partial translation into English of al-Marzūqī's argument in favor of prose, see Grunebaum, "Arabic Poetics," 38–39.

61. "Li-anna kull manẓūm aḥsan min kull manthūr min jinsihi fī muʿtaraf al-ʿāda." Ibn Rashīq, *ʿUmda*, 73.

62. Ibn Rashīq, *ʿUmda*, 74.

63. Ibn Rashīq, 75.

64. Ibn Rashīq, 77–78.

65. Ibn Rashīq, 83–84.

66. Ibn Rashīq, 84.

67. Weiss et al., "Poetry," 265. Scheindlin, "Rabbi Moshe Ibn Ezra on the Legitimacy of Poetry," 105.

68. Habermann, "Samuel Ha-Nagid," 776.

69. Ben Elʿazar was certainly skilled in Arabic, having composed works in Arabic and having translated *Kalila wa-Dimna* from Arabic to Hebrew.

70. Weiss et al., "Poetry," 267.

71. For a discussion of opposition to poetry, see Brann, *Compunctious Poet*; Rosen, *Unveiling Eve*, 74–81; Tobi, *Between Hebrew and Arabic Poetry*, 389–482.

72. Ibn Ezra, *Kitāb al-muḥāḍara wa-l-mudhākara*, 1:28–29 (14v–15).

73. Ibn Ezra, 1:26 (13v); 1:130–31 (63v–64).

74. For the word *connected*, ibn Ezra inserted the Hebrew word *ḥaruzim* in his Judeo-Arabic text, further explaining that ḥaruzim was taken from the expression *ṣavarekh ba-ḥaruzim* ("your neck strung with pearls") from Song of Songs 1.10. Readers with a robust adab education would recognize *ḥaruzim* as the equivalent of *naẓm*, the Arabic term for verse, which refers to the stringing of pearls.

75. Ibn Ezra, *Kitāb al-muḥāḍara wa-l-mudhākara*, 1:28–29 (14v–15).

76. Brann, "'Dissembling Poet' in Medieval Hebrew Literature," 54n80.

77. Scheindlin, "Rabbi Moshe Ibn Ezra on the Legitimacy of Poetry," 112–13.

78. Scheindlin, 106.

79. Ibn Ezra, *Kitāb al-muḥāḍara wa-l-mudhākara*, 1:292 (143). For a reading on how ibn Ezra contradicts his own position on this matter, see Brann, *Compunctious Poet*, 78. For Brann's analysis of ibn Ezra's stance on poetry, see 59–83.

80. Pagis, "Trends in the Study of Medieval Hebrew Literature," 140.

81. For a thorough discussion of Maimonides's attitude toward poetry, see Sáenz-Badillos, "Maimonides y la poesía." See also Schirmann, "ha-Rambam ve-ha-shira ha-ʿivrit"; Norman Roth, "Maimonides on Hebrew Language and Poetry"; Kozodoy, "Reading Medieval Hebrew Love Poetry"; Monroe, "Maimonides on the Mozarabic Lyric." For an overview of poetry as a topic of study, see Schirmann, "Function of the Hebrew Poet in Medieval Spain," 237.

82. Maimonides, *Maimonides' Treatise on Logic* (*Maqāla fī sināʿat al-mantiq*), 48–49.

83. Maimonides, *Mishna ʿim perush*, Avot 1:16; trans. in Monroe, "Maimonides on the Mozarabic Lyric," 20.

84. Maimonides, *Guide of the Perplexed*, 2:435 (3.8).

85. Maimonides, *Mishna ʿim perush*, Avot 1:16; trans. in Monroe, "Maimonides on the Mozarabic Lyric," 20.

86. Maimonides, *Mishna ʿim perush*, Avot 1:16; trans. in Monroe, "Maimonides on the Mozarabic Lyric," 20.

87. Roth, "Maimonides on Hebrew Language and Poetry," 97.

88. For excerpts, see Schirmann, *Ha-shira ha-ʿivrit bi-Sfarad uvi-Provans*, book 2, 1:331–42. For discussions of the work, see Brann, *Compunctious Poet*, 124–36; Rosen, *Unveiling Eve*, 75–77; Tobi, *Between Hebrew and Arabic Poetry*, 467–82.

89. Brann, *Compunctious Poet*, 126, 135.

90. "Kale yemotekha be-ḥadesh sod / ḥokhma ve-daʿat—lo be-divre shir, / va-ʿmod lehithḥakem ve-ladaʿat / daʿat qedoshim darkekha tayshir." Ibn Falaquera, *Sefer ha-mevaqesh*, in Schirmann, *Ha-shira ha-ʿivrit bi-Sfarad uvi-Provans*, book 2, 1:336, lines 35–37.

91. "Ze darko kesel lo ve-ḥema / ve-shav ve-divre khazav be-shirotav u-mezima; lo yeshamshu veʿaleha ela va-shemot ha-mushʾalim veha-moʿtaqim / asher hem me-horot ʿal ha-emet reḥoqim, / ve-lo yeshameshu va-shemot ha-muskamim / asher yishmerem pi ḥakhamim." Ibn Falaquera, *Sefer ha-mevaqesh*, in Schirmann, *Ha-shira ha-ʿivrit bi-Sfarad uvi-Provans*, book 2, 1:336, lines 40–41; 337, lines 50–51.

92. "U-leyased binyaneha ʿal yesod ha-shirim, lemaʿan yaʿamdu ba-lev yamim rabim vi-yhiyu nizkarim, vi-ysadetiha ba-sapirim, u-gezartiha li-shnei gezarim, u-lesader devareha ha-rishonim mi-divre ha-meshorerim, ledaber bi-lshon ha-meliṣim veha-shoʿarim, va-ʾeʿerokh devareha ha-aḥaronim, mi-divre ḥakhme lev ha-neʾemanim, u-lehaṣim ʿamudeha asher hi nishʿenet ʿalehem, me-ḥidot ḥakhamim ve-mishlehem." Ibn Falaquera, *Sefer ha-mevaqesh*, 8 (Warsaw 1924); trans. in ibn Falaquera, *The Book of the Seeker*, 3.

93. "Ve-ʿad hena higiʿu divre ha-igeret ha-rishonim, ve-ele divre shir ha-aḥaronim, umeha-yom ha-ze ve-halʿa en li ḥeleq be-shirot, ve-lo naḥala bi-zmirot, ve-ʿet lidrosh et ha-shem ve-hu be-ḥasdo yoreni ha-derekh ha-yeshara umi-ḥet bi-lshoni yishmereni." Ibn Falaquera, *Sefer ha-mevaqesh*, 87 (Warsaw 1924); trans. in ibn Falaquera, *The Book of the Seeker*, 91.

94. Brann, *Compunctious Poet*, 135. For a reading of ibn Falaquera's *Sefer ha-mevakesh*, see Salvatierra Osorio, "Shem Tov ibn Falaquera: A Redefinition of Poetry," 171–72.

95. Decter, *Iberian Jewish Literature*, 100.

96. Decter, "Belles-Lettres," 804.

97. Bedersi, *Sefer ha-pardes*, 22; for additional contextualizing, see Decter, "Belles-Lettres," 804.

98. See Harris, "Occitan Translations of John XII and XIII–XVII."

99. See Kelly, *Arts of Poetry and Prose*.

100. Murphy reminds the modern reader that authors such as Vendôme and Vinsauf were instructors of the *ars grammatica*, not the *ars rhetorica*, and that grammar, besides including correct speaking and writing, also encompassed literary analysis. *Rhetoric in the Middle Ages*, 135–36.

101. Translation of the text's title is from Kay, *Parrots and Nightingales*, 3.

102. [Cicero], *Rhetorica ad Herennium*, 252–53.

103. [Cicero], 258–59.

104. Cicero, *De Oratore*, 22–23, 138–39.

105. Horace, *Satires, Epistles and Ars Poetica*. "Telephus et Peleus, cum pauper et exsul uterque / proicit ampullas et sesquipedalia verba, / si curat cor spectantis tetigisse querella." "So, too, in Tragedy Telephus and Peleus often grieve in the language of prose, when, in poverty and exile, either hero throws aside his bombast and Brobdingnagian words, should he want his lament to touch the spectator's heart." Horace, lines 96–98, trans. 459. "Aut prodesse volunt aut delectare poetae / aut simul et iucunda et idonea dicere vitae. / quidquid praecipies, esto brevis, ut cito dicta / percipiant animi dociles teneantque fideles: / omne supervacuum pleno de pectore manat." "Poets aim either to benefit, or to amuse, or to utter

words at once both pleasing and helpful to life. Whenever you instruct, be brief, so that what is quickly said the mind may readily grasp and faithfully hold: every word in excess flows away from the full mind." Horace, lines 333–37, trans. 479.

106. Curtius, *European Literature and the Latin Middle Ages*, 75, 148–49, 151; Murphy, *Rhetoric in the Middle Ages*, 157.

107. Curtius, *European Literature and the Latin Middle Ages*, 75, 149. Curtius points out that John of Garland delineates "three poetic styles and four 'modern' prose styles" in his *De arte prosayca, metrica, et rithmica* (151). In classical Arabic, rhymed prose is considered to be a kind of prose, not a form that falls between prose and poetry.

108. Geoffrey of Vinsauf, *Poetria nova*, 100–101, 103.

109. John of Garland, *"Parisiana Poetria" of John of Garland*, 3.

110. John of Garland, 5.

111. Poe, *From Poetry to Prose in Old Provençal*, 3.

112. Vidal, *"Razos de trobar" of Raimon Vidal*, 22.

113. Trans. in Kay, *Parrots and Nightingales*, 29. "Et tuit li mal e·l ben del mont son mes en remembransa per trobadors. Et ia non trobares mot [ben] ni mal dig, po[s] trobaires l'a mes en rima, qe tot iorns [non sia] en remembranza, qar trobars et chantars son movemenz de totas galliardias." Vidal, *"Razos de trobar" of Raimon Vidal*, B text, 27–31, 2.

114. Kay, *Parrots and Nightingales*, 10–11.

115. Alighieri, *De Vulgari Eloquentia*, II.i.1, 47.

116. Alighieri, II.i.8, 49.

117. Alighieri, II.i.7, 53. Boccaccio expresses a similar sentiment regarding the aptness of contents in his 1360 Latin *Genealogia deorum gentilium* [*On the Genealogy of the Gods of the Gentiles*]; for a discussion of his comments on the roles of the vernacular and love in poetic composition and on his equating of prose and poetry with respect to "hermeneutical potential," see Eisner, *Boccaccio and the Invention of Italian Literature*, 16–17.

118. Alighieri, *De Vulgari Eloquentia*, II.i.8, 53.

119. Yosef Tobi argues that this maqama represents ben Elʿazar's opinion of poetry. *Between Hebrew and Arabic Poetry*, 469, 479.

120. Drory, "Maqāma," 197; Huss, "Status of Fiction in the Hebrew Maqama."

121. Levy, "Hybridity through Poetry," 133.

122. Drory, "Maqāma," 197. As Drory explains, "of all Arabic modes of writing, the Andalusi maqamas were the closest to poetry, which likewise operated within a social context and played on the opposition between reality and fiction." "Maqāma," 197. She also notes that the Hebrew maqama functioned slightly differently than the Arabic maqama, because of the resistance of the Hebrew language to representations of reality, noting that Hebrew maqamas "seem to be more successful in constructing non-realistic fiction than in constructing reality." "Maqāma," 200, 205.

2

THE MEDIEVAL JEWISH PROSIMETRIC POET-LOVER

An Anxious Student of Ethics

Before, my friend, you enter the room
lift your eyes and read the writing on the curtain . . .
Choose brief sayings and sweet matter and then
your soul will attract your darling

—Jacob ben Elʿazar, *Sefer ha-meshalim*

To succeed in love, read poetry and write poetry. These are the instructions that Jacob ben Elʿazar offers the readers of his love stories. Similar instructions appear in love-centric prosimetra composed in other literary traditions of the medieval Mediterranean, ranging from ibn Ḥazm's *Ṭawq al-hamāma* (*The Ring of the Dove*) to Dante's *Vita nuova* (*The New Life*). Even more revealing of the special connection between poetics and love is that ben Elʿazar chose to make this key statement in rhymed, metered verse rather than in rhymed prose, despite the preference for prose over poetry in formal writing in medieval Hebrew compositions of this period and despite the otherwise equivalent space given to prose and poetry in his prosimetrum. To interpret the epigram that he presents is complex enough, let alone to pinpoint the idea of love from which he draws his inspiration. The two verses deftly traverse Arabic and Romance literary customs and notions of love, combining poetic techniques and theories of love from a range of traditions: from the spoken (Romance vernacular) to the unspoken (secular medieval Hebrew), from quantitative meter (Arabic via Hebrew) to syllabic meter (Romance), and across cultural and theological borders.[1]

Jonathan Decter and David Wacks have both written in excellent detail about connections between Romance courtliness and ben Elʿazar's love stories, Decter with a focus on the Romance implications of the protagonists' "internal transformation" and Wacks on the story of Sahar and Kima as "a case of courtly ideals refracted through a diasporic experience, where courtly heroics are framed in terms of excellence with the pen, as opposed to the sword."[2] As I show in this chapter, it is ben Elʿazar's use of poetics (whether in prose or verse) to enact Romance courtliness that most distinctly characterizes and facilitates his embracing of a Romance approach to love and proper living. His writing exhibits a range of approaches to secular love, pairing love with education and etiquette and with ethics and the transcendent, pairings that I argue ultimately reflect on love's inextricable connection with the poetic itself, whether rendered in lyric or in prose: love draws attention to the use of verse and to the idea of poetry. To arrive at a deeper understanding of ben Elʿazar's notion of love, this chapter gauges how the author grapples with poetic formulations of love with respect to lyric and philosophical underpinnings of Arabic, Hebrew, and Romance prosimetra.

After contending with the first story, an opaque Neoplatonic disquisition on love, the reader encounters the testing of poetry's ability to save love and goodness in the sixth story, followed by the refining of poesy's potential to ennoble love in the seventh.[3] Finally, the reader reaps the great reward of the poetic process in the ninth story (perhaps not coincidentally nestled between two bleak stories having nothing to do with love): a mini-treatise on the poetics of courtly love in which both the form and contents of the story are an homage to love poetry as a guide to ethical living. Sahar survives a rough storm at sea and, as an outsider, courts Kima, the town's princess.[4] The story contains thirty-four poems: Sahar and Kima each recite fifteen, the king relates one, and Kima's handmaidens present three anonymous poems to Sahar. Kima lures Sahar with her compositions and uses poetry to instruct Sahar on how to be a virtuous lover, and Sahar, an eager student, offers his beloved poems that show his developing understanding of love.[5] Kima's father dies after giving the couple his blessing, leaving Sahar to rule as king and to continue the game of love with Kima. Love poetry, which is central to their game of love, not only serves as the story's thematic focus but also propels its plot.

Though formulations of love vary across traditions, the special bond between poetry and love is a constant in tenth- and eleventh-century al-Andalus and twelfth-, thirteenth-, and fourteenth-century Spain, Italy, and France. Why did authors across traditions single out verse as the form particularly suited to love, and why, in turn, did they figure love as especially at home in a lyric context? Across literary traditions, the poet-lover was a fixed model, acting within particular constraints depending on the given tradition. Such superficial commonalities perhaps explain why scholars across language boundaries have seized on the term "courtly love," problematic for more than mere anachronism.

Coined as "amour courtois" by Gaston Paris in the late nineteenth century to describe love in Chrétien de Troyes's late twelfth-century *le Chevalier de la charrette*, courtly love was quickly associated with the love in Occitan troubadour lyrics, and it just as quickly became controversial, particularly with regard to its heavily debated origins.[6] Opinions of twentieth-century scholars encompass a vast range: some find origins in classical Arabic; others look to Ovid; some cite the feudal society of Languedoc; others turn to cults; and still others invoke Christian teachings.[7] Some scholars object to the imposing of modern theory on medieval praxis, while others assert that such a notion was certainly in play in a variety of medieval settings, if not in the form of that specific phrase.[8] Still others, including scholars of both Romance languages and classical Arabic, prefer not to limit courtly love to historical and geographical constraints: Peter Dronke asserts that "the feelings and conceptions of *amour courtois* are universally possible, possible in any time or place and on any level of society." As an alternative to *courtly love*, Dronke proposes the term "the courtly experience," which is defined as "the sensibility that gives birth to poetry that is *courtois*" and may apply to poetry that is "either popular or courtly."[9] This distinction is applicable and important here, since Jewish authors in Christian Iberia were not necessarily employed by courts and since the addressing of the perceived hierarchical dichotomy between cultured and popular lyric is long overdue. Jean Claude Vadet similarly claims that "l'esprit courtois" is not bound to a particular genre, event, or philosophical leaning.[10] Rather than taking a position in the debate of origins, I instead explore the range of medieval theories of love in Occitan, Galician-Portuguese, Arabic, and Hebrew lyrics to map out how ben Elʿazar's poetics of ethical loving fits into this range of definitions.

Classical Arabic and Medieval Hebrew: Courtly Love Classics?

I begin with classical Arabic poetry (and its Hebrew iterations) for the sake of thorough comparison, though the very affiliation of Arabic with a notion of courtly love risks anachronism, because its love poetry flourished centuries before Romance lyric came into being and equally because Gaston Paris did not consider Arabic lyric when theorizing *amour courtois*. Still, scholars of classical Arabic literature sometimes invoke the terms *spiritual love* and *courtly love* with reference to classical Arabic lyrics that posit a spiritualized notion of love.[11] *Ghazal*, the general term for love poetry, can be dated to the last quarter of the sixth century. Sometime in the seventh century, poets began to incorporate into amatory verse elements of "ʿ*Udhrī* love or the courtly spirit," a term named after the Banū ʿUdhra, a nomadic pre-Islamic people known for their "passionate love and tender-heartedness."[12] The early ʿAbbāsid poets perhaps used the term more as a convenient vessel for their own courtly sentiment than as a genuine attribution to the Banū ʿUdhra: for these poets—who created such figures as love-crazed Majnūn—"love was imbued with a 'courtly' flavor and projected back into an idealized Bedouin past." Indeed, under the guise of the ʿUdhra affiliation, their poetry reflected "intellectual trends of later periods."[13]

Some of the poems that stemmed from this tradition, such as the following by al-ʿAbbās ibn al-Aḥnaf (c. 750–c. 808), express a kind of courtliness comparable to Romance courtly love, in which the beloved must remain distant and unattainable:[14]

> My princess, stingy with her letters, spends
> a lot on spurning me, hiding from sight.
> Thus is my soul submerged in passion's pangs;
> my eyes shed streams of tears incessantly.
> For how much longer will her anger last?
> I've melted from her anger and reproach.
> She seizes someone's heart, all of it; then
> she turns away, leaving him mindless, mad.
> So much have I endured from Love: woe Love!
> If Love had hands, it would cast out my soul.[15]

The tangibles in this poem—the unsatisfactory epistles of the beloved, the tears of the poet and personified Love—produce, rather than attainment of love, an utter absence that renders the poet-lover insane and chaste. Personified Love, which has complete control of the poet, is akin to a deity, a paradigm that appears regularly in both classical Arabic and Romance vernacular poetry that seeks spiritual fulfillment through love, such as Dante's *Vita nuova*. The beloved's identity as princess (*ʾamīratī*) situates the poem within a courtly milieu, whether al-ʿAbbās was depicting the ideal beloved or whether, as some scholars have supposed, he wrote his lyrics for Princess

ʿAyla.[16] It is just as likely that the poet was illustrating what Ross Brann terms "the ideal and objectified female" while warning the modern reader "not to be misled by the figure of a woman seemingly so empowered as to hold the poet's life in the balance."[17]

Hebrew poetry adopted and adapted Arabic poetry's treatment of the painful experience of love for use in secular lyrics, as in the following poem by Solomon ibn Gabirol (c. 1021–c. 1057):

> He watches me, his eyelids like an invalid's
> The goblet with the likeness of his cheek is filled;
> Behind his lips, his teeth are pearl on pearl;
> He smiles with a mouth more precious far than gold,
> His every tooth a word that murders me,
> Like a pitiless creditor dunning a penniless wretch.
> The goblet goes round like the sun in the sky;
> The day is departing: so friends disappear.
> My blood is raining all over me, rushing
> Down my cheek, to go up no more.[18]

Similar to al-ʿAbbās's poem, ibn Gabirol figures this beloved as the cause of the poet's pain and potentially his death. Though the poet bemoans the beloved's unattainability—which could lead the poet toward a kind of spiritual love—the tropes that ibn Gabirol employs place the poem more directly in the classical Arabic context, in which the poet-lover does not necessarily transcend to a spiritual level. The pearly teeth are a reference to naẓm (the Arabic term for verse), and the inflicting of physical pain by wine and love, each endemic to the Arabic tradition, points to an immediacy (albeit understood in the poet-lover's painful hindsight) that accentuates the humanness and worldliness of this poem. Ibn Gabirol's poem, however, does not exist in a vacuum. As the author of philosophical treatises that grapple with matter and form, the most cross-culturally influential of which is considered "almost pure Neoplatonic metaphysics," ibn Gabirol perhaps chose the tangible human and natural elements as a foil to the inexplicable, ineffable nature of love.[19]

Equally rich and complex, these two poems have nonetheless presented different portraits of the ideal beloved, and a moment to contextualize their gender formulae will add nuance to our overall understanding of how medieval Hebrew poetics engaged love. For the most part, classical Arabic poetry, and medieval Hebrew poetry, which followed suit in many ways, figured the beloved as a youthful male, and in this respect al-ʿAbbās's poem was more of an outlier than ibn Gabirol's.[20] While earlier scholarship tended to ignore or censor the paradigmatic youthful maleness of the beloved, modern scholarly debates vary in approach. Some insist that the Arabic pattern emulated the ancient Greek ideal in theory but not in practice, an explanation that conveniently maintains the propriety of women; indeed, the term *tashbīb* refers to the prohibition against addressing the other sex in verse. Further, this explanation downplays the carnal aspect by focusing on Plato's model in *Symposium*, in which male relationships were figured as an ideal path toward intellectual and spiritual enlightenment.[21] Others are more realistic: Jefim Schirmann's 1955 article, which granted that the male beloved was a literary convention that might have had some basis in reality, as poetic conventions often do, was, as Jonathan Decter notes, a critical moment.[22] As one must recalibrate one's notion of what literary criticism was in the Middle Ages or parse what exactly courtly love meant to medievals across traditions, readers must likewise contextualize poetic gendering to fully appreciate the complexity of medieval Jewish authors' literary creations.[23] Indeed, though the first and ninth stories of *Sefer ha-meshalim* mirror the heterosexual convention of Romance courtly love, the collection as a whole highlights a far more variegated range of loves—from the story of Sapir, Shapir, and Birsha to the story of Yashefe, Yefefiya, and Yemima.[24]

And the complexity continues: both Arabic and Hebrew love poetry developed devotional lyrics that invoke these same courtly themes—such as wine parties and the pain of love—a natural growth given the "concurrent development of the 'courtly' and mystical tendencies."[25] Within these lyrics seemingly grounded in human pursuits, mystic poets, such as female Sufi and saint Rābiʿa al-ʿAdawiyya al-Qaysīya (714 or 718–801), explored the comprehension of the divine, mystical union, and love's destruction of the soul:[26]

> My cup, my wine and the companion make three,
> And I, who long for the Beloved, am Rabiʿa, the fourth.
> The cup of joy and felicity is passed round,
> Again and again by the bearer of the wine.
> If I look, I am seen only *by* Him,
> And if I am present, I am seen only *with* Him.
> Oh, you who rebuke me—I love His beauty!
> By God, my ear does not heed your reproach!
> How many nights, burning with the ardor of my affection,
> Have fountainheads streamed from my weeping eyes?
> My tears do not dry, nor does my union with Him
> Endure, nor can my swollen eyes rest peacefully.[27]

Rābiʿa dwells on the physical and emotional experience of love, figuring this intoxicating moment to be a stepping-stone to mystical union. The stylistic and thematic correspondences to the profane lyrics are unmistakable, from the flames of love to the poet's unceasing tears. Only the poet's object of affection has been altered, conveying meaning of an entirely different nature.

In the following devotional poem composed in Hebrew, Judah Halevi (1057–1141) similarly presents the person seeking spiritual fulfillment as an unrequited lover wracked with pain, in this case positioning the lover and beloved as God and Israel, respectively:[28]

> Far-flown dove wandered to a wood,
> Stumbled there and lay lame,
> Flitted, flailed, and flustered
> Storming, circling round her love's head.
> A thousand years she thought would bring her time,
> But all her calculations failed.
> Her lover hurt her heart by leaving her
> For years; she might have died.
> She swore she'd never say his name again,
> But in her heart it burned like fire.
> Why so hostile to her?
> Her mouth is open always to your rain.
> She keeps her faith, does not despair,
> Whether in your name her lot is pain or fame.
> Let God come now, and not come quietly,
> But round him raging storms and wild flame.[29]

Just as Rābiʿa borrows the tropes of love lyric in her mystical poem, Halevi likewise draws on the same themes used in his secular love lyrics composed concurrently with this devotional poem, from the heart's burning to the lover's parched throat.

The profane love lyrics in Arabic and Hebrew (though perhaps not the mystical lyrics) satisfied a didactic need: the composition of and copying/anthologizing of such poems served the practical purpose of rounding out a thorough adab curriculum that any individual of means would have pursued.[30] Rather than, or perhaps in addition to, providing a means to reach physical or spiritual contentment, or even metaphysical understanding, these poems presented the reader with an opportunity to hone a technical skill. Accordingly, in his *Kitab al-zahra* (*The Book of the Flower*), ibn Dāwūd al-Ẓāhirī (d. 909) provides ample poetic depictions of lovers and beloveds as a useful rubric for aspiring lovers. Though ibn Dāwūd carried on the work of his father, founder of the Ẓāhirī school in Baghdad, he is best known for the *Zahra*, purportedly one of the earliest works to expound "courtly love."[31] Though many deem the *Zahra* an anthology, three elements reveal the ways in which the text develops and supports ibn Dāwūd's argument: the inclusion of prose chapter introductions that both hint at the main themes of his forthcoming argument and situate the poetic passages; the careful choice and ordering of verses, which indicate the path of his reasoning; and prose passages without interspersed verses.[32]

An examination of this first chapter of the *Zahra*—which is exceptional in that it contains more prose than the other chapters—explains ibn Dāwūd's approach to love lyric and defines what might be termed courtliness. He opens with a proverb that incorporates the words *ʿishq* (love, in the sense of passion) and *laḥẓa* (glance): "How many wars have been perpetrated because of one word, and how many a love has been planted by a glance."[33] In this opening, he does not indicate the importance of these words to the theme of the chapter, nor does he make clear the link between the two terms. Such explanations come forth in the verse passages that follow. The first three sets of verses introduce the following key terms: *qalb* (heart; poem 1, verse 1), *ḥubb* (love; poem 2, verse 1), *fuʾād* (heart; poem 2, verse 2), *dhikr* (memory; poem 2, verse 3), *hawā* (passion; poem 2, verse 4), *ʿayn* (eye; poem 3, verse 3), and *nafs* (soul; poem 3, verse 3).[34] In their verse contexts, these terms work to clarify the proverb's reference to passion and sight. The first set of verses presents the notion that the lover's very sight of the beloved immediately exerts power on his heart, and the second set spells out the distinction between love (*ḥubb*) and passion (*hawā*). The third set uses Aristotle's notion of the eyes as gateway to the soul to fuse the terms with concepts presented in the first two: passion-infused arrows shot forth from the beloved's eyes ensnare the lover, and not entirely uninvited, as the soul naturally seeks passion (*hawā*). The war imagery in these verses recalls the opening of the chapter and creates an association between the two components of the proverb: passion, the verses suggest, like war, may prove fatal.

Some poems that appear later in the chapter draw on the same key vocabulary as in earlier verses but move away from the trope of passion as the cause of pain. The tenth poem, for instance, without any connotation of peril, refers to the beloved's glancing (*naẓar*) at and salutation of the lover, while the eleventh contains the chapter's first mention of passion (*hawā*) as the cause of illness (*maraḍ*). The thirteenth echoes the sweetness of the tenth, depicting the tender parting of lovers, while the fourteenth returns to a meditation on passion as a sickness that culminates in death.[35] These poems oscillate in tone and serve as a perfect complement to the madness to which the author refers at the end of the chapter when he paraphrases Galen's pronouncement on the ailment of love: on seeing the beloved, the lover may die of either joy or sorrow.[36] In addition to relying on Galen (129 CE–c. 202 or c. 216 CE) in this chapter, ibn Dāwūd also refers to Plato, interspersing verse passages with paraphrases of two passages in Plato's *Symposium*, both of which address the union of souls.[37] Indeed, alongside his references to Greek philosophical opinions on love, repetition of poetic vocabulary works to create meaning, adding to the sensation of ibn Dāwūd's codifying of love poetry: these particular poems form a kind of rulebook that consolidates a definition of the ideal love, with its blend of dangers and delights.

The role of the Greek philosophical tradition deserves brief contextual mention here. No complete translation seems to have existed of the *Symposium* into Arabic from the original Greek, although fragments were preserved in Ḥunayn b. Isḥaq's collection of sayings, as were ideas on love from the *Phaedrus*, which ibn Ḥazm likewise incorporated into the *Ṭawq al-hamāma*, soon discussed in greater detail.[38] References here to Platonic views on love—which in medieval Arabic thought was considered a topic in both philosophy and medicine—have little to do with any consideration of the idea of poetry, as Arabic thinkers were unlikely to have linked love to the realm of literary criticism.[39] While there is certainly a link between philosophical considerations of love and love poetry (*ghazal*), this does not imply that poetry was contemplated as a topic in philosophy as was love. In this way, the classical Arabic poet functioned on two planes: that of the theorist on profane love, who would naturally turn to Greek concepts, and that of the literary theorist inquiring into the idea of poetry.

When assessing Aristotle in the context of medieval Islam, the modern reader must keep in mind that Arabic philosophers considered both *Rhetoric* and *Poetics* to be a part of the *Organon*: they were taken as components of the philosophy of logic and were not considered from the point of view of literary criticism.[40] Furthermore, Arabic literary critics were not interested in Greek poetry itself but rather in the fact that the Greeks had a poetic tradition. In the *ʿUmda*, ibn Rashīq creates a parallel between Greek and Arab cultures: he explains that Greeks used poetry to preserve information that might otherwise be lost and notes that Arabs should likewise consider their poetry a point of pride for its ability to preserve history. This comment does not in any way touch on Greek philosophy or poetry; it is simply an analogy that illustrates ibn Rashīq's broad admiration for Greek culture.

In his *Kitāb al-hayawān*, al-Jāḥiẓ makes the clearest statement about Arabic poetry and its relation to that of other peoples: "Excellence with regard to the art of poetry is limited to the Arabs and those who speak the Arabic language. Poetry cannot be translated and does not render itself to transmission. And whenever it is converted into another language its concinnity (*naẓm*) is broken, its meter is rendered defunct, its beauty evaporates, and that something that inspires wonder and admiration simply absents itself."[41]

Thus, while ibn Dāwūd might seem to be harmonizing poetics, love, and philosophy, he is instead using specific standard concepts; in turn, his compiling and ordering of poetic excerpts that draw on these fixed concepts constitute his vision of love poetry.

Ibn al-Washshāʾ (Abu ʾl-Ṭayyib Muḥammad b. Aḥmad b. Isḥāq al-Aʿrābī; c. 869–937), a grammarian, rhetorician, and lexicographer from Baghdad who was personally acquainted with ibn Dāwūd, was similarly devoted to commending the greatness and utility of Arabic poetics. He demonstrates a kindred approach to poetics and love in his tenth-century *Kitāb al-muwashshā* (The book of ornamentation): though the treatise aims to instruct readers on how to achieve *ẓarf* (elegance or refinement), al-Washshāʾ devotes a sizeable portion to love, its symptoms, and the rules by which it operates, since love is the essential quality of the elegant, well-educated person.[42] This structure has led scholars to term it "a code based upon civilized and chivalrous love" that constitutes a wistful recollection of *ʿudhrī* love.[43] Still, al-Washshāʾ's focus is seemingly didactic, especially in its final twenty chapters, which provide the reader aspiring to elegance with apt verse excerpts to confer on a beloved in a variety of situations. In fact, al-Washshāʾ's reader need not be a seasoned, or even promising, poet to be an ideal lover; rather, and in a manner perhaps opposed to a chivalrous vision of love, he must know how to select and employ poetry successfully.

Al-Washshāʾ also uses the prose portions of the chapter to develop and express his idea of love poetry: he lists famous figures who have been afflicted by love, and among these figures, he highlights poets as a special group. He first mentions that countless poets have been passionately in love

(*ʿishq*) and then offers a roster of figures famous for their "passion and love poetry."[44] Near the end of the passage, he provides another list, this one specifically dedicated to "Arab poets" famous for their "passion and love poetry."[45] Later in the chapter he again reflects on poetry in the context of prose, this time via a gloss of verses that he has just cited: he follows verses about Majnūn's experience in love with a brief explication and praise of their contents, commending in particular the poet's use of description. In this rare gloss, the author reveals his concern with the quality of the poetry he includes in the text; for him, poems serve not only to highlight the narrative role of poetry alongside the prose but also to measure its aesthetic virtue: the more beautiful and artistically sound the verses, the more successfully they will convey the poet's refinement in matters of love. This notion will become more apparent in the last twenty chapters of the treatise, not through the author's explanations but rather through his very choice of verses.[46]

Despite this disconnect between lover and poetry, the verses that al-Washshāʾ chose and incorporated into his treatise seem to expound a courtly message. In the chapter "The practices of elegance" (*Sunan al-ẓarf*), he cites passages from eighty-seven poems, all of which are devoted to the theme of love, except for the first two citations—versifications of definitions of *ẓarf* that the author provides in the opening prose. The three subsequent poems present an exchange between a young woman and a young man that allows the author to develop his discussion of the link between ẓarf and love: the woman complains that the man's glance will cause her demise (poem 3); the man blames the action of his eyes on her gaze and on her elegant poetry (poem 4); and the woman responds that she would like for him to embrace one gazelle (*ẓaby*, i.e., beloved) rather than to continue trifling with multiple offers (poem 5).[47] Though these three verse passages encapsulate the definitions of ẓarf offered thus far, they add an additional taste of a sort of courtly love: in the exchange, the female speaker attempts to teach her male interlocutor how to be a good lover by encouraging him to be eloquent and chaste. Without introducing any of the many terms for love and passion, al-Washshāʾ establishes proper courtship practice as the key to the courtier's attainment of ẓarf; he uses poetry not only as the medium of the didactic exchange—that which makes the expression of elegance possible—but also as one of the players. When the young man refers to the young woman's "elegant poetry" (*al-shiʿr al-ẓarīf*), he links poetry and ẓarf within the context of a lover's exchange.[48]

In a further espousal of a variety of lovers' code, al-Washshā' focuses on chastity (*ʿiffa*), a term that in ethical literature links the balance in the tripartite soul to moderation in one's behavior. (Chastity—in addition to signaling an overarching ethical construct—will likewise play a crucial role in Romance vernacular love lyrics.) To highlight the importance of chastity in love, al-Washshā' completes a group of verse citations (poems eight through fourteen) with a poem whose definition of love (*ḥubb*) applauds chastity (*ʿiffa*).[49] In the chapter's opening, al-Washshā' defines courtly behavior as man's possessing knowledge and culture (*adab*), and in the prose leading up to the eighteenth poem, he defines it as "being dressed in dignity or staidness."[50] The lyrics that follow reaffirm that "love is among the traits of those with noble characters," even as he admits that many such men have firsthand experience of passion (*hawā*).[51] For al-Washshā', poetry is the means to courtliness: the nobleman must be in love and must employ suitable poetry in order to achieve complete elegance.

Polymath ibn Ḥazm of Córdoba (994–1064) carries on the tradition of merging the rules of love and poetry in his Arabo-Andalusian treatise on love, *Ṭawq al-hamāma* (1022). Like al-Washshā' and ibn Dāwūd—whose *Kitāb al-zahra* he mentions in the prologue of the *Ṭawq*—ibn Ḥazm uses verses to instruct the aspiring lover on ways to employ poetry to achieve his amorous goals.[52] Still, the *Ṭawq*, a text riddled with anecdotes, autobiographical details, and lyrics primarily of the author's own composition, devotes less attention to laws of love than to laws of poetry, albeit poetry expertly exemplified by the causes and effects of love. In a manner akin to Dante's approach to love poetics in the *Vita nuova*, in the *Ṭawq* love becomes the subject matter through which ibn Ḥazm explores the creation of lyric rather than the principal objective of the narrative. Because of this blurred distinction between art of poetry and art of love, the *Ṭawq* provides a useful rubric with respect to ben Elʿazar's professing a code of love poetics.[53] One of the best places to ascertain ibn Ḥazm's advice to the poet-lover is in "The Signs of Love," the first chapter following the introduction to the treatise, in which ibn Ḥazm describes mannerisms that an observer can use as evidence that the observed is in love.[54] Beyond constituting a mere list, however, these signs provide the author with a medium to illustrate different styles of poetic composition, analogous to the kind of instruction that ben Elʿazar provides to the aspiring poet-lover. In the first four segments of prose and poetry, ibn Ḥazm shows how to transform a prose description of a sign of love into a poem that illustrates the sign, enlisting the didactic technique of naẓm al-ḥall (the versification of prose). He begins by describing how lovers frequently gaze at one another and accompanies his observation with a poem about a lover whose eye is drawn compulsively to the object of his affections: "My eye has no place to stop besides upon you."[55]

The passages that follow break from this technique to promote poetic instruction. In the fourth section of prose and verse, ibn Ḥazm claims to combine nine signs of love into one accompanying poem, and unlike the earlier portion of the text, the poem in question does not refer directly to each of the nine signs. Instead, it draws on the author's opening sentence in this prose passage, in which he implies that love changes man's behavior: "When he speaks I do not listen to those sitting near me, but only to his exquisitely coquettish words."[56] In a further abstraction, ibn Ḥazm investigates metaphor in the sixth, seventh, and eighth poems: he shows the reader how he succeeds in comparing two, three, four, and five elements within a single verse. He does this in part to display his own poetic prowess: after comparing five things in one verse of the eighth poem, he remarks in prose that no one can incorporate more than five such comparisons into a single verse. In this effort to create "a chain of similes conceived within the figure of 'enumeratio,'" ibn Ḥazm is not alone.[57] In fact, Dan Pagis discusses how our own ben El'azar's chains of similes in the third story of *Sefer ha-meshalim*, numbering up to seven images in a row, might have been inspired by ibn Ḥazm's example and explication in the *Ṭawq*.[58] Poetic feats aside, ibn Ḥazm nevertheless manages to figure prose on the subject of love as subservient to the poetry, as the prose informs the reader of the dexterous feat to follow.[59] Further, while love is the subject matter of all of the verse passages, it facilitates a crucial symbiotic relationship: the act of writing poetry is a key component to being a lover, and the theme of love is the ideal means through which to pursue an inquiry into poetic composition.

Ben El'azar's collection features cynical parables and lessons in love poetry, and though the former have little to do with love, they do not indemnify it. To the contrary, ibn Ḥazm firmly renounces profane love in the concluding chapter of the *Ṭawq*, a maneuver that perhaps reflects both a poetic convention and an advantageous deflecting of criticism to salvage his reputation as a prominent theologian. In the conclusion, ibn Ḥazm apologizes for any lies that his poems might have expressed and notes that it is poetic convention to overstate descriptions of lovers' ailments, "such as the exaggeration in the description of [the lover's] emaciation, the comparison of his tears to rain that quenches [thirst], his total lack of sleep, and the termination of all eating."[60] Even though ibn Ḥazm and his fellow intellectuals were familiar with Galen's medical approach to love, these exaggerated qualities of the lover across traditions had long been considered amorous tactics rather than innate symptoms; Ovid, for instance, recommends his pupils stop eating and sleeping to succeed in love.[61] Ibn Ḥazm nevertheless recants, concluding that "these things all lack reality; they are all lies."[62] Though ben Elʿazar makes a similar claim of the falsity of poetry in the second story of his collection, the claim is exclusive to that story. Further, ben Elʿazar's introduction represents the opposite kind of claim: he has revealed truths and subsequently placed the onus on the reader to understand or to fail to understand them. While ibn Ḥazm elaborates on the scientific implausibility of particular poetic tropes—despite the unlikelihood that this late disclaimer would placate those "bigots" who will find his treatise inappropriate—he in effect highlights the artistry and ingenuity of the poet (i.e., himself). He has managed to create a treatise dependent on the plausibility of love poetry, and even when love is exposed as a fabrication, a treatise on poetics nonetheless remains.[63]

Perhaps the Arabic rendering of love that, at least structurally and superficially, most closely resembles ben Elʿazar's formulation appears in *Ḥadīth Bayāḍ wa-Riyāḍ*, an anonymous early thirteenth-century Andalusian prosimetrum that centers on the all-consuming love between the son of a Damascus merchant, Bayāḍ, and an Andalusian slave girl, Riyāḍ, communicated via a female go-between. In her translation and explication of the text, Cynthia Robinson describes the poetry and primarily unrhymed prose of *Bayāḍ wa-Riyāḍ* as clumsy in comparison to compositions that constitute the "higher-end production" maqama and conjectures that the text more closely resembles the Romance *roman idyllique*, specifically *Floire et Blanchefleur*.[64] Aside from the *Taḥkemoni*, Hebrew prosimetra are equally difficult to classify and would be more precisely characterized as rhymed prose narratives with interspersed metered, rhymed poems than as maqamas. Still, such Hebrew texts hardly match the relatively simple register that Robinson ascribes to *Bayāḍ wa-Riyāḍ* with respect to the Arabic maqama; rather, what characterizes these Hebrew prosimetra is the explicit aim—so stated in their introductions—to achieve the "virtuosic manipulation" of language for which the Arabic maqama was renowned.[65] In addition to the seemingly comparable external prosimetric structure, the similar patterns of poetic exchanges in *Bayāḍ wa-Riyāḍ*, on the one hand, and ibn Ṣaqbel's

Ne'um Asher and ben El'azar's story of Sahar and Kima, on the other, would likewise seem to point to a commonality, but the substance and trajectory of these poems diverge decisively. In their poetic exchanges, Bayāḍ and Riyāḍ engage all tropes consistent with agonized lovers: the burning, wounded heart; loss of appetite; uncontrollable sighs; muddled thoughts; inability to sleep. But rather than leading the pair to heightened intellectual/spiritual consciousness by harboring a curated code of poetics, their lovesick lyrics lead to more poems lamenting more of the same symptoms. Finally, though the courtliness in *Bayāḍ wa-Riyāḍ*, described by Robinson as "as a path toward the achievement of noble status," seems to mirror the path that ibn Ṣaqbel's Asher and ben El'azar's Sahar seek, a distinction arises in the actions of the beloveds. While Asher's and Sahar's beloveds are both women who instigate an intellectualized poetics of love, Riyāḍ "is presented as the antithesis of proper, or 'courtly,' behavior in matters of love"—certainly not as the bearer of an ennobling poetic code.[66]

Leaving behind this superficial, if tempting, comparison, I return briefly to ibn Ḥazm, whose *Ṭawq* is a more likely point of comparison, despite the two centuries between it and *Sefer ha-meshalim*. Chronological gap aside, ben El'azar was indeed a reader, writer, and translator of texts in Arabic, and, as Pagis noted, ben El'azar employs specific poetic techniques that seem to echo those in the *Ṭawq*.[67] Indeed, ben El'azar's predecessors were just as likely familiar with ibn Ḥazm's treatise on love as with his polemic against Samuel ha-Nagid's critique of the Quran. Still, there is no precise medieval Hebrew or Judeo-Arabic equivalent of the eleventh-century *Ṭawq*, nor is there a Hebrew equivalent of Andreas Capellanus's twelfth-century *De Amore* (*On Love*; widely known in English as *The Art of Courtly Love*) or of Ramon Vidal's thirteenth-century *Razos de trobar*.[68] The closest text by a Jewish author is Moses ibn Ezra's twelfth-century Judeo-Arabic treatise on poetics, *Kitāb al-muḥāḍara wa-l-mudhākara*. Because of its numerous poetic citations, ibn Ezra's *Kitāb* is not only prosimetric like the *Ṭawq* but also notable for ibn Ezra's (like ibn Ḥazm's) self-citations: Joseph Dana's calculations show that 145 of the 207 quotations of Hebrew poetry in the *Kitāb* come from ibn Ezra's own compositions.[69] Yet of these citations, verses on secular love are far from the majority, a logical allotment given ibn Ezra's characterization of erotological poetry as an "error of youth."[70] Ibn Ezra's negative opinion of secular love lyric—however ironic given his own prolific contribution to secular Hebrew love poetry—means that his treatise is only a partially plausible source for ben El'azar's inspiration.[71] Still, as

Joseph Sadan has noted, both ibn Ezra and ben Elʿazar penned kindred defenses of the Hebrew language with respect to Arabic's claims of superiority stemming from the inimitability of the Quran (*iʿjāz al-Qurʾān*).[72]

Ben Elʿazar's knowledge of ibn Ezra's *Kitāb* and of ibn Ḥazm's *Ṭawq* and his potential awareness of *Ḥadīth Bayāḍ wa-Riyāḍ*—even when coupled with his encounters with Occitan and Galician-Portuguese troubadours and with day-to-day spoken Romance, discussed in the following pages—are only parts of the whole. Historical circumstances and literary evidence aside, no precise documentary evidence exists to prove these confluences. Still, as Rina Drory has posited, we can and should strive to learn from such "hidden contexts," even if common literary and historical circumstances defy the historian's desire for solid evidence and connected dots. The next places to map these potential dots are in Romance language lyrics.[73]

Romancing Courtliness

Before returning to *Sefer ha-meshalim* and the medieval Hebrew rendering of courtly love, I first describe Occitan and Galician-Portuguese courtly love traditions, both of which were already well established at the time of composition of *Sefer ha-meshalim*. Ben Elʿazar composed *Sefer ha-meshalim* within a couple of decades of Ramon Vidal de Besalú's Occitan *Razos de trobar*, the first vernacular art of poetry.[74] Both a theorist and practitioner of troubadour lyric, Ramon Vidal was born in Besuldu (Besalú) in Catalonia, a region that not only shares an expansive border with southern France but also possesses extensive political and blood ties to the birthplace of troubadour lyric: Ramiro II of Aragon, who ruled from 1134 to 1137, was married to Agnes of Aquitaine, the daughter of William IX "the Troubadour," who, in addition to being the Duke of Aquitaine (1071–1127), is the Occitan troubadour with the earliest extant lyrics. Petronilla, the daughter of Ramiro II and Agnes, strengthened the cultural bond her mother initiated when she married Ramón Berenguer IV of Barcelona, not only uniting Aragon with Barcelona but also firming ties with Provence, whose leader was Berenguer Ramón, her husband's brother.[75] In the next generation, Alfonso II "the Troubadour" of Aragon, son of Petronilla and Ramón Berenguer IV, who ruled from 1162 to 1196, formalized the role of the troubadours' language: he made Occitan the official language of the court of Barcelona "in order to bolster his claim to Provence," a task facilitated by the fact that Catalonia was much more politically unified than Occitania.[76]

To keep geographical and historical confluences in mind, it is helpful to note that during the years in which the Aragonese king strengthened ties with southern France, Hebrew literary production in southern France was thriving: the ibn Tibbons, the preeminent family of Jewish translators, sought to inculcate the educated Jews of Provence with Andalusi intellectualism via translations of texts from Arabic and Judeo-Arabic to Hebrew.[77] Judah ibn Tibbon, the merchant and physician who spearheaded these translations, was born in Granada around 1120 but relocated to Lunel, in Occitania, most likely because of persecutions inflicted on the Jewish communities of al-Andalus by the stringent Almohads. Judah's son Samuel, who lived from 1150 to roughly 1230, followed his father's lead by translating, among other works, Maimonides's *Guide of the Perplexed* from Judeo-Arabic to Hebrew. Samuel's son Moses and son-in-law Jacob Anatoli carried on the tradition. The ibn Tibbons were presumably communicating in the same Romance language as their Christian neighbors (even if their written language was Hebrew), though we have very little evidence that Jews were composing in Romance in this period. There is a curious exception to the seeming lack of Romance—which is perhaps not as exceptional as the manuscript tradition would have one believe: in *Sefer Ḥasidim* (*Book of the Pious*), a thirteenth-century compilation of ethical teachings from Germany, author Judah ben Samuel he-Ḥasid (Rabbi Judah of Regensburg; c. 1150–1217) rails against reading romances, transliterating the word *romances* into Hebrew letters to make his point crystal clear.[78] Though geographically and culturally distinct, southern France and Ashkenaz might have shared exposure to the northern French trouvère tradition, in which knights and ladies starred in myriad romances. If it were necessary to disparage the romance, it is accordingly appropriate to imagine that these Jews heard, read, and understood the lyrics of their Christian neighbors.

Ramon Vidal shares a kind of kindred outsider status with Jacob ben Elʿazar: both wrote in languages that varied from the spoken languages that surrounded them, even if Vidal's circumstance was decidedly subtler than ben Elʿazar's, given that Catalan and Occitan were so similar that they were perhaps at times indistinguishable.[79] While the text of the *Razos* follows in the tradition of the Latin arts of poetry, it diverges in a key way. Vidal considers the ideal language of composition—something a Latin or Arabic treatise would never need to do: "the Limousin idiom both is acquired naturally, and expresses itself by means of case, number, gender, tense, person, and word class, as you will be able to hear if you listen properly."[80] In pausing to discuss the innate grammatical merits of Limousin as a mother tongue (a status Latin cannot claim), Vidal echoes the political endorsement of Occitan by Alfonso II of Aragon, preceding not only Alfonso X's demarcation of the uses of Castilian and Galician-Portuguese but also, as Elizabeth Wilson Poe notes, Dante's pronouncement in the *De Vulgari Eloquentia* with respect to the various Romance dialects of Italy and France.[81] In a similar way, ben Elʿazar, like his fellow Hebrew maqama authors, fashions the introduction to *Sefer ha-meshalim* as a defense of Hebrew with respect to Arabic: he weaves into his opening invocation that God chose Hebrew above all languages and moves to a critique of Arabic and an affirmation of Hebrew's aptness to literary composition.[82] This focus on identifying the highest form mirrors ben Elʿazar's musing on the relative merits of poetry and prose in the second story. In the context of love, ben Elʿazar refocuses poetics—whether presented in rhymed prose or rhymed, metered verse—as a means to achieve an ideal, ethical love.

Love is undoubtedly an underlying force in the *Razos*. As Sarah Kay observes, the majority of the examples that Vidal cites for the purpose of explicating grammatical points are drawn from love poems: "The first person implied by lyric insertion is typically a subject of desire—for love or for social involvement—identified as a character within the fiction."[83] With more frequency than he cites other troubadours, Vidal draws on lyrics by Bernart de Ventadorn (1135–94) and Giraut de Bornelh (c. 1138–1215), the latter of whom spent significant time at the courts of Castile. Indeed, the first citation to appear in Vidal's treatise belongs to Giraut: "Boldness befits a lady well," a quotation that, as Kay remarks, conveys "the sense of touring obligatory landmarks in the ideological landscape of *cortezia*."[84] The treatise depends on the beauty and compositional dexterity of its chosen citations, most of which treat love in some way; indeed, as I likewise argue in the case of ibn Ḥazm's *Ṭawq*, love poetry forms the basis for Vidal's literary theory in the *Razos*.

Love and the spiritualization of love shaped the poet-lover from within the confines of the Occitan courtly poetic world, and before modern literary criticism termed this practice a kind of game, the poets themselves did: "Amics Bertran, ben es iocs cumunals," writes a *trobairitz*—the term for a female troubadour—in exchange with Bertran del Pojet.[85] For the Occitan troubadours, love underwent what Erich Auerbach termed a "process of sublimation of love which led to mysticism or gallantry" and which "led far from the concrete realities of this world," paving the way for the poetry of praise endorsed by the *stilnovisti*, poets of the late thirteenth- and early fourteenth-century who composed their sweet new style (*dolce stil novo*) in the Tuscan dialect.[86] This allegorical-spiritual impulse existed, of course, in tension with Christianity, though the vernacular is already in itself a kind of theological protest, distinctly beyond grace. One of the most conspicuous examples of potential blasphemy is in the Occitan tradition's recurrent notion of adultery as one of the prerequisites of the courtly love relationship—one that could be consummated solely by way of poetry. Even when this kind of relationship is rendered in poetry, its implications oppose religious and social norms, as in the following verses by trobairitz Castelloza (early thirteenth century): "For all the damage and the harm / that come to me from you / my family thanks you, especially my husband."[87] A more complicated rendition of impiety develops among the Italian poets of the *duecento* (thirteenth century): in his *canzone* "Al cor gentil rempaira sempre amore" (Love always returns to the gentle heart), Guido Guinizelli (1235–76) claims that God has noticed the perfection of the poet's lady and has asked the angels to bring the lady to sojourn in heaven. Iterations of this impulse played out in thirteenth- and fourteenth-century Italy as love became increasingly allegorical and less focused on obtaining the affections of the lady or on merely lamenting her unattainability.

Writing a few decades after Raimon Vidal's treatise and a few decades before Guinizelli's poetic pronouncement, ben Elʿazar put forth his own allegorically tinged collection, one in which physical attainment of the beloved is supplanted by a higher power: at the end of the first story of *Sefer ha-meshalim*, the Soul, unable to obtain the affections of her beloved, embarks on a journey of Neoplatonic inquiry. Likewise, though the ninth story has a more conventionally happy ending, it never completely concludes: the lovers are only able to sustain their love through regular exchanges of poetry, marking poetry, rather than physical connection, not only as the true conduit of love and lifeblood of the story but also as a kind of devotional practice.

These thematic confluences raise the question of ben Elʿazar's actual awareness of the Romance world, and geographical circumstances provide a favorable assessment: the travels of Occitan and Galician-Portuguese troubadours overlapped with ben Elʿazar in Toledo, making it possible that ben Elʿazar encountered the varieties and forms of love that these troubadours professed. Occitan and Galician-Portuguese troubadours alike frequented the courts of Alfonso VIII of Castile (king from 1158 to

1214); King Ferdinand III of Castile (from 1217 to 1251), León (from 1230 to 1251), and Galicia (from 1231 to 1251); and the son of Ferdinand III, King Alfonso X (from 1252 to 1284).[88] Alfonso VIII, in fact, proved crucial in the cross-pollination of Old Occitan and Galician-Portuguese lyrics: in 1170, he married Eleanor of England, Queen of Castile, who was the daughter of Eleanor of Aquitaine, the most famous patron of the Occitan troubadours, and the granddaughter of William IX "the Troubadour."[89] Alongside marriages that facilitated the spread of Occitan, the politics of religion also contributed: the Albigensian Crusade (1209–29), which aimed to rid Languedoc of the dualistic Cathar sect, displaced many individuals, among them troubadours who sought out more welcoming courts.[90]

Poetry shaped the cultures of these courts, culminating in that of Alfonso X, who established Toledo as the political center of his reign, which began a few decades after ben Elʿazar composed *Sefer ha-meshalim* in the same city. A ruler attuned to the political benefit of patronizing cultural production and establishing a unique vernacular corpus, Alfonso X not only encouraged troubadour presence but also quickly began a campaign to bolster the language and culture of Christian Iberia, in part through the translation of scientific and literary works from Arabic to Castilian, an effort in which Jews took part.[91] This program resulted in his creation of vernacular linguistic categories for particular literary genres, much as Alfonso II of Aragon had done for Occitan: Alfonso X deemed Galician-Portuguese the acceptable language for lyric poetry, while Castilian was relegated to prose.[92] It would be presumptuous to imagine that ben Elʿazar took part in this translation program, though he was an established translator from Arabic to Hebrew and is known for his translation of ibn al-Muqaffaʿ's eighth-century Arabic translation of *Kalila wa-Dimna* into Hebrew rhymed prose.[93] Speculation aside, ben Elʿazar and Alfonso X were clearly on the same literary wavelength: in 1251, a year before he was crowned, Alfonso X commissioned the Arabic to Castilian translation of the very same *Kalila wa-Dimna*, marking it the first translation of a text into Castilian.[94]

Occitan troubadour Giraut de Bornelh, who frequented the courts of Alfonso VII, Alfonso VIII, Alfonso IX, and Ferdinand III, makes recurring references in his lyrics to his sojourns in Spain while employing language and themes representative of the Occitan tradition: "And if she who is wise and courtly, and with whom I find comfort and consolation, sends me no help before I return from Spain in April, then do not imagine that blossom and orchard and meadow give me any help or pleasure, nor the song of birds in the hedgerows, and do not think that I have as much pleasure now in the company of other people or feel at home with them, so that on many occasions I abruptly take my leave of them."[95]

Aside from attesting to Giraut's travels in Spain (insofar as lyric poetry can be a credible source of historical information), this excerpt crystallizes many key features and vocabulary of Occitan courtly love. The poet depends on the lady for his well-being: her courtliness enables him to appreciate his interactions with other people and with his physical environs. Scholars have refuted the etymological connection between the Latin *dominus* and the troubadour's referring to the lady as *midons* or *domna*, which would position the poet as the lady's feudal subject; still, they do acknowledge the importance of this metaphorical hierarchy within the Occitan lyric: "The topos of equality symbolizes love's fulfillment, just as that of subservience expresses yearning. To conclude from the latter that the lady did in fact enjoy a social rank superior to that of the poet would be imprudent in the extreme."[96] Giraut's acute self-consciousness of his internal being, references to nature and birdsong, and uses of the words *cors*, *pratz*, *chanz*, and *plaiszatz*—vocabulary emblematic of the tradition's values—further place these verses precisely in the lyric orbit of the Occitan troubadours. The *tornada*, or final stanza, solidifies his adherence to this method of composition: "And I see from her how joy and happiness would come to me from all sides if she would accept this song without demur."[97] Joy and happiness, coupled with the reference to the song itself—which echoes the birdsong—round out the poet's rendering of courtly love.

Though Occitan and Galician-Portuguese troubadours overlapped at the thirteenth-century courts of Castile and León, and though scholars have claimed that Galician-Portuguese lyric is based primarily on Occitan motifs, there are notable autochthonous themes and forms in Galician-Portuguese lyrics, just as there are forms in the Occitan tradition that Galician-Portuguese composers did not adopt.[98] It is reductive to limit each tradition to a list of characteristics, but this kind of organizing allows certain aspects of each tradition to stand out. Accordingly, the Occitan and Galician-Portuguese lyric traditions both express the need for moderation in the process of courtship; the necessary suffering of the poet-lover; the courteous treatment of the beloved; and the feelings of love, joy, and youth. In Galician-Portuguese lyric, however, the lady is a less distant and prideful figure than she is in the Occitan tradition and tends not to be figured as the poet's superior, even in a metaphorical sense.[99] Rather, she seems to possess a more candid intimacy with the beloved, as in the following *cantiga d'amigo* by Pedr'Amigo de Sevilha, who spent time at the court of Alfonso X:[100]

—Tell me, mother, why did you put me
In such a prison, and why did you deprive me
Of being able to see my boyfriend?
—Because, daughter, since you met him
He's done nothing but try to steal you from me.[101]

Indeed, this poem bears more of a resemblance to the following verses from an early twelfth-century Arabic muwashshaḥ, an Arabic strophic poetic form invented in al-Andalus, than to Occitan counterparts:

Will you rebuke me,
or will you pity me,
stop the wasting away
of a lover
when he ails?
  Woe unto me! Imprisoned in
  my sea of fears
    with far-off shore
    I cling to waves.[102]

In a further distinction, references to nature, which feature prominently in both Occitan and Galician-Portuguese, tend to focus on the sea in the latter and often coincide with the repetition found in Galician-Portuguese lyric, known as *leixa-pren*. Both of these elements—the sea and leixa-pren—appear in the following cantiga d'amigo by Galician-Portuguese troubadour Pae Gomez Charinho, who likewise frequented the court of Alfonso X:[103]

They told me today, oh friend, that my boy
Is no longer an admiral of the sea
And now my heart can finally be calm
And finally sleep, for this reason;
The one who plucked my boy from the sea—
May God pluck him from sorrows, since he played
Very fairly by me, since I'll no longer be
Sad because of the winds I see
And now I won't have to lose sleep
Over storms, friend, but if it was the king—
The one who plucked my boy from the sea—

May God pluck him from sorrows, since he played

Very fairly by me, since now each time I see
Someone arrive from the border
I won't be afraid he'll tell me bad news,
But since he did me a favor without my asking—
The one who plucked my boy from the sea—
May God pluck him from sorrows, since he played

<Very fairly by me . . .>.[104]

With these varieties of early Romance courtly love lyric in mind, I return to Hebrew.

Medieval Hebrew Prosimetra: Courtliness or Courtly-Not

In Arabic prosimetra such as the *Zahra* and the *Ṭawq*, poems expounding proper comportment in love might build theories of poetics via lyrics that represent incrementally appropriate approaches to the beloved, but they do not ask the poet-lover to grow and change. In the prosimetric context of Occitan and Galician-Portuguese lyrics found within the *vidas* and *razos*, the poet-lover is similarly static. Yet some Romance prosimetra and anthologies refashioned the role of the poetry with respect to narrative progression. For instance, Nicolette of the thirteenth-century French prosimetrum *Aucassin et Nicolette* enlists poetry to help her reunite with her lover: she disguises herself as a minstrel and sings to Aucassin about their relationship.[105] As in Dante's *Vita nuova*, the anonymous author of *Aucassin et Nicolette* uses the prose of the prosimetrum to graft new meaning onto the poetry. Dante's lyric recontextualization—discussed in the fourth chapter with respect to Immanuel of Rome—is further developed in Petrarch's *Canzoniere*, in spite of its lack of prose.[106] As Schirmann, Pagis, Scheindlin, and Decter theorize, what differs in ben Elʿazar's text with respect to stand-alone Hebrew love poems and to most fellow Hebrew maqamas is the fact that even though the characters in *Sefer ha-meshalim* are idealized types, they nevertheless grow through the course of the narrative. I contend that the poems in ben Elʿazar's collection—their ordering and accruing of meaning in the narrative framework—are the catalysts of this growth, such that each poem is particular to a given moment.

In this poetic effort in Hebrew, ben Elʿazar is not alone; while the characters in Judah al-Ḥarizi's *Taḥkemoni* remain unchanged over the course of the narrative, Asher from *Ne'um Asher ben Yehuda* also changes, though perhaps not as profoundly as ben El'azar's characters do. Asher—the protagonist from the earliest extant Hebrew maqama, written by Solomon ibn Ṣaqbel sometime during the first half of the twelfth century—is a key to the development of the poetics of love in maqamas by Jewish authors.[107] For ibn Ṣaqbel and ben El'azar, the right poem at the right moment can make Asher's regret palpable, haunting the reader beyond the story's close, and can make Sahar into a proper poet-lover.[108] In the first poem he recites after seeing Kima, Sahar says:

> Yesterday she rebuked the poor with abuse, / and now today she abused me
> She dissuaded me and made me weary, / crushes me and blots me out
> The day of my death; know, please, that / her farewell killed me.[109]

This singular moment in Sahar's broader trajectory as student of love is not so unlike the experience of the disconsolate poet-lover in the earlier verses by ibn Gabirol or of Heman in the *Maqama of the Seven Virgins* in the *Taḥkemoni*.[110] The difference is that while Sahar moves on and learns from this period of painful love, the poet-lover of ibn Gabirol's verses remains forever unrequited, hemmed in by constraints of meter, verse, theme, and convention, just as Heman and Ḥever of the *Taḥkemoni* maintain their fixed roles as narrator and trickster protagonist throughout, not allowing poetry to sway their course as they move toward the inevitable anagnorisis of each maqama.

This fixity, however, does not precisely capture the trajectory of Asher, who, though blinded by stubbornness, does not remain completely static throughout the course of the narrative: regret colors his forward motion. Further, as Scheindlin claims, it is the theme of love that facilitates ibn Ṣaqbel's character study of Asher, a connection I argue is made possible by poetry.[111] Frivolous Asher returns home penniless after pursuing girls, only to become embroiled again in matters of love when a lady throws him an apple engraved with a poem. Congratulating himself on being irresistible to females, Asher walks away without responding but later regrets his decision and recites a poem for her, to which she does not respond. Now forlorn, Asher eventually receives a poem rebuking him for not responding sooner and is escorted to the lady's chambers, where the master of the house appears and threatens him. The master (who turns out to be a maiden in disguise) agrees to introduce him to the lady, but when Asher removes her veil, he sees a decrepit old man who reveals himself to be Asher's dear friend and promises Asher his daughter's hand in marriage. Where Asher fails in matters of love and love poetry, Sahar learns and ultimately succeeds, but Asher's failure is not without remorse and effort—indeed, not without growth.

Certain uses of poetry in *Ne'um Asher* create a connection between love and poetry that informs the plot of the story.[112] For instance, Asher converses with his personified heart in verse. When Asher blames his heart for flirting indiscriminately, his heart fails to move beyond this superficial interaction and refuses to take responsibility. Then, employing a trope that the reader has seen in ibn Dāwūd's *Zahra* with respect to the potency of the *laḥẓa* (glance), Asher tries to calm his heart with verses that denounce the soul for succumbing to the eye's wiles:

> My soul—your handmaid—is alarmed / she fell into a snare, ambushed.
> What is the use in berating me— / I, who have been ensnared by the love of a gazelle?
> What am I to do? / My eyes have harmed my soul![113]

Despite Asher's attempts, his heart "refused to be comforted."[114] His temperamental heart is eager to blame others and, in particular, to pick a fight with the superior soul. This style of interaction, which in ibn Ṣaqbel's story consists of a prose passage and poem (both brief), forms the backbone of ben Elʿazar's entire first story and is likewise rehearsed in the *Taḥkemoni* in the *Maqama of the Dispute of the Soul with the Body*.[115] Though this is a common debate in Neoplatonic discourse, it plays out differently in ibn Ṣaqbel's and ben Elʿazar's texts than in al-Ḥarizi's: in the *Taḥkemoni*, the personified Soul, Body, and Intellect are general ideas and do not belong to Heman, Ḥever, or any other particular individual, while in *Ne'um Asher* and *Sefer ha-meshalim*, the components of the self belong to the characters in the narrative. This kind of fracturing of the fictional character into basic components so that he can communicate with his heart and soul (though not perhaps with the illusive intellect) is rare in medieval Hebrew literature but not absent. In fact, it appears in one of the most important medieval Jewish texts: in his Judeo-Arabic *Kitāb al-hidāya ilā farā'id al-qulūb* (*Book of Direction to the Duties of the Heart*; in Hebrew *Ḥovot ha-levavot*), eleventh-century philosopher Baḥya ibn Paquda describes man as "'a small city,' since man is a world in miniature. His limbs and character are alluded to by the term 'with few inhabitants,' since they are few, compared to the capabilities of the human heart with its many worldly desires and inabilities to satisfy them."[116] Aside from Baḥya's use of bodily divisions, this same phenomenon is much more at home in the Romance tradition, particularly when it blossoms into a favorite metapoetic trope among the Italian stilnovisti, most notably Guido Cavalcanti.[117] Despite the difference in scale, given that ibn Ṣaqbel only has one such poem and ben Elʿazar builds the whole first maqama on this conceit, it seems that ibn Ṣaqbel privileges the heart in granting it a poetic voice. After all, only those characters with principal involvement in the story recite poems: the narrator, the lady, Asher, the master/maiden figure, and the heart.

Ibn Ṣaqbel again relies on poetry to inform the plot of *Neʾum Asher* when he employs an apple as a surface for poetic inscription and as a conduit between lovers.[118] The apple, which will be discussed in greater detail in the next chapter, is scented with myrrh and encapsulates the lady's flirtation with her lover: the lady puts forth the first love poem, to which the male protagonist responds. In initiating an exchange of love poems, this poem sets a standard for poetic composition that exists within the realm of courtly love: the verses are poised to instruct the protagonist on how to comport himself in matters of love and poetry. Indeed, the Romance concept of courtly love is relevant to a discussion of ibn Ṣaqbel's writing, since the love poetry of the Occitan troubadours was emerging at the very time *Neʾum Asher* was composed.[119] It is entirely possible that ibn Ṣaqbel would have been aware of "the rules of love," and his story accordingly displays clear characteristics of courtly love and courtly love poetry: ibn Ṣaqbel refers to "the etiquette of nobles" (*berit nedivim*), a phrase that simultaneously recalls al-Washshāʾ's "those of noble characters" (*shiyami al-kirāmi*) and looks toward the Romance poet-lover's goal of personal betterment.[120] Rather than characterizing the ideal qualities of an enduring beloved, Asher's story teaches how not to behave; the master reprimands Asher's misunderstanding of love/lust—the very error that has led him to seek entrance into the harem. While the master's reproach regards the social norms surrounding the harem, in the larger context of the story it also alludes to Asher's amorous blundering, which begins with his literal mishandling of verse, when he waits too long before responding to the apple poem, a poem addressed more thoroughly in the next chapter.

Unlike the love stories of *Sefer ha-meshalim*, *Neʾum Asher* does not conclude in the manner apropos to courtly love: Asher fails in all aspects of courtship, exposing himself to be, as Scheindlin remarks, "a ridiculous parody of a courtly lover."[121] The poem that prompted Asher's adventure was nothing but a ruse, and in this sense ibn Ṣaqbel ignores the ennobling course of courtly love, in which poetry allows the lovers to develop their relationship, and instead follows the path of the Arabic maqama:

> Heed well, my friends, my pleasant discourse / but please take note lest you're fooled:
> This is nothing but a mockery of lovers and their words, / devised in your friend's heart![122]

Even though ibn Ṣaqbel discloses that the whole story, flirtation and all, was a trick, this tactic ultimately mocks Asher more than any institution of love, and Asher has nonetheless changed through the narrative, moving from arrogant to regretful. Moreover, the apple poem remains a testament to the use of poetry in the process of courtship, and the three poems with which Asher attempts to respond to the apple poem play a similarly crucial role in the development of the story: they uncover Asher's increasing panic as he realizes he has fumbled his opportunity with the maiden.[123] In a final effort to save Asher from being termed a fool, the reader must bear in mind that *Ne'um Asher* was likely part of a larger collection of stories—one that ben El'azar might have known in its potential entirety; other conceivable maqamas in the collection might have moved Asher (or another character) away from a life as an unteachable simpleton to a proper courtly lover who behaves in a way that mitigates the need for regret.[124]

Whether honoring or mimicking courtly love, love poetry plays a crucial role in the plot and itself becomes a motif in the love stories of *Sefer ha-meshalim* and in *Ne'um Asher*. This is decidedly not the case in the *Taḥkemoni*, which more closely follows the Arabic model of the maqama and does not broach notions of poetic courtliness, though it does thematize poets and poetics. Indeed, although the poetry does not influence the plot as it does in *Ne'um Asher*, it is nonetheless important to the *Taḥkemoni*: al-Ḥarizi shows his admiration for poetry by writing poetry and writing about poetry in a number of his maqamas. In the third maqama, for instance, he discusses the Hebrew poets from Spain, and the eighteenth continues with this subject. In the third maqama, Ḥever's poem acts as the exclamation point at the end of his excursus on Spain's Hebrew poets but does not alter the course of the story since Ḥever's prose has sufficiently convinced the audience of his wit. The poem manages to make Ḥever's discourse all the more dramatic and makes known al-Ḥarizi's wish to impress the reader with his ability to compose in a style true to that of the poets he praises.

In this way, al-Ḥarizi's poetry fits with most critics' assumptions about the function of poetry in prosimetric texts: verses act as peripheral insertions that reiterate the contents of the prose or provide emotive interludes. This interpretation seems shortsighted, however, given that al-Ḥarizi himself lists both metered poetry and rhymed prose equally among components of the exemplary compositional style. But even if al-Ḥarizi recognizes the importance of poetry in his text, he does not employ it in a context of love as ibn Ṣaqbel and ben Elʿazar do.

Still, the *Taḥkemoni* includes stories about, if not love, something akin to desire—a quality on display in the thirteenth (twentieth in the old numbering) story of the collection, which clearly mirrors *Neʾum Asher.* In the maqama, rogue Ḥever, disguised as a beautiful maiden in the company of six other maidens, deludes narrator Heman into courting him and mocks Heman on unveiling his identity.[125] Of the six women, Heman is most attracted to the disguised Ḥever, who is a head taller than the others, like the "lady" in *Neʾum Asher.* Ḥever initiates communication with Heman in prose, and Hever responds, also in prose. The story contains two poems, the first one recited by Heman and the second by the disguised Ḥever. Heman's verses make use of tropes common to courtly love—the pain of love and the danger of females—and Ḥever's poem also employs courtly vocabulary, but neither poem advances the courtship (or the plot) of the story.[126] Unlike in *Neʾum Asher,* the poems are not well integrated into the prose text, and the story would function adequately without them. It is accordingly difficult to assess Heman's knowledge or ignorance of courtly customs on the basis of his one brief poem, as the reader may do with poems that Asher recites, nor is this even an apt assessment, since Heman's courtliness is not at stake. In Asher's case, his *uncourtliness* is at stake, a fact that reflects—and then lampoons—some of the so-called tenets of courtly love. His ridiculing of the rules of love suggests that ibn Ṣaqbel knew that such rules surrounding the practice of love lyric existed; indeed, it would not be too early to mimic the ideal, as Andreas Capellanus arguably did in the late twelfth century in his Latin treatise *De Amore.*

Courting Loftiness

Authors from traditions as varied as the Arabic *ghazal,* Occitan *cansos,* and certain Hebrew maqamas endorse the notion of courtship as a process in which the lover must dedicate himself to learning how to be a model lover, particularly when this learning includes knowing when and how to draw on a fitting poem: the better one is equipped with the tools of a poet, the more likely he will be to succeed in love and in life. In this way, ben Elʿazar's poetic trajectory matches his surrounding literary currents. There is, however, a difference between becoming a better-educated individual in society and becoming a worthier member of a courtly society. Both Arabic and Romance traditions imply that if the aspiring lover learns how to be a better poet-lover, he will in turn be a more accomplished individual, but while this general betterment seems to be the goal of the Arabic tradition, it is more of a secondary consequence for the lover in the Romance tradition, who treats love as something "more-than-human" and has loftier goals for his honed skills as poet-lover.[127] Such skills will not merely grant him the attention of a beloved for a moment in time, however exquisite; rather, the Romance poet-lover continues to refine his art out of a desire to improve beyond the requisite elegant application of appropriate verses, as described by Auerbach: "The personal element in the courtly virtues is not simply a gift of nature; nor is it acquired by birth; to implant them now requires, besides birth, proper training too, as preserving them requires the unforced will to renew them by constant and tireless practice and proving."[128] This, as Scheindlin and Decter note, is precisely how ben Elʿazar depicts Sahar's ongoing romance with Kima in the ninth story: even after Sahar marries Kima and inherits the throne, he continues to renew "the words of their love, for quarreling of lovers sharpens love."[129] Crucially, it is poetry that enables this perpetuity: from his opening allegory and personified debate on the merits of prose and poetry to his whimsical love stories, ben Elʿazar relies on the poetics of love—expressed in poetry and in rhymed prose—to illustrate proper ethical comportment.

The first story, a Neoplatonic allegory that uses love to discuss the relationships among the self, the heart, the soul, the intellect, and wisdom, sets the stage for considering ben Elʿazar's treatment of love lyric.[130] The Soul's beloved, the Intellect, referred to as the Commander of the Army, leads a procession through town while the Soul sleeps. When the Soul wakes up and recounts her dream, the Heart—considerably evolved with respect to the personified Heart in *Ne'um Asher*—is irate and hides the Soul "in the chamber of his heart" to prevent the Intellect from seeing her.[131] When the Soul thus fails to greet the Intellect, the Intellect departs angrily. The Soul accuses the Heart of causing the Intellect's departure, and the two demand that the narrator—who at that moments awakens from his dream—arbitrate.[132] The narrator sides with the Soul, who despairs on learning that her lover is busy wooing another beloved, Wisdom, in the "garden of delight."[133] The narrator initially claims to be too feeble to accompany the Soul on her quest to the garden, but she ultimately persuades him and launches into a Neoplatonic description of the nature of the soul.

A love story provides the premise for the plot, and a lovers' quarrel prompts the anthropomorphized characters to engage in recitations of courtly love poetry and philosophical discourse. Love thus serves as the common bond between the text's poetry and the subject of Neoplatonism, a connection made evident by the story's four philosophically minded poems, particularly its climactic penultimate poem, which solidifies the connections among love, poetry, and ethics. As the following examples suggest, ben Elʿazar's use of poetry to treat both love and medieval philosophical thought highlights the importance of love lyric to the story's plot and to its underlying allegorical meaning. The first poem, spoken by the Soul, begins to illustrate how ben Elʿazar uses love poetry to develop the plot of the story:

> I slept but my Heart was awake / hark, the voice of the gazelle knocks.
> Doe, stop dozing; / go and cling to your love.
> When he heard this, he trembled / and he could not control himself. [134]

Here, he allows poetry to convey narrative meaning without stripping it of its uniquely lyrical characteristics, such as the Soul's referring to her lover as a gazelle and to herself as a doe (in the first and second verses, respectively), which are conventional names for the lover and beloved in Arabic and Hebrew love poetry.[135]

In addition to developing the story's plot, poetry also serves to define ben Elʿazar's notion of courtly love in the story. In the third poem, the Soul recites a lover's lament:

> Take, O my eye, the view of the doe as provisions: / this is your only portion from the beloved!
> And you also, my mouth, bid your heart to kiss her: / the intended one will praise you every day.
> These are the rules of the lovers of wisdom; / this is indeed the practice.
> What bitterness is the departure of the graceful doe, / and what hardship to eulogize the separation.[136]

The first verse continues the lover's farewell, begun in the preceding prose passage—a mixed-form cooperation that is absent in the Arabic maqama tradition and in al-Ḥarizi's *Taḥkemoni*—and creates narrative continuity across the two forms. While the first two verses of the poem carry on from where the prose passage ended, the third and fourth meditate on proper practices in love, anticipating the ninth story of the collection, in which ben Elʿazar elaborates on the rules of love: the third verse refers to "the rules of the lovers of wisdom," and the fourth describes the phenomenon of the separation of lovers. The fifth poem likewise employs the phrase "the instruction of lovers"—something akin to a code—and highlights the negative effects of love, a subject that receives ample attention in love poetry in both Arabic and Romance traditions:

> Can a lover be angry at his beloved and swear / on the life of love? Were it not for my Heart I would have killed you.
> My Soul lied to her. I am not like a lover: / only yesterday I knew you as the most faithful.
> This is the instruction of lovers: if the doe curses / her lover responds: I ransomed you in my soul![137]

The presence of a lovers' code allows poetry to provide the basis of the rules of love, as it is through verse that the poet-lover puts these rules into action.

Ben Elʿazar draws candidly on love and on love's dependence on poetry to link love to his philosophical allegory—an affinity likewise at home among his contemporary Romance-language thinkers.[138] In the third poem, the author applies the rules of lovers to "the rules of the lovers of wisdom" to move the reader from the realm of courtly love to that of Neoplatonism, using the mode of poetry to literalize this shift. In the fifth poem, he portrays the characters of his philosophical allegory as players in the game of love: the poetic *I* figures himself as the jealous lover of the Soul, who is beholden to his Heart. In the final poem of the story, the narrator announces, "The parable of the Intellect is complete / it has been made using the themes of love."[139] This interweaving of the allegory and love poetry suggests that ben Elʿazar was familiar enough with the Romance scheme of a lovers' code to borrow it as a medium for the philosophical context of the first story while also anticipating the extensive discussion of the rules of lovers in the ninth story of the collection.

While the third and fifth poems of this first story impress on the reader the importance of courtly love poetry to the prosimetrum, the fourth poem elaborates on the ability of verse to create a connection among prose, poetry, and the philosophical core of the story.[140] The third prose passage and fourth poem work together to draw a distinction between the Heart—the anthropomorphized, allegorical figure in the story who argues with the Soul—and the metaphorical heart—the emotional core of the lover.[141]

In the prose, the Soul blames the Heart for hiding her from her lover: "My Soul arose and bowed toward him and cried and begged him and said, 'Are you not aware that my Heart is my own and that when I talk with anyone he seeks to quarrel with me, and then the vigor of his face changes? He saw me, took me, brought me to his room and hid me in his heart; now nobody can see me.'"[142] The Heart, it seems, is keeping the Soul from pursuing the Intellect. In the selected verses from the poem that follows, the Soul complains that her lover has run off with her heart:

> O lovers, tell me / how can a lover live without his love?
> My heart was placed in the hand of the gazelle; / the gazelle is his keeper.
> Can a man without a heart live / when the gazelle carried it off in his hand?[143]

This distinction between the "two hearts" facilitates the comingling of courtly love (heart) and Neoplatonic allegory (Heart); love provides not only a means of exploring proper comportment in love but also a premise for philosophical exploration.

The ninth story shifts the paradigm from love lyric as messenger of philosophical enlightenment to love lyric as teacher of moral instruction and law giving, culminating in the moment in which Sahar and Kima must prove their love to the king. Kima recites a poem that captures the tenets of ben El'azar's courtly love, a feat manipulating poetry, poetic tropes, and the figure of the poet-lover:

> We wrapped ourselves in the cloak of beauty and humility / and dressed in clothes of love and fear;
> we wrote a covenant of love without blemish / in which there does not arise quarreling and envy;
> we bear the yoke of innocence and desire. / Has the heart that bears these two ever been seen?
> The spirit of love is aroused to cause harm / but the spirit of wisdom blocks it.
> The spirit of my love is conquered in me / and wisdom dresses itself in splendor and pride.
> Our enviers thought we were sated with sensual love / but lo, our throat is dry with thirst.[144]

The stunning courtly aspects of this poem must be parsed in the context of metaphor, which acts as a kind of go-between in the prosimetrum. Indeed, as the next chapter suggests, ibn Ṣaqbel and ben El'azar engaged metaphor in experimental and unexpected ways in efforts to stretch the capacity of Hebrew to encompass the dictates of a Romance vision of courtly love.

Ashkenazi Analogues?

Was this impetus toward an ideal love, codified in verse, particular to Jews of the Mediterranean, or did Jews of northern France and Ashkenaz experiment with similar literary angles with parallel outcomes? *Sefer ha-maʿasim*, an anonymous late thirteenth-century collection of prose narrative tales from northern France, is geographically poised to answer this question, given the influence of the troubadours of southern France on the trouvères of northern France and given the wide dispersion of frametale narratives, such as *The Thousand and One Nights* and *Sindibad*, throughout the Mediterranean and northern Europe.[145] In her comprehensive study of *Sefer ha-maʿasim*, Rella Kushelevsky identifies both the reworking of Jewish sources and the incorporation of non-Jewish sources into the tales, which draw on a variety of literary forms, including the exemplum, the romance, the fabliau, and the parable.[146] Even more compelling, she notes "traces of romances of chivalry" and "courtly love" and identifies themes that a few of the tales share with the prosimetric *Aucassin et Nicolette*.[147]

The most obvious disjuncture between *Sefer ha-maʿasim* and the Hebrew prosimetra from the Mediterranean is in form: *Sefer ha-maʿasim* consists entirely of prose narrative. The dearth of poetry seems to suggest that this narrative collection has a completely divergent purpose from that of our prosimetra, one that is more in line with widely circulating didactic tales that conveyed both wisdom and entertainment to broad audiences. To be fair, this is perhaps too simplistic an approach and does not do justice to the potential richness of formal and thematic linkages, especially since poetic elements can certainly be present in prose—a phenomenon discussed in the next chapter.[148] Kushelevsky identifies five tales in the collection (28, 52, 55, 66, 67) that interweave non-Jewish motifs and points out in the tale of "The Poor Bachelor and His Maiden Cousin" the presence of the quest motif—a motif "typical of the romance [that] entails a process of the development of self-awareness and the overcoming of obstacles."[149] In the tale, the rabbi advises a young Torah scholar to win his cousin's hand away from her uncle-suitor, an effort that leads him to seek a fortune in faraway lands. The young man's adventure recalls Sahar's leaving home at the opening of ben Elʿazar's ninth story, but with a difference: one of the many remarkable aspects of ben Elʿazar's story is its lack of reference to any Jewish elements aside from its repurposed biblical language; indeed, Sahar seems to encounter Kima in a harem. This likewise holds true in Immanuel's third maḥberet (addressed in the fourth chapter), in which Immanuel pursues a nun. In comparison, the story from *Sefer ha-maʿasim* is a carefully constructed version of the romance quest narrative that squares with its Jewish audience, from its entirely Jewish cast of characters to its deference to halakha. Still, the story undoubtedly displays its borrowing from the broader cultural context, prompting Kushelevsky to draw on Hans Robert Jauss's theoretical framework to relate this element of the tale to "the existence of a unique horizon of expectation of a Jewish audience in medieval France."[150]

In the sixty-sixth tale, "The Prophecy of the Ravens," which draws its motif from the Sindibad story cycle—whose contested origins in the East branched into Eastern (*Sindibad* in Arabic; *Mishle Sendebar* in Hebrew) and Western versions (*The Seven Sages of Rome*)—a young man leaves home in search of wisdom, eventually gains knowledge and wealth, and marries the daughter of the king. In *Sefer ha-meshalim*, Sahar likewise leaves home, not to seek wisdom (though this is what he eventually gains), but rather to have a youthful adventure far from the critical gaze of his father. While it is true that he also marries the daughter of the king, his marriage is a sign of his continuous ethical enrichment via poetic inquiry, not, as in the case of "The Prophecy of the Ravens," a vindication of his decision to leave home to study Torah, much to the vexation and disapproval of a wealthy and impious father. Indeed, familiar plots fueled narratives of the medieval world, just as poetic tropes seemed to exist on a conveyor belt. Further, while both *Sefer ha-maʿasim* and the secular Hebrew prosimetra of the Mediterranean interwove recontextualized biblical phrases, the practice had varying purposes: in *Sefer ha-maʿasim*, these phrases further supported the Jewish morality of the tale, whereas in the prosimetra of the Mediterranean, they were a sign of literary ingenuity that consciously risked irreverence. Their authors did not strive to reconcile the frametale narrative du jour with their daily practice of Judaism but rather to reinvent the Jewish literary landscape by illuminating the profound creative capacity of the Hebrew language, as al-Ḥarizi informs the reader of his *Taḥkemoni*. This effort, which likewise conveniently highlighted the talent of the author-manipulator, amounts to a kind of proto-cultural Judaism that reflects the somewhat diaphanous distinction between secular and religious studies that emanated from al-Andalus.

How does the thirteenth-century prosimetric *Aucassin et Nicolette* fit into this literary network? Kushelevsky notes the prominence of the female characters in some of the tales, even if the tales tend heavily toward misogyny; there are likewise myriad misogynistic elements in some Hebrew maqamas, most notably in Judah ibn Shabbetai's seemingly parodic *Minḥat Yehuda sone ha-nashim* (The offering of Judah, hater of women).[151] *Sefer ha-meshalim*, *Ne'um Asher*, and, to a lesser extent, Immanuel's third maḥberet feature unusually influential female characters who, as talented poets, strive to teach their male counterparts the arts of poetry and, in so doing, directly influence the plot. Nicolette likewise recites poetry and affects the course of the narrative by helping Aucassin, even if she does so without the goal of his ethical-spiritual betterment. To be fair, the maiden of the "Poor Bachelor and His Maiden Cousin" is bold enough to assure her cousin of her feelings by embracing him before he goes to seek his fortune, and the wife in "A Slave for Seven Years," another story from *Sefer ha-maʿasim*, plays an even more active role in the plot by planting crops and building a city in anticipation of famine, thus saving not only her husband but many others.[152] Indeed, the deeds of these women are remarkably productive, but, to draw on a crucial medieval paradigm, their words matter very little; neither woman recites or teaches poetry—a practice that distinguishes the virtuous, courtly woman—nor is this her purpose.[153] Nicolette, who is active in both poetic words and influential deeds, is thus a kind of go-between across the Hebrew narratives of northern France found in *Sefer ha-maʿasim* and the Hebrew prosimetra of the Mediterranean; the *chantefable* (itself a formal anomaly in its romance milieu) possesses formal characteristics of both realms.

Still, it is worth questioning whether love and poetry might constitute distinct categories in Romance literature, even if contrary to the crucial linking of poetry and love that Nicolette Zeeman has described: "From an early period the 'sentement' or 'matere' of love was inextricably associated with certain kinds of courtly poetry. On the one hand, the Occitan and French love poets describe singing or composing as virtually synonymous with loving; they imply that the poet is inevitably a 'lover.' Whatever extra-textual form of love this may refer to, in many texts 'love' seems to become a metaphor for 'poetry.' On the other hand, love can be viewed from two vantage-points provided by the structure of the love lyric, as the source of poetic inspiration and even 'sincerity.'"[154]

Putting aside this established intertwining of love and poetry, perhaps it is true that where poetry is lacking, there might exist some common ground in the formulation of love. Accordingly, Kushelevsky asks, "Does *Sefer ha-maʿasim* suggest that feelings of passionate love between men and women are acceptable, an approach that may be ascribed to the courtly love discourse?"[155] A careful examination of the texts, however, reveals that the terminology of courtly love may be out of place. These women are active, righteous, and even passionate, but they are not paradigms of spiritual and intellectual betterment through a deified vision of love.[156] Their steady love, candidly expressed in the prose of proper behavior, is so distant from both the erotic Hispano-Hebraic lyrics and the troubadour's at times playful and at times miserably unrequited eros that it seems to be an entirely different kind of love—poetic or not. Social obligation, not ethical love, drives these tales; the love matches are wrapped up tidily at the conclusion, having lacked all of the elements that define the all-encompassing love we have been tracing: "a love with an endlessly receding goal, which finds fulfillments only in longing, striving, aspiration."[157] Indeed, even with the help of *Aucassin et Nicolette* as textual mediator, there seems to be a profound divide between the richly intellectualized and self-consciously literary poetics of love emanating from these Hebrew prosimetra, on the one hand, and the appropriately and cleverly adapted didactic narratives of *Sefer ha-maʿasim*, on the other, even if some of the tales do indeed fulfill the purpose of allowing the audience to escape the mundane for the marvelous.[158]

Perhaps a more fitting parallel might be drawn from poetry, and yet neither medieval Ashkenaz nor northern France produced a secular erotic lyric corpus in Hebrew. Still, as earlier examples in this chapter have shown, distinctions between secular and devotional lyrics from al-Andalus that share thematic, formal, and linguistic elements can be profoundly subtle. Susan Einbinder describes the reception of Jewish martyrological poetry from medieval northern France as follows: "Medieval Hebrew poetry from Ashkenaz and northern France has rarely been deemed 'good' poetry by readers attuned to the elegance of the medieval Hebrew poetry written in Islamic settings . . . yet these aesthetic and historical judgments have been hasty, as this poetry yields a wealth of beauty and information about the historical conditions in which it arose and flourished."[159]

This assessment mirrors the general opinion of the Hebrew poetry and prosimetra of Christian Spain, which was considered less eloquent and masterful than the poetry of the great Jewish poets of al-Andalus that Einbinder likewise references. On closer examination, it becomes clear that the Hebrew poetry and prosimetra of Christian Spain fulfilled different purposes than the earlier poems, aimed at readers living amid different cultural and political realities. It is, then, less productive to search for stock signs of "courtliness" across geographically distinct medieval Jewish textual traditions than to acknowledge the kindred striving for beauty inherent in some of these traditions. Where Ashkenazi poetry lacked a secular erotic tradition, its tradition of liturgical poetry (*piyut*) was robust and deep: "The pain and anguish of the poets find expression in verses of unadorned language which, coming from the heart, touches the heart" to capture "the profound religious emotion which pervades and distinguishes them."[160] Perhaps, by extension, it is not too indelicate to suggest a common desire in these northern French and German poetic traditions and in our love-themed prosimetra to stir Jewish audiences and readers by plumbing the depths of Hebrew for new poetic meaning. For Ashkenazi poetry, this entails "adoption and adaptation" of "early Christian images of martyrdom," a parallel to the infusion of Arabic theme and style into Hispano-Hebraic poetry.[161]

Indeed, there is something particularly meaningful that poetry can generally more deeply convey than prose, as Einbinder explains: "Prose commemoration accounts for only a small proportion of Jewish writing about persecution and martyrdom, whereas non-narrative writing exerted an abiding influence in the creation and sustenance of martyrocentric attitudes among medieval Jews. The fact remains that most medieval Jews did not encounter martyrological texts in prose, but in verse—and moreover, verse that was performed in a liturgical setting."[162]

Hebrew verse allowed for a continuously meaningful profundity in northern liturgical traditions that prose could not match; in a comparable way, poetry, poetics in prose, and the very idea of poetry inspired the prosimetra of Christian Spain: ben Elʿazar fashioned characters who continuously hone their arts of poetic love, and ibn Ṣaqbel characterized Asher's poetic remorse as ongoing. Beyond confirming what the reader knows to be correct and righteous, as is the case in *Sefer ha-maʿasim*, these Iberian prosimetra and Ashkenazi devotional lyrics offer philosophical approaches to beauty, bound in an economy of language and with the hope of reshaping the reader's outlook and way of being. This does not necessarily mark a particular Jewish literary trend, but it does reveal interesting and diverse combinations of Hebrew language and Jewish content across various Jewish cultural regions.

Accordingly, Einbinder's comment on the reception of martyrological poetry also rings true for our prosimetra: "Lyric is hardly exempt from the questions we pose of other forms of cultural production. The social importance of this poetry lay in part in its ability to respond to real and perceived changes in the conditions of Jewish life. The literary conventions that characterize this poetry are not static but dynamic, and change as these conditions changed."[163]

Without the erotic, the poetry of Ashkenaz and northern France captured the same impulse toward beauty that the authors of prosimetra in the Mediterranean region sought, allowing their poets to rejuvenate the Hebrew language and to innovate their poetic practices. This effort requires a kind of love on the part of the poet—not the all-consuming love of eros, but a love nonetheless particular to the designer of verse, one so attuned to matters of words that the deeds they recount resonate both affectively and intellectively.

Notes

1. See chap. 1, note 5 for scholarship on Arabic and Romance elements in *Sefer ha-meshalim.*

2. Decter, *Iberian Jewish Literature*, 124, 156; Wacks, *Double Diaspora*, 34–63.

3. For the ability of love to ennoble the protagonists in *Sefer ha-meshalim*, see Schirmann, *Toledot ha-shira ha-ʿivrit bi-Sfarad ha-noṣrit uvi-drom Ṣarefat*, 237–38; Decter, *Iberian Jewish Literature*, 138–41; Levy, "Hybridity through Poetry."

4. *Sahar* means "moon" and *kima* means "the Pleiades." In the story, ben Elʿazar plays with the celestial meanings of the characters' names. Although the word sahar is found in the Song of Songs, there it means "round goblet," not "crescent moon." It developed the meaning of "moon" and was used frequently as such in medieval poetry. Ben Yehuda quotes a poem by Samuel ha-Nagid as an example. *Milon ha-lashon ha-ʿivrit ha-yeshana veha-ḥadasha*, 8:8975–77. It has equivalents in Akkadian and Arabic.

5. Scheindlin proposes that Sahar is tested both as poet and lover. "Sipure ha-ahava shel Yaʿaqov ben Elʿazar," 17. Decter notes that Sahar "learns the art of courtly love from Kima." *Iberian Jewish Literature*, 147.

6. Paris, "Etudes sur les romans de la Table Ronde," 519. Although Paris notes the similarity between troubadour lyrics and Chrétien's romances, John C. Moore notes that Paris does not specifically associate the troubadours with the term *amour courtois*. "'Courtly Love,'" 622. Still, the Occitan troubadours used terms that may loosely be translated to courtly love: *cortez'amor*, *fin'amor*, and *amor veraia*. See Cherchi, *Andreas and the Ambiguity of Courtly Love*, 4.

7. For discussions of potential Arabic influences on Romance literature, see Menéndez Pidal, *Poesía árabe y poesía europea*; Menocal, *Arabic Role in Medieval Literary History*. For the opposing opinion, see Dozy, *Spanish Islam*. For a consideration of Ovid's influence, see Schrötter, *Ovid und die Troubadours*. For a bibliography of the origin theories, see Boase, *Origin and Meaning of Courtly Love*.

8. For a skeptical view of the term, see Denomy, "Courtly Love and Courtliness," 46; Donaldson, "Myth of Courtly Love." For approval, see Ferrante, "*Cortes' Amor* in Medieval Texts."

9. Dronke, *Medieval Latin and the Rise of European Love-Lyric*, 2, 3.

10. Vadet, *L'Esprit courtois en Orient*, 18.

11. See Vadet, *L'Esprit courtois en Orient*; Pérès, *Poésie andalouse en arabe classique au XIe siècle*; Robinson, *In Praise of Song*; Robinson, *Medieval Andalusian Courtly Culture in the Mediterranean*. For a rich historical background on love—including religious, allegorical, erotic, and more—see Nirenberg and Capezzone, "Religions of Love."

12. Jacobi, "ʿUdhrī"; Lecker, "ʿUdhra."

13. Jacobi, "ʿUdhrī."

14. See Sells, "Love"; Blachère and Bausani, "Ghazal"; van Gelder, *Classical Arabic Literature*, 44. Some scholars have noted the profound influence of the poetry of al-ʿAbbās on the love poetry of al-Andalus, noting that ibn Ḥazm refers to al-ʿAbbās in the *Ṭawq*. Blachère, "al-ʿAbbās b. al-Aḥnaf"; Pérès, *La poésie andalouse en arabe classique au XIe siècle*, 54, 411.

15. Trans. in van Gelder, *Classical Arabic Literature*, 44. For the Arabic, see al-ʿAbbās ibn al-Aḥnaf, *Dīwān*, 72–73.

16. Blachère and Bausani, "Ghazal."

17. Brann, "He Said, She Said," 11. See also Scheindlin, *Wine, Women, and Death*, 80–86.

18. Ibn Gabirol, trans. in Scheindlin, *Wine, Women, and Death*, 130–31. For Hebrew and notes, see Schirmann, *Ha-shira ha-ʿivrit bi-Sfarad uvi-Provans*, book 1, 1:215.

19. The work in question, most commonly known as *Fons Vitae* (*The Fountain of Life*), was composed by ibn Gabirol in Judeo-Arabic, parts of which are contained in Moses ibn Ezra's *Maqālat al-ḥadīqa fī maʿnā al-majāz wa-l-ḥaqīqa*; see Fenton, "Gleanings from Môseh ibn 'Ezra's *Maqâlat al-Hadîqa*." See Goodman, "Editor's Introduction," 6; Pessin, *Ibn Gabirol's Theology of Desire*.

20. For an overview, see Wright and Rowson, *Homoeroticism in Classical Arabic Literature*.

21. *Symposium* was known in the classical Arabic world. See Gutas, "Plato's *Symposion* in the Arabic Tradition."

22. Decter, "Hebrew 'Sodomite' Tale from Thirteenth-Century Toledo," 188; Schirmann, "Ephebe in Medieval Hebrew Poetry." For grammatical and linguistic arguments, see Roth, "Deal Gently with the Young Man." Roth explains that when transliterated to Hebrew, *ṣabī*, an Arabic word for male youth, resembles *ṣevi*, the Hebrew word for male deer, which is fitting because deer was the most common poetic proxy for the beloved. "Deal Gently with the Young Man," 28. Others have argued that the second-person male endings more conveniently accommodated the rules of quantitative meter, which were an artificial fit for Hebrew and which warranted grammatical creativity. Roth followed Schirmann's example and advised that homoeroticism was a cultural norm in poetry and in life, citing evidence from responsa regarding actual cultural practices of the period. Pagis returns to the earlier argument that this was a poetic convention. *Hebrew Poetry*, 68. In his study of the story of Sapir, Shapir, and Birsha (another story contained in ben Elʿazar's *Sefer ha-meshalim*), Decter traces medieval poetic examples and theological opinions alongside twentieth-century scholarly debate on medieval homoeroticism, detailing how male-male eroticism, documented in classical Arabic culture, can likewise be found in medieval Christian Europe. "Hebrew 'Sodomite' Tale from Thirteenth-Century Toledo," 198–99.

23. As C. Stephen Jaeger reminds the reader in *Ennobling Love*, Eve Kosofsky Sedgwick's term "homosocial" can be productive in the medieval context and allows for "sexuality as the grounding of love, desire, and friendship." Jaeger, *Ennobling Love*, 15; Sedgwick, *Between*

Men. Jaeger cites and explicates a plethora of homoerotic lyrics in medieval Latin and Romance languages. He distinguishes between homosexuality in practice and in poetry as follows: "Very few texts of any genre from any milieu in the Middle Ages represent sex between males as ennobling or exalting. They are, however, only slightly fewer than the texts which represent sex between men and women as exalting. But putting aside the virulently antihomosexual literature (like Peter Damian's Book of *Gommorrha* or Alan of Lille's *Complaint of Nature*), the moral hesitations, the taboos, the circumscriptions and proscriptions relate to sexual intercourse, and not to the choice of gender in friendship and love relationships." *Ennobling Love*, 25.

24. For readings of these stories, see Decter, "Hebrew 'Sodomite' Tale from Thirteenth-Century Toledo"; Rosen, *Unveiling Eve*; Levy, "Hybridity through Poetry."

25. Arkoun, "ʿIshḳ."

26. Sells, "Love," 134; Smith and Pellat, "Rābiʿa al-ʿAdawiyya al-Ḳaysiyya."

27. Trans. in Coffin, *Princeton Online Arabic Poetry.*

28. Scheindlin, *The Gazelle: Medieval Hebrew Poems on God, Israel, and the Soul*, 73.

29. Judah Halevi, trans. in Scheindlin, *Gazelle*, 70–71. For Hebrew and notes, see Schirmann, *Ha-shira ha-ʿivrit bi-Sfarad uvi-Provans*, book 1, 2:471.

30. For a detailed discussion of the relationship between love and adab, see Vadet, *L'Esprit courtois en Orient*, 18. With regard to the spirituality of love in the Arabic tradition, Vadet brings up the "culte d'amour" found in the *ẓāhiri* tradition, which he compares to "l'union mystique," 438.

31. Raven, "al-Washshāʾ, Abu ʾl-jayyib Muḥammad b. Aḥmad b. Isḥāq al-Aʿrābī" and Vadet, "Ibn Dāwūd, Muḥammad b. Dāwūd b. ʿAlī b. Khalaf." For further discussion of the notion of "courtly love," see Vadet, "Littérature courtoise et transmission du ḥadit." For comments on the potentially problematic nature of this term, see Giffen, *Theory of Profane Love*, 14. For a thorough survey of ibn Dāwūd's life and of the *Zahra*, see Raven, "Ibn Dāwūd al-Iṣbahānī and his *Kitāb al-zahra*."

32. Vadet, "Ibn Dāwūd, Muḥammad b. Dāwūd b. ʿAlī b. Khalaf." Nykl defines the *Zahra* as a compilation: "a well-chosen collection of excellent verses on one subject." Preface to Ibn Dāwūd's *Kitāb al-zahra*, 6. García Gómez also considers the *Zahra* an anthology. "Un precedente y una consecuencia del *Collar de la paloma*," 312.

33. Ibn Dāwūd, *Kitāb al-zahra*, 8.

34. Ibn Dāwūd, 8.

35. Ibn Dāwūd, 10.

36. Ibn Dāwūd, 18. For background on Galen in classical Arabic, see Biesterfeldt and Gutas, "Malady of Love."

37. Ibn Dāwūd, *Kitāb al-zahra*, 15–16.

38. Gutas, "Plato's *Symposion* in the Arabic Tradition," 36; Rosenthal, "On the Knowledge of Plato's Philosophy in the Islamic World," 419.

39. Biesterfeldt and Gutas, "Malady of Love," 22.

40. Black, *Logic and Aristotle's Rhetoric and Poetics in Medieval Arabic Philosophy*, 1, 5.

41. Trans. in Jackson, "Al-Jahiz on Translation," 101.

42. Giffen, *Theory of Profane Love*, 14.

43. Giffen, 14. Further, Giffen includes *Kitāb al-muwashshā* in her study on treatises on profane love for the following reasons: "The *ẓarf/adab* ideal imposes standards of decency, manners, and emotional behavior. Integral parts of this code were the concepts of idealized and chaste (ʿ*Udhrī*) love." *Theory of Profane Love*, 14.

44. "Bi-l-ṣabwa wa-l-ghazal." al-Washshā', *Kitāb al-muwashshā*, 83.
45. "Shuʿarā' al-ʿarab." al-Washshā', 84.
46. This kind of collecting appears across literary traditions, from al-Washshā''s *Muwashshā* and Petrarch's *Canzoniere* to Walter Benjamin's practice of collecting quotations, as Hannah Arendt describes it: "Benjamin's ideal of producing a work consisting entirely of quotations, one that was mounted so masterfully that it could dispense with any accompanying text, may strike one as whimsical in the extreme and self-destructive to boot, but it was not, any more than were the contemporaneous surrealistic experiments which arose from similar impulses." Arendt, "Introduction," 47.
47. al-Washshā', *Kitāb al-muwashshā*, 67, poems 1–2; 67–68, poems 3–5.
48. al-Washshā', 67, poem 2, verse 2.
49. al-Washshā', 69–71.
50. "Wa-min ziyyahim al-waqar." al-Washshā', 74. Many thanks to Andrew McLaren for discussing this passage with me.
51. "Bi-anna al-ḥubba min shiyami al-kirāmi." al-Washshā', 74, poem 18, hemistich 2. Contrary to the popular view of prose as providing the substance of a prosimetrum, poetry here establishes the narrative's link between noblemen and love. Brogan notes that the verse components of a prosimetrum have been traditionally defined as "lyric, emotive, or personal insets within a philosophical or narrative frame." Brogan, "Prosimetrum," 1115.
52. Ibn Ḥazm, *Ṭawq*, 21. Giffen notes the following: although ibn Ḥazm refers to ibn Dāwūd to disagree with his position on a particular matter, ibn Dāwūd is not responsible for the position with which ibn Ḥazm disagrees, since ibn Dāwūd attributes this stance to "one of the philosophers." She speculates that ibn Dāwūd was referring to Aristophanes's speech in Plato's *Symposium*. Giffen, *Theory of Profane Love*, 79–80. Nykl comments in the foreword to his edition of the *Zahra* that ibn Ḥazm must have been quite familiar with the *Zahra* and indicates in the textual notes whenever it seems that ibn Ḥazm has drawn on a particular passage for use in the *Ṭawq*. Dāwūd, *Kitāb al-zahra*, 4.
53. The *Ṭawq* begins with a prologue in which ibn Ḥazm situates the treatise as his response to a friend's inquiry. He follows with a description of the text's contents, explaining that he has divided it into thirty chapters: ten on "the principles of love," twelve on "the accidents of love" and its praiseworthy and blameworthy qualities, six on "the misfortunes" pertaining to love, and two closing chapters that praise God and honor good over evil. "uṣūl al-ḥubb; aʿrāḍ al-ḥubb; āfāt." Ibn Ḥazm, *Ṭawq*, 17–18.
54. "Bāb ʿalāmāt al-ḥubb." Ibn Ḥazm, *Ṭawq*, 17–35; trans. Arberry, in Ibn Ḥazm, *The Ring of the Dove*, 33–45.
55. "Fa-laysa li-ʿaynī ʿinda ghayraki mawqif." Ibn Ḥazm, *Ṭawq*, 27.
56. "In qāla lam astamiʿ mimman yujālisunī illā siwā lafẓihi l-mustaṭrafi l-ghunujī." Ibn Ḥazm, *Ṭawq*, 28. In verse: A man [in love] becomes generous, spending all he could from that which was prohibited to him before that: "Wa-minhā an yajūd al-mar' bi-badhl kull mā kāna yaqdir ʿalayhi mimmā kāna mumtaniʿ bihi qabl dhālika." Ibn Ḥazm, *Ṭawq*, 28.
57. Pagis, *Hebrew Poetry of the Middle Ages and the Renaissance*, 30.
58. Pagis, 32–36.
59. Arberry translates the third verse of the eighth poem, in which ibn Ḥazm incorporates five comparisons into a single verse, as follows: "It was as if myself, and she, / The cup, the wine, the obscurity, / Were earth, and raindrops, and pearls set / Upon a thread, and gold, and jet." Ibn Ḥazm, *The Ring of the Dove*, 41. "ka-annī wa-hiya wa-l-ka'sa wa-l-khamra wa-l-dujā tharan wa-ḥayan wa-l-durru wa-l-tibru wa-l-shabajū." Ibn Ḥazm, *Ṭawq*, 31.

60. "Mithl al-ifrāṭ fī ṣifat al-nuḥūl, wa-tashbīh al-dumūʿ bil-amṭār wa-anna-hā tarwī al-sifār, wa-ʿadam al-nawm al-battatan, wa-inqiṭāʿ al-ghidhāʾ jumlatan." Ibn Ḥazm, 195.

61. "But let every lover be pale; this is the lover's hue. Such looks become him; only fools think that such looks avail not. Pale over Side did Orion wander in the woods, pale was Daphnis when the naiad proved unkind. Let leanness also prove your feelings; nor deem it base to set a hood on your bright locks. Nights of vigil make thin the bodies of lovers, and anxiety and the distress that a great passion brings." Ovid, *Art of Love and Other Poems*, 62–63.

62. "Illā anna-hā ashyāʾ lā ḥaqīqa lahā, wa-kidhb lā wajh lahu." Ibn Ḥazm, *Ṭawq*, 194, 195.

63. Ibn Ḥazm, 196.

64. Robinson, *Medieval Andalusian Courtly Culture in the Mediterranean*, 127–29, 175.

65. Robinson, 129.

66. Robinson, 97, 103.

67. Pagis, *Hebrew Poetry of the Middle Ages and the Renaissance*, 30.

68. While classical Arabic treatises on profane love proliferated and seem to have offered relevant insight into the nature of love and the process of courtship, the only widely studied Latin or Romance vernacular equivalent is of dubious import: scholars question the reliability of Andreas Capellanus's *De amore* as an authority on the topic of courtly love. Cherniss, "Literary Comedy of Andreas Capellanus," 223. Peter Dronke likewise views the treatise as an unsuitable source for considering courtly love poetry: Capellanus's treatise "is a clerical *jeu d'esprit*, not a guide to the interpretation of love-lyrics." Dronke, *Medieval Latin and the Rise of European Love-Lyric*, 1:47. Indeed, while poetry is the backbone of the analogous Arabic texts, Capellanus does not discuss the role of poetry at all in his treatise.

69. Dana, "Who Is Moses Ibn Ezra's 'Jewish Poet'?," 281.

70. Ibn Ezra, *Kitāb al-muḥāḍara wa-l-mudhākara*, 1:117.

71. For instance, consider ibn Ezra's poem in which the speaker encourages youths to seek worldly pleasures:

> "Caress a lovely woman's breast by night, / And kiss some beauty's lips by morning light . . . Immerse your heart in pleasure and in joy, / and by the bank a bottle drink of wine, / enjoy the swallow's chirp and viol's whine. / Laugh, dance, and stamp your feet upon the floor! / Get drunk, and knock at dawn on some girl's door. / This is the joy of life, so take your due . . ."

Ibn Ezra, trans. in Scheindlin, *Wine, Women, and Death*, 90–91. For the Hebrew and notes, see Schirmann, *Ha-shira ha-ʿivrit bi-Sfarad uvi-Provans*, book 1, 2:370–71.

72. Sadan, "Identity and Inimitability." Ben Elʿazar's defense of Hebrew is in the preface of *Sefer ha-meshalim*.

73. Drory, "Hidden Context," 9.

74. Guerau de Cabrera's *Ensenhament* (c. 1145–1170), perhaps a precursor to Vidal's treatise, is a 216-verse poem that offers compositional advice. For the text, see Riquer, *Los cantares de gesta franceses*, 378–406. For background on the *artes de trobar*, see Johnston, "Literary Tradition and the Idea of Language in the *Artes de Trobar*."

75. Chaytor, *History of Aragon and Catalonia*, 52–65, 292–93.

76. Kay, *Parrots and Nightingales*, 12.

77. For a study of the ibn Tibbons and Andalusi intellectualism in southern France, see Pearce, *Andalusi Literary and Intellectual Tradition*.

78. Marcus, "Jewish-Christian Symbiosis," 486. A graphical convention of Judeo languages, the use of Hebrew letters in Judeo-Romance dialects was used in translations of the Hebrew Bible and soon after in secular texts, such as mid-fifteenth-century *Poema de*

Yuçuf (Poem of Joseph), a rhymed rendering of the Joseph story that scholars have deemed the earliest secular Ladino text. Lazar, *Sephardic Tradition*, 16.

79. Kay, *Parrots and Nightingales*, 12.

80. Trans. in Kay, *Parrots and Nightingales*, 29. "car tota la parladura de Lemosyn se parla naturalmenz et per cas et per [nombres et per] genres et per temps et per personas et per motz, aisi com poretz auzir aissi si ben o escoutas." Vidal, *"Razos de Trobar" of Raimon Vidal*, B text, lines 86–89, at 6.

81. Deyermond, "Juan Ruiz's Attitude to Literature," 122; Poe, *From Poetry to Prose in Old Provençal*, 93.

82. "Va-yivḥar bi-lshon ha-qodesh leshon ha-ʿivrim." Ben Elʿazar, *Sipure ahava shel Yaʿakov ben Elʿazar*, ed. David, 13, line 8.

83. Kay, *Parrots and Nightingales*, 15–16. Kay further links Occitan poetics and desire: "From the very beginning, troubadour lyrics intertwine desire and knowledge. They express desire; they lay claim to knowledge of desire; they inspire, in different proportions in different listeners, the desire to desire and the desire to know; these in turn fuel the desire for lyric as both a vehicle and an object of knowledge; and a discursive field is created in which different subjects of desire/knowledge are supposed," 17.

84. "Bien s'escai [a] dompna ardimenz." Trans. in Kay, *Parrots and Nightingales*, 34.

85. Singleton, "Dante," 47; "Friend Bertran, this is a game we share." Bruckner, Shepard, and White, *Songs of the Women Troubadours*, 52–53, line 36.

86. Auerbach, *Mimesis*, 141.

87. "Tot lo maltraich e.l dampnatge / que per vos m'es escaritz / vos grazir fan mos lignatge / e sobre totz mos maritz." Bruckner, Shepard, and White, *Songs of the Women Troubadours*, 24–25, lines 41–44.

88. Lang, "Relations of the Earliest Portuguese Lyric School with the Troubadours and Trouvères," 105; Mermier, "Diaspora of the Occitan Troubadours," 69.

89. Interestingly, Eleanor is rendered as the ice queen protagonist in Lope de Vega's (1562–1635) play, *La judía de Toledo* (*The Jewess of Toledo*).

90. Fidalgo, *De amor y de burlas*, 24.

91. See chap. 1, note 6 for sources on Jews as translators.

92. Deyermond, "Juan Ruiz's Attitude to Literature," 122. This is analogous to the "division of labor" of Latin, Greek, and Arabic in twelfth-century Sicily. Mallette, *Kingdom of Sicily, 1100–1250*, 7.

93. *Kalila wa-Dimna* is a collection of didactic animal fables originally composed in Sanskrit as *Panchatantra*. Ben Elʿazar translated ibn al-Muqaffaʿ's Arabic unrhymed prose version of the text into Hebrew rhymed prose. The other translation of ibn al-Muqaffaʿ's version, by Rabbi Joel in the early twelfth century, was rendered in Hebrew unrhymed prose. Although this means ben Elʿazar took artistic liberties, it does not necessarily mean that his translation was more "poetic" because of its use of rhymed prose. In the Arabic tradition of literary criticism, rhymed prose (*sajʿ*) was classified as prose—albeit eloquent prose—and not as a halfway point between prose and poetry. For further discussion of the transmission and translations of *Kalila wa-Dimna*, see Brockelmann, "Kalila Wa-Dimna." For ben Elʿazar's version of *Kalila wa-Dimna*, see Elʿazar and Jacob, *Deux versions hébraïques du livre de Kalīlah et Dimnāh*. For a fascinating comparative analysis of ben Elʿazar's translation and the Castilian rendering, see Girón-Negrón, "How the Go Between Cut Her Nose."

94. For an edition of the Castilian, see Cacho Blecua and Lacarra, *Calila e Dimna*.

95. E s'acors del cors adreig
Ab que'm conort e'm refraing
No mi ven sai part l'abril,
Al torn que farai d'Espaigna,
I alai non creszatz
Que flors ni vergiers ni pratz
Gaire m'aiut ni bo'm sia,
ni'l chanz pels plaiszatz,
ni d'autrui paria
no m'a grat tant quon solia
ni'm tenc per assolassatz,
per qu'eu prenc mains breus comiatz.

Giraut de Borneil, trans. in Sharman, *Cansos and Sirventes of the Troubadour, Giraut de Borneil*, 212–14.

96. Paden et al., "Troubadour's Lady: Her Marital Status and Social Rank," 38.

97. "E mostra'm com m'en venria / Iois e bes devas totz latz, / Si'l chan me sufri'en patz." Giraut de Borneil, trans. in Sharman, *Cansos and Sirventes of the Troubadour, Giraut de Borneil*, 212–14.

98. Lang, "Relations of the Earliest Portuguese Lyric School with the Troubadours and Trouvères," 209–11; Mermier, "Diaspora of the Occitan Troubadours," 67–91.

99. Shapiro, "Provençal Trobairitz and the Limits of Courtly Love," 568. For a similar list of these characteristics, see Dronke, *Medieval Latin and the Rise of European Love-Lyric*, 7.

100. Lang, "The Relations of the Earliest Portuguese Lyric School with the Troubadours and Trouvères," 222.

101. —Dizede, madre, por que me metestes
en tal prison, e por que mi tolhestes
que non possa meu amigo veer?
—Por que, filha, des que o [vós] conhocestes,
nunca punhou erg' en mi vos tolher.

Cohen, *500 Cantigas*, 453–54; trans. in Cohen, *Poetics of the "Cantigas d'Amigo,"* 18.

102. Trans. in van Gelder, *Classical Arabic Literature*, 71. For the Arabic, see ibn al-Khaṭīb, *Jaysh al-tawshīḥ*, 273–74.

103. Mermier, "Diaspora of the Occitan Troubadours," 80; Frenk, *Lírica española de tipo popular*, 13. Frenk also notes the depiction of natural elements as magical in the Galician-Portuguese tradition as opposed to that in the Occitan tradition (80). Lang, "Relations of the Earliest Portuguese Lyric School with the Troubadours and Trouvères," 212; Cohen, *500 Cantigas*, 299.

104. Disseron m' oj', ai amiga, que non
é meu amig' almirante do mar,
e meu coraçon ja pode folgar
e dormir ja, e, por esta razon,
o que do mar meu amigo sacou
saque o Deus de coitas, ca jogou

mui ben a min, ca ja non andarei
triste por vento que veja fazer
nen por tormenta non ei de perder

o sono, amiga, mais, se foi el rei,
o que do mar meu amigo sacou,
<saque o Deus de coitas, ca jogou>

mui ben a min, ca, ja cada que vir
algun ome de fronteira chegar,
non ei medo que mi diga pesar,
mais, por qu m' el fez ben sen lho pedir
o que do mar meu amigo sacou,
<saque o Deus de coitas, ca jogou>

Cohen, *500 Cantigas*, 299; trans. in Cohen, "*Cantigas d'Amigo*," 90–91.

105. Schirmann, "Les Contes rimés de Jacob ben Eléazar de Tolède," 295; Scheindlin, "Sipure ha-ahava shel Yaʿaqov ben Elʿazar," 17; Decter, *Iberian Jewish Literature*, 152. Schirmann, Scheindlin, and Decter relate the love stories of *Sefer ha-meshalim* to *Aucassin et Nicolette*, a topic that I address more thoroughly in chap. 3, in the discussion of concrete metaphors. The work is often referred to as a *chantefable*, since this is the term the anonymous author coined to describe it: "no cantefable prent fin, / n'en sai plus dire." *Aucassin et Nicolette*, 40. Mason translates the term *chantefable* as "song and tale." *Aucassin and Nicolette*, 72. Scheindlin compares Nicolette's prominence in the story to that of Yemima and Yefefiya in the seventh story of *Sefer ha-meshalim*. "Sipure ha-ahava shel Yaʿaqov ben Elʿazar," 19.

106. Barolini, *Dante and the Origins of Italian Literary Culture*, 175–92.

107. Although *Sefer ha-meshalim* does not mimic the framework of the canonical Arabic maqama, it shares the impulse to defend the merits of the Hebrew language with its fellow Hebrew maqamas. Given that the *Taḥkemoni* is the only example of a "canonical" Hebrew maqama—that is, a maqama that follows the narrator-hero/trickster framework established in the Arabic maqama—the preoccupation among authors of Hebrew prosimetra with defending Hebrew is perhaps a more fitting unifying trait and may be regarded the true hallmark of the genre. For comparisons of *Neʾum Asher* and *Sefer ha-meshalim*, see Scheindlin, "Sipure ha-ahava shel Yaʿaqov ben Elʿazar," 16; Decter, *Iberian Jewish Literature*, 152–54.

108. Decter points out the importance of poetic education, or lack thereof: "Asher never learns to recite poetry, as is demanded of the lover. Sahar, on the other hand, undergoes a process of maturation, largely through the instruction of his wise and more sophisticated beloved." *Iberian Jewish Literature*, 152.

109. "Temol tigʿar be-ʿosheq dal / ve-sham hayom ʿashaqatni // heniʾatni ve-helʾatni / meḥaṣatni meḥaqatni // ve-yom mati deʿu-na ki / feridatah hemitatni." Ben Elʿazar, "Sipure ha-ahava shel Yaʿaqov ben Elʿazar," ed. Schirmann, 251, lines 102–4.

110. This is the twentieth maqama in the old numbering and the thirteenth in Yahalom and Katsumata's numbering.

111. Scheindlin, "Asher in the Harem," 256.

112. *Neʾum Asher* and *Sefer ha-meshalim* share other motifs that do not appear in the context of poetry, such as the twinkling eye behind the wall. For this motif in *Neʾum Asher*, see ibn Ṣaqbel, *Neʾum Asher ben Yehuda*, in Schirmann, *Ha-shira ha-ʿivrit bi-Sfarad uvi-Provans*, book 1, 2:557, lines 22–23. For this motif in Sahar and Kima, see ben Elʿazar, "Sipure ha-ahava shel Yaʿaqov ben Elʿazar," ed. Schirmann 249, line 59. In addition to noting the apple poems, discussed in the third chapter, Decter also points out the lovers' waiting to meet and the figure of the "older man" as traits that the two texts share. *Iberian Jewish Literature*, 152.

113. Nafshi—amatkha—nivhala / uve-faḥ me'arevim nafela.
ma tigʿara vi—va-ani / nilkad be-ḥesheq yaʿala?
ma yesh be-yadi laʿasot? / ʿeni le-nafshi ʿolala!

Ibn Ṣaqbel, *Ne'um Asher ben Yehuda*, in Schirmann, *Ha-shira ha-ʿivrit bi-Sfarad uvi-Provans*, book 1, 2:559, lines 60–62.

114. Ibn Ṣaqbel, book 1, 2:559, line 64.

115. This maqama is thirteen in the old numbering of the *Taḥkemoni* and ten in the new numbering by Yahalom and Katsumata in their 2010 edition of the *Taḥkemoni*.

116. Ibn Paquda, *Duties of the Heart*, 246.

117. Scheindlin notes the rarity of this event. "Asher in the Harem," 265n17. Schippers mentions Judah Halevi's discussion with the "walls of his heart," but the heart does not respond as a personified character. He also comments on the theme of the "heart as prisoner." Schippers, *Spanish Hebrew Poetry and the Arabic Literary Tradition*, 160–61, 170–73.

118. Ben Elʿazar also includes poems written on a variety of objects, including apples and curtains, in his ninth story. Poems written on objects will be discussed in detail in the following chapter.

119. However, the notion of Castile's vernacular as a literary tongue was still on the horizon. Scheindlin finds elements from the Romance tradition in *Ne'um Asher*. "Fawns of the Palace and Fawns of the Field," 200.

120. Ibn Ṣaqbel, *Ne'um Asher ben Yehuda*, in Schirmann, *Ha-shira ha-ʿivrit bi-Sfarad uvi-Provans*, book 1, 2:563, line 146.

121. Scheindlin, "Fawns of the Palace and Fawns of the Field," 199–200.

122. "Sheʿu, dodai, yefi siḥi ve-tuvo / ve-shimru-na, leval tinaqeshu vo: / halo hem laʿage ʿogevim u-milim / asher bada yedidkhem mi-levavo!" Ibn Ṣaqbel, *Ne'um Asher ben Yehuda*, in Schirmann, *Ha-shira ha-ʿivrit bi-Sfarad uvi-Provans*, book 1, 2:565, lines 197–98.

123. For analyses of these poems and their progression of "mood and theme," see Scheindlin, "Fawns of the Palace and Fawns of the Field," 192–94.

124. Schirmann and Fleischer studied a fragment by ibn Ṣaqbel that likewise began with "Ne'um Asher ben Yehuda," which attests to the possibility of additional stories by ibn Ṣaqbel. Schirmann, "Poets Contemporaneous with Moses ibn Ezra and Judah Halevi"; Fleischer, "Studies in Liturgical and Secular Poetry."

125. For a discussion of the similarities between ibn Ṣaqbel and al-Ḥarizi's versions, see Dishon, "Ne'um Asher ben Yehuda li-Shlomo ibn Ṣaqbel ve-ha-maqama ha-ʿesrim be-Taḥkemoni li-Yhuda al-Ḥarizi."

126. Heman's poem:
yaʿla asher libi ka-ḥuṭ meshakhathu / uve-gaḥale ḥishqah hayom serafathu.
ḥimli ʿalai ḥosheq nafsho mekharathu / uve-ma'asar ahav ʿeno netanathu
na raḥami ʿalav u-feni be-ḥen elav / pen yomeru ʿalav isha haragathu.

al-Ḥarizi, *Taḥkemoni*, ed. Yahalom and Katsumata 236–37.

"Fair maid, who has drawn my heart like a cord, / And with coals of longing for her this day has burned it, / Have pity on one, the lust of whose soul has sold him, / And whose eyes have landed him over into the prison of love, / Pray, have compassion on him and turn in grace to him, / That man say not of him: 'A woman slew him,'" al-Ḥarizi, *The Book of Taḥkemoni*, trans. Reichert, 81.

Verses 1–2 and 15–16 from Ḥever's poem: "ṣeviyat ḥen levana kha-levana / ve-saʿrah ʿal me'or leḥyah ʿanana // sefatah ṣuf ve-leḥyah man ve-ruqah / ke-ṭal orot u-faneha ke-gana." al-Ḥarizi, *Taḥkemoni*, ed. Yahalom and Katsumata, 238–9. "Graceful damsel, white as the moon, / Whose hair is a cloud upon the light of her cheek!" and "Her lips are flowing honey;

her cheeks are manna; and her kisses / Are the dew of lights, and her face as a garden," al-Ḥarizi, *The Book of Taḥkemoni,* trans. Reichert, 83–84.

127. Dronke, *Medieval Latin and the Rise of European Love-Lyric,* 7.

128. Auerbach, *Mimesis,* 134. Scheindlin and Decter note that the notions of the testing and proving of the lover come from the Romance tradition. Scheindlin, "Sipure ha-ahava shel Yaʿaqov ben Elʿazar," 17; Decter, *Iberian Jewish Literature,* 156.

129. "Ve-divre ḥishqam meḥadesh / ki riv ahavim ha-yedidot loṭesh." Ben Elʿazar, "Sipure ha-ahava shel Yaʿaqov ben Elʿazar," ed. Schirmann, 265, lines 457–58. Scheindlin and Decter refer to the lovers' quarrels in the story of Sahar and Kima as a characteristic of Romance courtly love. Scheindlin, "Sipure ha-ahava shel Yaʿaqov ben Elʿazar," 17; Decter, *Iberian Jewish Literature,* 146, 155–56. Bibring discusses these lovers' quarrels with respect to the medieval literature of northern France in "Fairies, Lovers, and Glass Palaces."

130. For a more detailed summary and explication of the story, see Rosen, "Story of Maskil and Peninah by Jacob ben Elʿazar." For a translation and commentary, see Levy and Torollo, "Romance Literature in Hebrew Language with an Arabic Twist."

131. "Va-yaḥbi'eni be-ḥadre morashav." Ben Elʿazar, *Sipure ahava shel Yaʿakov ben Elʿazar,* ed. David, 15. In Hebrew, soul (*nefesh*) is feminine, heart (*lev*) is masculine, and commander of the army is masculine (*sar ha-ṣava*).

132. The *I* who awakens is Jacob, not Lemuʾel ben ʾItiʾel, the fictional narrator of all ten stories. For a discussion of the roles of narrator and author, see Rosen, *Unveiling Eve,* 97.

133. "Gan shaʿashuʿim." Ben Elʿazar, *Sipure ahava shel Yaʿakov ben Elʿazar,* ed. David, 19.

134. "Ve-yashanti ve-libi ʿer / ve-hine qol ṣevi dofeq // ṣeviya, dai leheradem, / lekhi ʿal dod lehitrapeq // vekhi-shmoʿa levavi zaʿ / ve-lo yakhol lehitʾapeq." Ben Elʿazar, 15; trans. in Levy and Torollo, "Romance Literature in Hebrew Language with an Arabic Twist," 289. The tone of the three verses is confusing at first glance, since the supposed speaker, the Soul, refers to the narrator's heart as "my Heart" in the first and third verses. The reader would expect the narrator—and not his soul—to speak about the heart in this manner, but this construction appears again in the story and might reflect the Soul's Neoplationic vision of herself as superior to (and possessor of) both the Heart and the narrator (i.e., the body). See ben Elʿazar, *Sipure ahava shel Yaʿakov ben Elʿazar,* ed. David, 17, line 52 for another example of the Soul's reference to "my Heart."

135. There is also a precedent for the beloved as a deer in the Song of Songs, a fact that complements the reference to the Song of Songs, 5.2 in the first verse. For an explanation of the deer as a reference to the beloved, see Schirmann, *Le-toledot ha-shira veha-drama ha-ʿivrit*; Scheindlin, "Fawns of the Palace and Fawns of the Field," 81. For speculation on the deer as an allegorical figure, see Tobi, *Between Hebrew and Arabic Poetry,* 127–30.

136. "Qeḥi ʿeni reut ʿofra le-ṣeda / ve-ze ḥelqekh levad min ha-yedida // ve-gam at, pi, yeʿad libekh lenasheqah / tehalelkha be-khol yom ha-yeʿuda // ve-zot torat yedide ha-tevuna / u-venehem halo zot ha-teʿuda // u-ma mara peridat yaʿalat ḥen / u-ma qashe sefod ʿal ha-perida." Ben Elʿazar, *Sipure ahava shel Ya'akov ben El'azar,* ed. David, 16; trans. in Levy and Torollo, "Romance Literature in Hebrew Language with an Arabic Twist," 291.

137. "Dod hayiqṣof ʿal raʿayato ve-nishbaʿ / ḥe yedidot, lule levavi haragtikh // kazva lah nafshi ve-eni ke-ḥosheq / hen temol baʿlat emunim yedaʿtikh // zot teʿudat dodim: ṣeviya teḥaref / yaʿane dodah: hen be-nafshi peditikh!" Ben Elʿazar, *Sipure ahava shel Yaʿakov ben Elʿazar,* ed. David, 18; trans. in Levy and Torollo, "Romance Literature in Hebrew Language with an Arabic Twist," 293.

138. "That the critic most attentive to the rhetorical and formal structures operative in the troubadour and trouvère lyric should have so insisted on the need to consider the medieval

love poets in relation to the philosophical tradition attests to the degree to which poetic and philosophical production in the eleventh and twelfth centuries cannot easily be separated. The unity of literary form and philosophical discourse in the twelfth century . . . has been repeatedly stressed by historians of medieval philosophy." Heller-Roazen, "Matter of Language," 853.

139. "Meshal sekhel kevar nishlam / be-ʿinyan ahava naʿsa." Ben Elʿazar, *Sipure ahava shel Yaʿakov ben Elʿazar*, ed. David, 22; trans. in Levy and Torollo, "Romance Literature in Hebrew Language with an Arabic Twist," 301.

140. The third poem draws attention to the voice of the poet, who laments the difficulty of writing poetry about separation yet manages to do precisely that. The purpose of this seems not to be an assertion of ben Elʿazar's authorship. The story does include two references to Jacob—the first name of the author but not of the narrator. In at least one of these instances, Jacob might refer to the people of Israel. See Isaiah, 39.22. In Isaiah, Jacob refers to the people of Israel, but as David mentions in his notes to the edition of *Sefer ha-meshalim*, in this context, Jacob might also refer to the author himself. Notes to ben Elʿazar, *Sipure ahava shel Ya'akov ben Elʿazar*, ed. David, 120, note to line 156. Rosen also considers the role of "Jacob" in the story in *Unveiling Eve*, 97. Rather than drawing attention to himself or to the Soul, he instead seems to highlight the trope of the difficulty of versification, one that features prominently in love poems across traditions as the lover strives to capture the attention of his beloved.

141. Rosen terms the Heart a "synecdoche for the whole body." *Unveiling Eve*, 96.

142. "Va-taqom nafshi va-tishtaḥu lemulo / va-tevkh va-titḥanen lo / va-tomer: ha-lo yadaʿta ki libi li uv-dabri ʿim adam yitʾane / ve-ʿoz panav yeshune / uvi-rʾoto oti leqaḥani / vela-ḥadarav heviʾani/ uv-morashav heḥbiʾani / ve-omnam en ʿata roʾani." Ben Elʿazar, *Sipure ahava shel Yaʿakov ben Elʿazar*, ed. David, 17; trans. in Levy and Torollo, "Romance Literature in Hebrew Language with an Arabic Twist," 291.

143. "Libi beyad ha-ṣvi sam / gam ha-ṣevi hu feqido // adam beli lev hayiḥye / u-ṣevi nesaʾo ve-yado." Ben Elʿazar, *Sipure ahava shel Yaʿakov ben Elʿazar*, ed. David, 17; trans. in Levy and Torollo, "Romance Literature in Hebrew Language with an Arabic Twist," 292.

144. "Ve-yaʿaṭnu meʿil-ḥen gam ʿanava / ve-lavashnu levush-ahav ve-yirʿa // ve-kharatnu berit-ḥesheq beli mum / asher lo yaʿalena riv ve-qinʾa // anaḥnu nosʾe ʿol tom ve-ḥesheq / ve-lev nose shete ele hanirʾa // ve-ruaḥ ahava teʿor leharaʿ / aval ruaḥ ḥakhama hi meniʾa // ve-ruaḥ ahavati nikhbesha vi / ve-ḥokhma lavesha gaʾon ve-geʾa // reve dodim ḥashavunu meqaneʾim / ve-he yavesh geronenu be-ṣimʾa." Ben Elʿazar, "Sipure ha-ahava shel Yaʿaqov ben Elʿazar," ed. Schirmann, 264; translations of the ninth story are my own.

145. The travels of the Occitan troubadours "contributed to the diffusion of the artform into other languages such as Northern French, starting at the end of the 12th century." Paden, "Occitan Poetry."

146. Kushelevsky, *Tales in Context*, 51. For an overview of these tales and their context, see Yassif, *Hebrew Folktale*.

147. Kushelevsky, *Tales in Context*, 17–18; Kushelevsky, "Chastity versus Courtly Love."

148. The romance as a genre does not necessarily necessitate poetry: "By the 13th century, however, any tale of adventure, whatever the origin of its matter and whether in verse or prose, could be romance. The earlier examples are mainly in verse; hence medieval romances are often called 'metrical romances,' though after 1400, variant forms, continuations, or new subjects were mostly in prose, the dominant medium from the 13th century." Varty, "Medieval Romance."

149. Kushelevsky, *Tales in Context*, 545. For background on the quest as a part of the romance, see Varty, "Medieval Romance."

150. Kushelevsky, *Tales in Context*, 549; Jauss and Benzinger, "Literary History as a Challenge to Literary Theory."

151. For a discussion of the parodic intent in the maqama, see Fishman, "Medieval Parody of Misogyny."

152. Kushelevsky, "Chastity versus Courtly Love," 74. For the texts, see Kushelevsky, *Tales in Context*, 292–303, 276–81.

153. For a discussion of women as teachers of poetry within the context of courtly love, see Jaeger, *Ennobling Love*, 77, 88: "It is important to note that at the same time woman becomes virtuous, she also becomes a poet. The image of the virtuous woman is coupled with learning virtue, but also with learning and practicing poetry."

154. Zeeman, "Lover-Poet and Love as the Most Pleasing 'Matere,'" 821. Zeeman refers the reader to *Las Leys d'amors* as the text that established "amours" as a metaphor for poetry.

155. Kushelevsky, "Chastity versus Courtly Love," 64–65.

156. Varty describes the role of women in a romance as follows: "Women always play important roles, allowing authors to depict, analyze, and celebrate matters of the heart. Indeed, love often ennobles the hero, spurring him on to deeds of prowess which confirm him as the ideally chivalrous knight, wonderfully good-mannered, brave beyond belief, acutely conscious of honor and loyalty, ever merciful to his enemies, helpful to the oppressed." "Medieval Romance."

157. Jaeger, *Ennobling Love*, 109.

158. Rotman, "At the Limits of Reality," 128. Thirteenth-century *Sefer Ḥasidim*, mentioned earlier in this chapter, does refer to knights and thus demonstrates an awareness of courtly culture, but such references are used as *in malo* examples. See Marcus, "Why Is This Knight Different?"

159. Einbinder, *Beautiful Death*, 22.

160. Habermann, "Beginning of Hebrew Poetry in Italy and Northern Europe," 272.

161. Shepkaru, "To Die for God," 334.

162. Einbinder, *Beautiful Death*, 102.

163. Einbinder, 19.

3

LOVE BETWEEN POETRY AND PROSE

Concrete Metaphors

In poetry it is all right to speak of "white milk," but in prose this kind of thing is rather inappropriate and, if overdone, it gives the game away and exposes the writing as poetic in nature.

—Aristotle, *The Art of Rhetoric*

The reflective medium of poetic forms appears in prose; for this reason, prose may be called the idea of poetry.

—Walter Benjamin, "The Concept of Criticism in German Romanticism"

As love and poetry take center stage as paths to transformation, prose must adapt to new roles. Accordingly, this chapter delves more deeply into the intricate balance between prose and poetry in medieval prosimetra by Jewish authors via a study of metaphor. After examining the practices of writing poetry about objects that are metaphors for the beloved and writing poetry about writing on these same objects, I turn to a discussion of the literalizing of poetic metaphors in the prose found in medieval prosimetra. I pay particular attention to the intersections among metaphor, love, and form in *Ne'um Asher ben Yehuda* and *Sefer ha-meshalim*. I see the prosification of metaphors traditionally found in poetry—not to be confused with the didactic practice of turning verse to prose discussed in the first chapter—as a defining element of some Jewish authors' developing visions of fictional worldly love as being steeped in poetics even when articulated in prose. I compare these literal or concrete metaphors in ibn Ṣaqbel's and ben Elʿazar's compositions to those in al-Ḥarīrī's and al-Hamadhānī's classical Arabic maqamas, al-Ḥarizi's *Taḥkemoni*, Tibaut's polymetric *Li romanz de la poire*, and *Aucassin et Nicolette*, whose thematic and structural similarities to *Sefer ha-meshalim* Schirmann and others have noted.[1] Further, I discuss ways in which this literary concept differs from its didactic or theoretical counterparts and what these differences indicate with regard to the meaning of metaphor.

The Prosification of Metaphor

Though the phenomenon of metaphors in prose bears resemblance to *metalepsis/transumption*, *metonymy*, and *synecdoche*, no rhetorical term seems to fit it perfectly.[2] Instead, I use the term *concrete metaphor* to represent this particular use of metaphor in this particular literary time and space. I define this practice via both textual examples and a discussion of relevant medieval theories of metaphor. It is easier to explain what a concrete metaphor is *not* than what it is: it is *not* an instance of *concrete poetry*—"a work that has been composed with specific attention to graphic features such as typography, layout, shape, or distribution on the page"—nor is it *carmina figurata* (Lat. "shaped songs"), the equivalent of concrete poetry in reference to ancient and medieval poems whose graphical features partner with the words, such as the Hebrew tree-shaped poem by twelfth-century poet and exegete Abraham ibn Ezra.[3]

A concrete metaphor might be termed the opposite of a *dead metaphor*, "an expression that was originally metaphorical but no longer functions as a trope and is not understood literally."[4] In fact, a concrete metaphor stands opposite the dead metaphor Mordechai Cohen detects in Maimonides's *Guide*, used there to distinguish between metaphor and allegory so that the reader can immediately accept scriptural metaphor and move on to deeper understanding.[5] In the case of our Hebrew maqamas, the prose halts this process: it brings to life the dead metaphor in the process of transferring it from poetry to prose. Phrases in prose that have long since lost their literal meaning in poetry, such as the burning liver as a sign of lovesickness, are reappropriated when translated across forms, and in the new context, they urge the reader to pause and reconsider the meaning.

This rebirth in metaphorical prose is analogous to that in the earliest devotional Hebrew lyrics of al-Andalus that incorporated themes and meters from secular poetry, which initially came as a shock to the uninitiated. When moved out of its original genre or form, a dead metaphor comes to life and jars the reader, momentarily allowing the unexpected to enter, as in Aristotle's "white milk" example.[6] Aristotle goes on to say that once the novelty wears off, the metaphor in prose can linger as artificial and clumsy, even if it is laudable for its unpredictability: "There is certainly a need for such epithets, because they give language the qualities of unfamiliarity and novelty, but a speaker should aim for moderation, because excess artificiality does more damage than no preparation at all. The latter is merely not good, but the former is actually bad."[7] But medieval Jewish authors toying with metaphors in the context of amorous prosimetra did not necessarily aim for moderation—especially when the worth of Hebrew as a literary tongue was at stake. They instead aimed for something new, perhaps counting on the fact that once the reader exposed the artifice of the unexpected metaphor, the metaphor would again return to its figurative meaning, as they tend to do over time, for "there is no clear-cut boundary between literal and figurative usage. Phrases and word couplings that were once either literal or figurative are now usually or always figurative—making them, in effect, literal."[8] Perhaps Sahar's liver was actually burning.

Classical Arabic literary theorists considered metaphor to an extraordinarily complex degree, the likes of which was again achieved only in the twentieth century. Even if such theorizing is generally formulated with poetry in mind, and even though touching on this topic only briefly and only partially runs the risk of being reductive, such mention is nevertheless a crucial step toward considering the theoretical backdrop of Jewish authors in Iberia. In his eleventh-century treatise on metaphor, *Asrār al-balāgha* (*The Mysteries of Eloquence*), al-Jurjānī (d. 1078) writes that a metaphor is formed when "someone, whether poet or not, then uses that vocal form somewhere other than in that original lexical place. This person transfers the vocal form to a new place in a move that is not strictly necessary."[9] Al-Jurjānī's limpid explanation perfectly captures the creation of metaphor, even if by the time readers encountered the umpteenth gazelle, twinkling star, and burning liver, such theorizing was perhaps taken for granted, right alongside the now-dead comparison. Yet al-Jurjānī complicates (and revives) the metaphor in his discussion of make-believe (*takhyīl*) as a category of metaphor that, as Alexander Key explains, "has to start in sensory reality but then escape it."[10] Lara Harb further describes *takhyīl*—which al-Jurjānī terms "trickery of the mind (*khidāʿ li-l-ʿaql*)"—as "a kind of poetic construction that tricks one into accepting a false claim," not for the purpose of embracing falsehood but rather to evoke "a new understanding of poetic beauty, one that is based on the ability of a poetic representation to evoke wonder in the listener."[11] She further remarks that "al-Jurgānī credits make-believe imagery with the ability to breathe new life into old ideas," noting that make-believe "is also adduced as a way of reinvigorating overused similes in the science of eloquence."[12] Although al-Jurjānī's formulation of the make-believe applies to poetic metaphors, the perseverance that they demand of the reader or listener resembles the kind of shock value inherent in the prosified metaphors of certain Hebrew maqamas, rendering the category of make-believe a fitting theoretical precursor.

In his early twelfth-century Judeo-Arabic *Kitāb al-muḥāḍara wa-l-mudhākara*, Moses ibn Ezra does not limit the implementation of metaphor to poetry: "One must know that, among all of the rhetorical devices that are necessary for whomever composes poetry and which beautify the words of whomever writes prose, the metaphor is one of the most beautiful things one can use."[13] As previously discussed, despite ibn Ezra's overt preference for poetry over prose at the outset of the treatise, his overall posture toward poetry is complex and fraught. His chapter on metaphor is no exception; he relies heavily on metaphors found in the Bible and the Quran, noting that metaphor is so abundant in scripture that his citations hardly scratch the surface. He draws the remaining examples from contemporary Arabic and Hebrew metered and rhymed poetry. Readers might thus intuit his scriptural examples as potentially representative of the theoretical possibility of metaphorical prose, though such references are certainly distinct in nature from the prose of ibn Ezra's world. At the very least, ibn Ezra's reliance on compositional styles aside from poetry certainly broadened the category of metaphor for his readers.

Poems as Objects of Love

Poetry about the inscribing of poems onto objects (i.e., a poem in which someone writes on an apple) and poetry that turned these same objects into poetic subjects with metaphorical meaning (i.e., a poem that treats an apple as a symbol of love or of a woman's breasts) were both established literary practices in ancient Greek: two epigrams attributed to Plato treat the "apple as love token," another "is spoken by the lover who throws the apple," and a fourth is figured as "an inscription on the apple itself."[14] Plato was in good company: fruit poetry with varying metaphorical connotations abounds, from Sappho's apple-as-desire fragments (fragments 2; 105a) to the Apple of Discord, an inscribed apple from Greek mythology that appears in around thirty classical sources.[15] The fruit need not be an apple to have the same effect: in Greek and Roman literature, the apple "is used throughout as a generic term to cover the apricot, quince, citron, peach, and most other fruits, except nuts, in addition to the genuine apple."[16]

Authors of classical Arabic works likewise composed poems about particular objects and treatises about inscribing poems onto objects. Beginning with Abū Nuwās (b. 747–62, d. 813–15)—arguably the most famous classical Arabic poet—versifiers compared their beloveds to fruits and precious stones.[17] Scholars have discussed the possible metaphorical meanings of these apple poems: the apple is what Arie Schippers terms a "go between in the love affair," such that the beloved's biting into the apple amounts to a kiss.[18] One such fragment by Abū Nuwās provides the rubric for many Arabic and Hebrew poems:

> (The apple) promised me a kiss of my beloved. Thus my beloved owed
> ten kisses.
> Never saw I the biting in an apple without becoming greatly disturbed.
> Such a bite is not a shame for (the apple), but it is a forerunner of kisses.[19]

Jewish poets writing Hebrew poetry in al-Andalus and Christian Spain would have undoubtedly been familiar with the classical Arabic paradigm. In tracing the spread of fruit metaphors from Abū Nuwās to medieval Hebrew poetry, Schippers notes fourteen Hebrew poems that Samuel ha-Nagid composed that include the apple-as-go-between motif and one in which Solomon ibn Gabirol figured the apple not only as a virgin girl but also as a lactating mother.[20] Judah Halevi likewise equated apples and breasts in his poetry, and Moses ibn Ezra figured the beloved as an apple lying next to the poet-lover, who is presented as a different kind of fruit.[21]

While this link is crucial, biblical precedent is simultaneously compelling: setting aside comparisons to spices, animals, and other natural elements, all of which likewise serve metaphorical purposes, consider the abundant apple, pomegranate, and grape metaphors in the Song of Songs (2.3, 2.5, 4.3, 4.13, 6.7, 7.8, 7.9, 8.2) and the apple as metaphor in Proverbs 25.11, among many other instances.[22] It is only natural, given the multiple sources with these metaphors, that medieval Hebrew poems abound with similar uses.

With Greek, Latin, and biblical precedents available, fruit was also a popular vehicle for romance in Romance-language poetry and prosimetra. For instance, the mid-thirteenth-century polymetric *Li romanz de la poire*

(*The Romance of the Pear*) derived its title from the poem's description of the beloved's tearing a pear with her teeth to share with her lover, a conspicuous modification of the Edenic apple, which preoccupied medieval Christian theology.[23] Beyond its titular fruit, Thibaut's text echoes many of the allegorical underpinnings of *Neʾum Asher* and *Sefer ha-meshalim*, such as the personified Love and Hope who engage in battle within the body of the poet-lover.[24] Still, despite its seemingly tangible nature, the pear is understood as metaphorical throughout and does not break away from the allegorical framework of the narrative as do the apples in the stories by ibn Ṣaqbel and ben Elʿazar.

Concrete Metaphors: Theory and Practice

The ways in which medieval literary theorists approached fruit-as-metaphor suggest additional literary-historical nuances. Amid the changing attitudes toward poetry and prose among classical Arabic theorists and poets, al-Washshāʾ (d. 937) began to challenge the boundaries between prose and poetry via his implementations of both written forms. The final twenty chapters of his *Kitāb al-muwashshā*, a didactic work on how to achieve elegance (*ẓarf*), discussed in the second chapter, are almost entirely devoted to poetic passages that treat particular themes, each defined in a prose chapter heading. The forty-fifth chapter, for instance, presents a series of verses that one might encounter written on curtains, pillows, rugs, cushions, and seats (*mā wujida ʿalā al-sutūr wal-wasāʾid wal-basaṭ wal-marāfiq wal-maqāʿid*). In addition to the thirty-third chapter—on reasons why the well-mannered man should avoid eating apples—the fifty-first chapter offers a collection suited for inscribing on a variety of fruits, including apples, grapefruits, and melons. Here, al-Washshāʾ tweaks the paradigmatic theme in Arabic poetry—that of writing poems about apples as an embodiment of the beloved. He shifts the fruit-as-metaphor motif that once existed in the body of the poem to the world outside the poem, which now provides the poem with a physical surface. While poetry constitutes more of the text in these twenty chapters than do prose and rhymed prose (sajʿ) passages, the prose headings place the poetic passages that follow into a material setting, providing the aspiring poet-lover with a tangible surface for his art, which in turn commends the notion of preservation via gathering of poetry.[25] In this way, al-Washshāʾ mimics the body of his treatise itself, which has largely been termed a compilation of poetry.[26] It seems that he literalizes this shift in accordance with his contemporaries' growing regard for prose;

even while his text clearly favors poetry and while the poetry provides all of the substance of the argument, the prose provides the crucial context that explains what he instructs.[27]

The prosimetric Arabic maqama seems to follow al-Washshā'’s lead in experimenting with the uses of objects as metaphors, though not in the context of the poet-lover's search for apt ditties. For instance, in al-Ḥarīrī's fourth maqama, the narrator comes across verses composed on a horse's saddle:

> Then I rose to equip my camel and lade for the departure; and I found that Abū Zayd had written on the pack saddle—
>
> Oh thou, who wast to me an arm and a helper, above all mankind!
> Reckon not that I have left thee through impatience or ingratitude:
> For since I was born I have been of those who when they have eaten separate.
>
> Said Al Ḥarith: "Then I made the company read the words of the Koran that were on the pack saddle, so that he who had blamed him might excuse him.—And they admired his witticism, but commended themselves from his mischief.[28]

In accordance with al-Ḥarīrī's regard for poetry as the ultimate intellectual achievement, the narrator praises the saddle poem, but neither the poem nor its jokingly insolent, if not overtly blasphemous, placement on the saddle is crucial to the story; the saddle poem is a flourish that confirms the wittiness of the characters and, ultimately, the learned status of the author. This prose does not undercut the power of poetry, and neither form, in turn, becomes increasingly metaphorical; the two fulfill distinct purposes.

No such collaboration could be further from the reality of ben Elʿazar's second story, discussed in the first chapter, in which the tension between poetry and prose is brought to life in Hebrew. Aside from treatises on the relative merits of prose and poetry, this anthropomorphized debate seems to be the most potent example of the anxiety of literary form; indeed, a century before ben Elʿazar composed his debate, Moses ibn Ezra discussed the human need to "elevate the . . . status [of inanimate objects], and speak of them in human terms." Mordechai Cohen further highlights ibn Ezra's uncannily modern intuition on anthropomorphism when he recalls George B. Caird's late twentieth-century statement that "anthropomorphism in all its variety is the commonest source of metaphor."[29]

However, not everything can be as clearly figurative as a story in which Prose engages Poetry in a battle of wits; when love is as crucial to the text as the status of poetry, the metaphor becomes increasingly complex, such as in the breaking of the self into disparate anthropomorphized components, a phenomenon discussed in the second chapter. In the Romance context, the formal tension has a different meaning, since prose was readily acknowledged to be subservient to poetry; more than merely insisting on the legitimacy of poetics, such concrete metaphors seem to illustrate the literalizing of courtly love. As if synthesizing the metaphor of the beloved as object and the prose instructions al-Washshāʾ prescribes, some Hebrew maqama authors brought this phenomenon to life via prose and poetry and in the process pushed the metaphor into the realm of courtly love rendered in prose. The following examples from medieval Hebrew elucidate the formal jostling within Hebrew prosimetric love stories, a tension most apparent when poems become tangible. If a character merely recites a poem, the poem lacks physical form to warrant much attention, but if the poem appears on a curtain, a pillar, or a piece of fruit, it suddenly takes up physical space within the jurisdiction of the prose narrative, becoming at once object and subject of the narrative. Accordingly, in ibn Ṣaqbel's *Neʾum Asher ben Yehuda* and in the ninth story of ben Elʿazar's *Sefer ha-meshalim*, instances of writing on objects seem to refer both to the status of poetry and to the acknowledgment of a Romance-esque vision of courtly love, which seeks to educate readers rather than provide them with fodder for memorization.[30]

As discussed in the previous chapter, a poem that the lady inscribes on an apple initiates the flirtation that plagues immature protagonist Asher in ibn Ṣaqbel's maqama. Aside from the author's opening epigram, this is the maqama's first poem and is prefaced by prose in which Asher describes the lady's throwing of the physical apple on which the poem appears:

> An apple fell by me, anointed with the fragrance of myrrh, / these words written on one side:
>
> > You who run to capture gazelles / in the desert, sea or cleft mountains
> > Stop, for they are caged inside the palace / inside in the harem's rooms
>
> And on the second side was written:
>
> > O you, intoxicated with wine, that vintage grape, / swaying like the date tree and cypress
> > My heart is drunk like you and reels: / love has overpowered me, silenced me.[31]

The poem is no longer merely a poem that refers to the beloved as an apple but rather a physical apple that possesses lyrics of its own, as al-Washshāʾ

instructed two centuries earlier in Arabic. If one follows the paradigms of ancient and medieval lyric precedents, the lady is throwing a piece of herself at Asher. The literalizing of the metaphor in prose makes explicit the seductive element of the lyric motif of the apple, but the purpose of the prose is not to make the poetic gesture vulgar; rather, it is a breaking apart of the metaphor to instruct Asher in the more accessible mode of prose. Even if the very act of holding the poem in his hands is not initially enough for him to understand how to proceed in the game of love, it is a start. The physicality of the metaphor in prose is, in other words, what gets through to Asher, as the verses themselves seem to have very little effect. The lady's poems on opposite sides of the apple, both of which employ tropes consistent with classical Arabic and medieval Hebrew lyrics, tell Asher that she is the one he seeks, for not only is she accessible, unlike the teases in the harem, but she also loves him as much as he loves wine. When Asher reads these poems, he commends his own attractiveness; only later, on rereading the poem, does he rethink his failure to respond. Memorization aside, such rereading could not have happened if the lady had not inscribed the verses on something with physical weight. Unable to sleep or eat, delirious Asher returns again to the apple as his sole connection to life and love: "When my strength failed / and my spirit hewn / I took the apple in my hand / and brought it to my nose, / sniffed its perfume / and was revived by its delights."[32] The apple now occupies its own role as subject, one capable of swaying the protagonist's feelings and actions—and thus the course of the narrative.

Poems written on objects likewise play a crucial, didactic role in the ninth story of *Sefer ha-meshalim*, both in terms of the story's development and in its application of courtly love motifs: rather than illustrating Sahar's amorous competence as one of al-Washshāʾ's stock poems would do for an aspiring poet-lover, these poems counsel Sahar on how to pursue Kima. The third poem comprises verses Kima engraves onto an apple and tosses over a wall to Sahar; the fifth and fourteenth poems are verses that Kima writes and Sahar recites; the eighth and eleventh are poems written on curtains; and the thirteenth is a letter Sahar is instructed to read. Although the identity of the poet in the latter three is ambiguous, Kima is a plausible composer, given that the verses advance her goal of instructing Sahar on how to court her properly and given her clear facility with love compositions within the world of the story.

As in *Ne'um Asher*, the beloved in ben El'azar's story is the first to initiate the exchange by way of a poem inscribed on an apple, which, like Asher's, both is scented with myrrh and becomes a physical symbol of the lady. Indeed, the apple enables Kima's handmaiden to confirm Kima's identity in the prose that follows: "Kima is the name of your fair beloved, the owner of the apple anointed with the oil of myrrh."[33] Later, it allows Sahar to distinguish among the maidens: "Who among you is my lady Kima, the creator of the lovely poem inscribed on the apple that was left beside the wall?"[34]

The other poems inscribed on objects in ben Elʿazar's ninth story are increasingly metapoetic and didactic—a shift that correlates with the increasingly metaphorical prose. Sahar must read the eighth poem, rendered on a curtain, before advancing. The verses themselves encourage Sahar to "bow down with your intellect and speak a choice poem," promising him that "if your words please her / you have hope of the beloved."[35] The eleventh poem (the next curtain poem) offers Sahar similar advice pertaining to composition and comportment:

> Before, my friend, you enter to the room / lift your eyes and read the writing on the curtain.
> Come in humility to her inner sanctum and then / you will have access to the house of the doe.
> Choose brief sayings and sweet matter and then / your soul will attract your darling;
> then you will have joy in the doe and please your soul / and she will rule over all your desire.
> Sit among the delicacies, breathing the myrrh / of her name with a mouth that kisses and a hand that caresses.[36]

The metapoetic element in the third verse echoes the practice in the Arabic tradition of winning the beloved's affections through the delivery of clever verses, such as those al-Washshāʾ provides. But the other verses add an ethical element that moves beyond the realm of party trick: in a shifting of functions, the poem provides—rather than the requisite rhetorically dense verses of a sweet exchange—practical instruction on composition that will aid Sahar's quest for Kima's love. The curtain poem continues by enumerating that which the lover will reap if his beloved accepts these verses, but what he gains in the penultimate verse seems to be an all-encompassing, deified love, which moves beyond the goal of obtaining a well-rounded adab education. While the last verse perhaps literalizes the interaction, it is all frustratingly hypothetical, in stark opposition to the tangible form of the poem's inscription; Sahar must, after all, succeed as a poet before even contemplating the rewards of the final verse. In this case, the concrete metaphor functions as does the promise of physical love: it is a tease, concealing deeper layers of meaning buried in the poem.

This sitting and contemplating (or perhaps fantasizing) complements Kima's instruction of Sahar on the customs of gentle lovers and recalls the ennobling ideal of the Romance courtly love tradition, discussed in the second chapter. When Sahar later bemoans Kima's mere kiss on the hand, Kima informs him of the following: "People like us [i.e., noble people] sit together, not to kiss or embrace but so that one heart is attached to another heart, for the love of people of dignity requires right conduct, righteousness and lawfulness and uprightness."[37] In verse, the same sentiment is repeated:

> I kissed him by means of an intermediary / and he answered me: "Indeed my mouth is a faithful messenger:
> to kiss someone like me by means of an intermediary— / this is the doctrine of gentle lovers."[38]

The hand kiss is another version of the apple, another messenger in the courtship. Examples of this modest hand kiss are found in Andalusian Hebrew poetry.[39] Moreover, "kissing the hand" was a customary opening formula in formal epistles in Arabic and Judeo-Arabic.[40] Yet the underlying custom to which Kima refers echoes the spiritual love that Romance courtly love favors over physical demonstrations; far from bemoaning the physical distance and unattainability of the beloved (whether figured as human or divine), these characters find spiritual fulfillment in enacting the regulations that maintain this distance. Ben Elʿazar has moved the expression from Arabic epistolary context to a poem that appears on a curtain. He thus literalizes the possibility of the hand kiss within the fictional narrative, shifting its meaning from customary nicety to a sign of ethical comportment. His recasting of meaning foreshadows the trajectory of the courtship—one that is inextricably bound to poetic exchange: "They stayed overnight, speaking all the best of words, and they did not come close to one another the whole night."[41]

The thirteenth poem, a letter Sahar is instructed to read, counsels him to "look at the doe / but be faithful to the secret" and concludes by noting that "the measure of beauty is signaled in poetry."[42] This poem, like the curtain poems, instructs Sahar on how to compose poetry that will win the affections of his beloved. When these poems become useful objects with practical (albeit intellectual) information to convey, the prose is left without a particularly plot-driven function and turns to the extraordinary.

Poetic Elements as Prose

In their canonical Arabic maqamas, al-Hamadhānī's and al-Ḥarīrī's protagonists regularly expound an array of precise literary phenomena, including metaphorical prose, as in the following passage from al-Hamadhānī's fifteenth maqama: "'Verily Jāḥiẓ limps in one department of rhetoric and halts in the other. Now the eloquent man is he whose poetry does not detract from his prose and whose prose is not ashamed of his verse: Tell me, do you know of a single fine poem of Jāḥiẓ?' We said: 'No!' He said: 'Come let us consider his prose. It consists of far-fetched allusions, a paucity of metaphors and simple expressions. He is tied down to the simple language he uses, and avoids and shirks difficult words.'"[43]

Following this critique of the dearth of metaphors in al-Jāḥiẓ's prose, the narrator and his friends respond that they would like to hear the stranger before them recite "a sample of speech." The stranger then presents a rhymed and metered poem, merely underscoring that—metaphor or no metaphor—prose is less eloquent than poetry.

The thirteenth maqama of al-Ḥarīrī's collection has a similar moment in which the narrator comments that "we were astonished at the excellence of her signifying and at the beauties of her metaphor,—So we said to her, 'Thy prose has enchanted us, but how is thy versifying?'"[44] Despite the fact that both al-Hamadhānī's and al-Ḥarīrī's collections showcase rhymed prose that displays the utmost dexterity and complexity, both passages emphasize that poetry, not metaphorical prose, is the ultimate measure of compositional achievement.

To be fair, al-Hamadhānī not only discusses metaphor in prose but also renders metaphors in prose from time to time, though these instances seem to amount to stock adjectival or verbal phrases that describe the wondrous qualities or accrued, past actions of a particular character and are not meant to be taken literally in the context of the passage. Thus, when the character whom the narrator chances on in al-Hamadhānī's fourth maqama says that in his youth "I have embraced supple forms, and plucked the rose from the crimson cheeks," he employs these euphemisms for youthful love affairs as a contrast to his comportment in later years: "But, now that the morn of hoariness has dawned and the dignity of old age has come upon me, I have resolved to make wise provision for my journey to the next world."[45] Even when the protagonist says, "I was roasting and grilling on the live coal of rage," the reader understands from the context that this is an expression of exaggerated anger.[46] The roasting and grilling of the protagonist is a self-contained narrative moment and does not have an effect on the storyline.

There is likewise an analogue in the Romance context: the author of *Aucassin et Nicolette* incorporates elements traditional in poetry into prose passages. This is perhaps a more intriguing comparison to the use of concrete metaphors in Hebrew maqamas, given the shared preoccupation with courtly love. In a prose passage, the author compares the beloved's body parts to fruits and nuts: "With lips more vermeil than ever was rose or cherry in the time of summer heat; her teeth white and small; her breasts so firm that they showed beneath her vesture like two rounded nuts."[47] These seem to be straightforward metaphors; the cherry, rose, and nuts are not inscribed objects, nor do they accrue additional meanings over the course of the narrative. In this way they are flourishes that function as dead metaphors. Perhaps more compelling to the case of metaphors moved from poetry to prose is the following example: when investigating what Nicolette's guardian has done with Nicolette, Aucassin says, "Be sure that should I die hereof, my blood will be required of you, as is most just, for I am slain of your two hands, since you steal from me the thing that most I love in all the world."[48] Though the reader would be accustomed to hearing such a statement about death in the context of poetry rather than in prose, the resulting prose is not exactly jarring or menacing when removed from the context of poetry, likely because the metaphor ends there; Aucassin is not slain. In fact, this instance might corroborate some scholars' speculations as to the chantefable's parodic intent.[49] The narrator again renders in prose a trope common to Occitan troubadour lyrics when he describes how Nicolette lies in bed in the summer heat, listening to a nightingale.[50] The nightingale echoes the poems that the lovers exchange, and Nicolette's nighttime sleeplessness signals her frustration as she longs for Aucassin. The reader or audience would have easily recognized these details as common components of Occitan cansos and might have found their articulation in prose unexpected, but because the metaphor ends there and has no plot-related repercussions, the resulting metaphor was most likely humorous or delightful rather than unsettling.

In contrast (though in the case of ibn Ṣaqbel, the element of parody is relevant), in ibn Ṣaqbel's and ben Elʿazar's compositions, the metaphors in prose exert physical control over the protagonists and influence the subsequent actions of the narrative. Although the prose passages of the two prosimetra directly address the topic of poetry via references to poems and poetry, the authors also manipulate the language of prose, imbuing it with language most often associated with poetry. The reader might expect that, as a result of the tangibility (or objectification) of poems that focus on the importance of composing the right poem at the right moment, the prose passages would become even more plot driven, enacting the compositional rules set forth in the poetry. In a way, the prose passages do enact the compositional rules, in that they recount the protagonists' efforts to write poetry, but more curiously, they do so by getting swept up in the language traditionally associated with love poetry, at times conveying metaphors for extended prose passages that are distinctly mimetic.

The beloveds in both prosimetra are first presented in the prose not as women but as twinkling stars, presumably figures moving slightly behind a latticework harem wall. In *Ne'um Asher*, Asher explains, "I was watching them / and listening to their voices / when hark, a star appeared from the windows, peeking from the corners."[51] Similarly, in the second prose passage of ben El'azar's story, Sahar laments having been saved in a storm only to be captured in a net by two men with bows and arrows, as the narrator describes: "He saw glowing faces and twinkling eyes, and two black warriors treated him bitterly, angrily shot arrows at him and concealed a trap for him, the archers finding him with their bow."[52] The "two black men" (*shene vene kushim*) are none other than Kima's twinkling eyes, a trope that Hebrew poetry adopted from Arabic verse.[53] Though they fulfilled their function as signifying Kima's flashing eyes, the arrows return again much later in the prose, acting, much like the apple, as an extension of Kima: one of Kima's handmaidens says to Sahar, "Here are the arrows that tired you," and indeed the arrows continue to act on him, leaving "his heart and soul, crushed by arrows and divided."[54]

Judah al-Ḥarizi likewise draws on this metaphor in the prose of his *Taḥkemoni*, but, as in the instances of metaphorical prose in the Arabic maqamas, al-Ḥarizi's use serves to embellish the prose in an exaggerated manner for the sake of exhibiting the author's compositional dexterity—a component to impress, not instruct, the reader. For instance, in the following passage, al-Ḥarizi explains metaphorical speech, informing the reader about the ways in which the two poets resembled warriors: "In my boyhood days and in the time of my youth my eyes beheld two men of the Hebrews striving together as armed warriors. In their mouths were cutting words and sharp themes, and on their tongues spears and arrows."[55] Thus, when one of the competitors says to the other, "How can you equal me, even in your race to reach the dust of my metaphors (*mashal*), while in my tongue is a fountain of understanding and of counsels, and in my heart a spring of poetry (*meliṣa*)," the reader understands the exchange as a display of poetic language in prose that ultimately reflects on the author, whose brilliance is never far from mind.[56] Al-Ḥarizi peppers the prose throughout the *Taḥkemoni* with similar metaphors (such as "a day on which he will burn with fiery coals"), but these instances seem to embellish rather than control the narrative.[57] At the end of al-Ḥarizi's maqama, the reader learns that, far from helping others learn versification, Ḥever and his son must alone restore the "scattered ruins of song" that generally characterize poetry: "I am Heber and this is my offspring; / But I and he are the whelps of rhetoric: / The paths of understanding, broken-down. / I build once more."[58] In contrast, the artifice at work in the ninth story of *Sefer ha-meshalim* is almost completely buried in the fictional construct; the reader is not referred back to the author but rather deeper into the world of the narrative, in which the protagonist is striving toward personal betterment, without a neat and inevitable anagnorisis in sight.

In *Neʾum Asher*, after ibn Ṣaqbel anthropomorphizes Asher's heart and soul via lyric exchange, these very components of the self become living characters, a reality that means these characters are subject to mortality as defined by the narrative framework. On reading the lady's poetic reproach, Asher describes his physical discomfort in prose: "When I read and understood these lines and recognized them to be a rebuke, my insides burst into flames, and my heart turned upside down, and my innards were overwhelmed with regret."[59] Though the bursting of the insides into flames has lyric precedent, it is uncomfortably out of place in the context of prose. Indeed, before this moment Hebrew prose was essentially devoid of fiction, and such forceful language would beg the reader to worry not only about Asher's well-being but also about that of his anthropomorphized heart. In another moment, Asher follows the lady's handmaidens, which leads to even greater bodily distress: "As soon as I crossed the door I was in fire and water."[60] Fire and water is a biblical pairing at home in the world of poetry but jarring in the context of prose narrative.[61]

Sahar faces similar predicaments in the prose of *Sefer ha-meshalim*. After he receives the apple poem and glimpses his beloved, the castle doors "were closed before him, and he was left with his ribs aflame and in pain, burning like the sight of a torch."[62] Of course, ben Elʿazar has embedded a simile within the tangible metaphor of Sahar's flaming ribs, softening the effect of the realistic fire.

But the next instance of burning in prose is more pronounced and prolonged: "He came to the palace and came close to the door and sparks came from his liver. Kima came out scurrying and barefoot to see where the fire was. She said to her maidens, 'What is the fire that is burning at the door?' They quarreled with him forcefully, and he replied, saying, 'Indeed this is the burning of coals of my liver. Why are you quarreling with me?'"[63] The fire in Sahar's liver, of course, is not a real fire but a symbol of Sahar's desire and a common trope in Hebrew and Arabic love poetry.[64] The physiological effects of love were also addressed in medical treatises, a natural counterpart to literary expression given the perceived connection between physical and emotional states. The Arabic translation of Galen's description of love characterizes the liver's role as follows:

> Love is one of the activities of the soul. The soul has its seat in the brain, in the heart, and in the liver. There are three dwelling places in the brain: imagining in the front part, thinking in the middle, and remembering in the rear part. A person can be said to be in love in the full sense of the term only if, should his lover leave him, his imagination, his thought, his memory, his heart, and his liver are preoccupied with the lover, so that he can neither eat nor drink because his liver is too busy, nor can he sleep because his brain is too busy imagining [him], thinking about him, and remembering him.[65]

Yet there is a subtle difference between a medical opinion on the condition of the love-laden liver and an overtly fictional literary treatment of the condition, even if the metaphor is based on the scientific data of the period. And further, while it would be easy to accept that the author employed this fictional metaphor to describe Sahar's yearning for his beloved, the reader cannot ignore Kima's role in this moment of the narrative. Indeed, perhaps more remarkable than the burning of Sahar's liver is Kima's ability to see the fire burning, a reality that propels the fire—and the intensity and reciprocity of Sahar and Kima's love—into the narrative plot. Ben Elʿazar continues the metaphor in prose, blending it with that of the arrows: "When Kima saw this, the love inside her became very angry, and the arrow of anger punctured her liver."[66]

Although removing metaphors from the realm of poetry and inserting them into the context of prose results in confused materializations of metaphors, in the make-believe world of the story, these literal tropes are feasible. Particularly in the case of *Sefer ha-meshalim*, rather than capturing the limitation of prose to operate the language of poetry, these passages reflect the great power of love poetry in the fictional world of the text: when the poetry becomes increasingly metapoetic and didactic, the prose is thrust into the world of love poetry. Further, a pattern emerges wherein a metapoetic/didactic poem precedes or follows these unusual prose moments, as in the metapoetic love poem that immediately precedes the prose describing the liver incident:

> O beloved! On the day of quarreling and bickering / time comes to an end while we quarrel.
> Are we alone tortured? Are lovers / like this? Or is this the rule of love?
> He answered: a lover without quarrel is like a neighbor / with his neighbor. Where is the sweetness of love?
> If there is no quarreling and strife / there is no sweetness of song or sweetness of love.[67]

In other words, prose has taken up the standard function of poetry that poetry itself has abandoned. Ben Elʿazar's concretizing of metaphors allows the text's prose to enact particular elements of poetic composition, which in turn allows poetry to assume a didactic function. In this way, the text touches simultaneously on the Romance vernacular link between love and poetry and on the Arabic/Hebrew preoccupation with the status of poetry.

Poetry of Virtue and the Vernacular

If it is true that poetry is more virtuous than prose, as some of these authors posit, then the link between poetry and metaphor is striking, signaling efforts of al-Washshāʾ, ben Elʿazar, and ibn Ṣaqbel to save the metaphor by extracting it from its typical setting, in the event that poetry might eventually fall by the wayside. Though his particular use of love-themed, nonparodic concrete metaphors is unusual, ben Elʿazar's close attention to prose places his work precisely within his historical context: as prose became the favored medium of the period for Hebrew, he sought to keep up with compositional trends, balancing this turn to prose with Romance courtly love, which in the Romance context is eminently more at home in poetry than in prose. Like other proto-novelistic authors of this period and later, ben Elʿazar seems to have reacted to the decreasing popularity of poetry (or increasing acceptance of prose) by imbuing his prose with love-laced poetic attributes.

On an oversimplified level, the issue of prose and poetry comes down to the question of theology. Debates regarding Arabic prose and poetry discussed in the first chapter frequently pounced on scripture or religious virtue as a deciding factor, one way or another, as to the aptness of form. On the Romance side of the discussion, the vernacular allowed authors to create a separation between religion and composition, as David Wacks and Sarah Kay, among others, have explained.[68] Without religion's constant intervening in and setting limits on literary expression—whether in prose or poetry—articulations of love flourished. While much of al-Washshā''s text is certainly devoted to etiquette in matters of love—including the final twenty chapters in which poems are inscribed on physical objects—he presents it as a work on how to achieve elegance and addresses a variety of topics in addition to love. For this reason, his concretizing of metaphor seems more forcefully linked to the question of poetry's status than to the presence of the love thematic. In the Romance vernacular texts, poetry was undoubtedly viewed as superior, but the newness of the language, combined with the all-encompassing theme of love, outweighed a preoccupation with formal constraints and in turn allowed for a relatively fluid use of metaphor across forms—though in prose such metaphors tend toward the humorous.

Medieval and early modern Romance texts that contain moments in which metaphors are taken out of poems and inscribed on objects, such as Petrarch's *Canzoniere* (mid-fourteenth century) and Ariosto's *Orlando Furioso* (1516), are decidedly focused on the subject of love. Indeed, one might consider all of Petrarch's sonnets as concrete metaphors, in that the name of Petrarch's beloved, Laura, is a reference to the laurel tree (though Laura is, of course, the simultaneously intangible air, *l'aria*). *Orlando Furioso* and Cervantes's *Don Quixote* (1605/15) offer more direct examples of this phenomenon: in both texts, lovers inscribe the names of their beloveds on trees. Even in *Don Quixote*, which, as a whole, reaches well beyond the theme of love, Cervantes employs this practice as a pointed nod to (and parody of) courtly love. In these Romance works, the poetic practice is intimately linked with love and love poetry, not with the status of poetry with regard to prose, as it is in the Arabic and Hebrew contexts. This distinction in attitude toward poetry is, naturally, intimately connected to the newness of vernacular composition: the very novelty of writing in the vernacular and the accepted notion of poetry's superiority seem to overshadow any potential sparring between poetry and prose. Regardless of the form a composition takes, there is much at stake in the vernacular, with its promise of freedom, which, in a relatively short period of time, led to novelesque (perhaps maqama-esque?) experimentations. Indeed, there is a distinction between writing on a tree or an apple to explore the power of man over nature and doing so as a manifestation of love and poetry. These expressions of love poetry are grounded in the worlds of the vernacular and courtly love, which blossomed interdependently, and which our authors writing in Hebrew manipulated to explore new literary forms, stretching both the Hebrew language and the significance and boundaries of their Jewish literary world.

The poems in *Ne'um Asher* and *Sefer ha-meshalim* establish poetry as more than a literary mode. It becomes a component that shapes the story; the lover needs to know how to compose poetry in order to win his beloved. Such instances of metapoetic instruction lack the spontaneity of moments in which a character extemporaneously recites verses of his own composition. In turn, this premeditated quality works to heighten the sense that such instructional moments are not mere afterthoughts or insertions, as poems in the prosimetric context are so often regarded; rather, these poems control the plot in their demand that the character read (or listen to) and comprehend their contents to progress toward the beloved. Although references to the act of writing across medieval traditions often serve to draw attention to the author of the text, here such references apply only within the world of the narrative and reflect the extent to which the beloved's culture equates an individual's ability to compose love poetry with social potential by way of ethical comportment. Our innovative Jewish authors' inspiration to harness the power of courtly poetry in the mixed form for loftier ends—beyond the mere achievement of love and righteousness—moves us to Italy, as it prefigures the waning of courtly love and the future of the love lyric, which plays out spectacularly in the *Maḥberot Immanuel* and in Immanuel of Rome's unprecedented and audacious lyric experiments in vernacular Italian.

Notes

1. Schirmann, "Les Contes rimés de Jacob ben Eléazar de Tolède," 295; Scheindlin, "Sipure ha-ahava shel Ya'aqov ben El'azar," 17; Decter, *Iberian Jewish Literature*, 152.

2. Umberto Eco ("Metaphor, Dictionary, and Encyclopedia") and Gérard Genette ("Rhetoric Restrained") both discuss the potential ambiguity of the name of the trope, summarized as follows: "the name of the trope can depend on how the example is interpreted." W. Martin, "Synecdoche."

3. McFadden, "Metalepsis or Transumption," 862–63; Drucker, "Concrete Poetry," 294; Drucker, "Carmina Figurata," 20; Friedman and French, "Dead Metaphor," 337. Abraham ibn Ezra's tree poem is found in Rosin, *Reime und Gedichte des Abraham Ibn Ezra*, 146. For analysis and instances of such poems, see Davidson, "Eccentric Forms of Hebrew Verse"; Pagis, "Shire temuna ʿivriyim ve-ʿod ṣurot melakhutiyot."

4. Friedman and French, "Dead Metaphor," 337.

5. Mordechai Cohen, "Dimyon ve-higayon," 436. For further discussion of Cohen's interpretation of Maimonides's use of dead metaphor, see Roberts-Zauderer, *Metaphor and Imagination in Medieval Jewish Thought*, 46–48.

6. Aristotle, *Art of Rhetoric*, trans. in Waterfield, 3.3, 1406a10, at 125.

7. Aristotle, 3.3, 1406a10, at 125–6.

8. W. Martin, "Metaphor," 868.

9. al-Jurjānī, *Asrār al-balāgha*, 29.1–3; trans. Key, *Language between God and the Poets*, 213. For further reading on al-Jurjānī's theory of metaphor, see Abu Deeb, *Al-Jurjānī's Theory of Poetic Imagery*; Heinrichs, *The Hand of the Northwind*; and Harb, *Arabic Poetics*.

10. Key, *Language between God and the Poets*, 213; al-Jurjānī, *Asrār al-balāgha*, 31.9–10. For further classical Arabic scholars on *takhyīl* and present-day comments on these theories, see van Gelder and Hammond, *Takhyīl*. For a translation of chaps. 16–18 of the *Asrār* into English, see van Gelder and Hammond, 29–69. Al-Jurjānī was not the first to use the term *takhyīl* with respect to poetry: al-Fārābī first combined the terms *poetry* (*shʿir*), *takhyīl*, and *imitation* (*muḥākāt*) in *Kitāb al-shiʿr* (*The Book of Poetry*); see Heinrichs's introduction to van Gelder and Hammond, *Takhyīl*, 6.

11. Harb, *Arabic Poetics*, 52; al-Jurjānī, *Asrār al-balāgha*, 253.6.

12. Harb, *Arabic Poetics*, 57–58.

13. Ibn Ezra, *Kitāb al-muḥāḍara wa-l-mudhākara*, vol. 1, 118v, lines 6–8, at 243.

14. Page, *Further Greek Epigrams*, 163; epigrams 1–5 are found at 162–64. One could also consider the telling of stories on ancient Greek vases as an analogue to this practice. Indeed, scholars have long debated the difference between inscriptions and epigrams; for instance, see Bing, "Between Literature and the Monuments." For analysis of the Plato epigrams, see Scodel, "Two Epigrammatic Pairs."

15. Littlewood, "Symbolism of the Apple in Greek and Roman Literature," 156, 150–51. Littlewood divides the symbolism of the apple into forty-four sections in the article, which also includes an annotated bibliography of other articles on apple symbolism. For Sappho, see *If Not, Winter*, trans. Carson 6–7, 214–15.

16. Littlewood, 147–48.

17. See Schippers, "Hebrew Andalusian and Arabic Poetry," 219–32.

18. Schippers, 222.

19. Trans. in Schippers, 222.

20. Schippers, 227–29. For commentary on such apple metaphors, see also Pagis, *Hebrew Poetry of the Middle Ages and the Renaissance*, 38.

21. Schippers, 230.

22. Littlewood refers to some of these biblical passages in his discussion of the apple in Greek and Roman literature. "Symbolism of the Apple in Greek and Roman Literature," 158.

23. Thibaut, *Romanz de la poire*; see editor's note on the pear, 59. See also Hunt, "Precursors and Progenitors of 'Aucassin et Nicolette,'" 17.

24. Thibaut, *Romanz de la poire*, 68. The thirteenth-century Old French allegorical poem *Roman de la Rose* (*Romance of the Rose*; ca. 1230, Guillaume de Lorris and ca. 1275, Jean de

Meun) also offers many intriguing points of comparison, though more for its overarching symbolism than for uses of concrete metaphor.

25. For commentary on apple-themed poetry in the *Muwashshā*, see Schippers, "Hebrew Andalusian and Arabic Poetry," 223–24.

26. In the introduction to her Spanish translation of the *Muwashshā*, *El libro del brocado*, Garulo describes the text as an anthology, crediting the abundance of verse citations to the text's status as a work of adab, though she allows that al-Washshāʾ employs verse citations as his "fundamental authority" when attempting to prove his opinions. Garulo, xlix, l; Giffen, *Theory of Profane Love*, xvii, 27, 57.

27. Leder and Kilpatrick allow that despite the profusion of poetry, al-Washshāʾ manages to maintain control over the trajectory of the text's argument. "Classical Arabic Prose Literature," 16.

28. al-Ḥarīrī, *Assemblies of al-Ḥarīrī*, trans. Chenery, 126. For the Arabic, see al-Ḥarīrī, *Assemblies of al Ḥarīrī*, ed. Steingass, 35.

29. Mordechai Cohen, *Three Approaches to Biblical Metaphor*, 87; Caird, *Language and Imagery of the Bible*, 173–74.

30. Thirteenth-century Toledan poet Todros Abulafia invoked a similar trope in presenting a poem inscribed on a goblet to King Alfonso X. For the poem, see Schirmann, *Ha-shira ha-ʿivrit bi-Sfarad uvi-Provans*, book 2, 2:441, poem 388. See note 14 for references regarding poems inscribed on ancient Greek vases. For a thorough consideration of the heart as a metaphorical poetic object in the Latin and Romance Middle Ages, see Jager, *Book of the Heart*.

31. "Va-yipol ʿalai tapuaḥ / be-shemen mor mashuaḥ, / ʿal ṣido ha-eḥad katuv lemor: / asher yaruṣ leṣoded ha-ʿofarim / be-midbar yam ve-hare ha-betarim— / ḥadal, ki hem keluʾim ba-ḥaṣerim / ve-nimṣaʾim be-ḥadre ha-ḥadarim! / uva-ṣad ha-sheni katuv lemor: asher shakhar be-yen ḥamar ve-tirosh / ve-yanuaʿ keʿeṣ tamar vekhi-vrosh— / lekha yishkar ve-yanuaʿ levavi / veha-ahva tesaded-bi ve-taḥrosh!" Ibn Ṣaqbel, in Schirmann, *Ha-shira ha-ʿivrit bi-Sfarad uvi-Provans*, book 1, 2:557, lines 28–34.

32. "Ve-khaʾasher kashal koḥi / ve-qaṣera ruḥi, / hoṣeti et ha-tapuaḥ be-khapi / ve-higashtihu le-ʾapi, / hariḥoti vesamav / ve-ḥayiti ve-manʿamav." Ibn Ṣaqbel, ed. Schirmann, book 1, 2:560, lines 83–84.

33. "Halo Khima shem ahuvatekh ha-neʿima / baʿalat ha-tapuaḥ / asher be-shemen ha-mor mashuaḥ." Ben Elʿazar, "Sipure ha-ahava shel Yaʿaqov ben Elʿazar," ed. Schirmann, 250, lines 88–89.

34. "Mi mikem gevirti Khima / baʿalat ha-shira ha-neʿima / ha-ḥaquqa va-tapuaḥ ha-mushlakh beʿad ha-ḥoma?" Ben Elʿazar, 252–53, lines 141–42.

35. "Be-sekhel bo ve-hishtaḥve; u-mivḥar shir tehaḥave." Ben Elʿazar, 253, lines 148b, 149b. "ve-ʾim teṭiv devarekha / beraʾya yesh lekha miqve." Ben Elʿazar, 253, line 155.

36. Ṭerem yedidi voʾakha la-ḥeder / sa ʿenkha u-qera khetav parokhet
bo vaʿanava el-devireha azai / eten be-vet ʿofra lekha mahlakhet
u-veḥar qeṣar omer ʿarev ʿinyan ve-az / nafshakh levav raʿya tehi moshakhet
tismaḥ be-ʿofra az ve-tinʿam nafshekha / uve-khol-asher titʾav tehi molakhet
teshev be-maʿdanim u-meriaḥ be-mor / zikhrah be-fe nosheq ve-yad moʿakhet.

Ben Elʿazar, 254–55, lines 188–92.

37. "Ki yeshvu yakhad lo lenasheq ve-lo leḥabek / aval lev [ze] be-lev ze doveq / ve-khen sibat ahavat bene ha-yeqarim/ laqaḥat musar haskel ṣedeq u-mishpaṭ u-mesharim." Ben

El'azar, 258. See Proverbs 1.3. The kiss on the hand refers to Kima's kissing her own hand as a signal of her affections for her lover; she does not kiss Sahar's hand. Schirmann addresses the hand kiss ("L'Amour spirituel dans la poésie hébrïque du moyen âge," 318), as does Decter, *Iberian Jewish Literature*, 140.

38. "Neshaqtiv 'al-yede mal'akh yedidim / ve-'anani 'ha-lo fi ṣir emunim // ha-khamoni ve-yad mal'akh lenasheq / hazot torat yedidim ha-'adinim.'" Ben El'azar, "Sipure ha-ahava shel Ya'aqov ben El'azar," ed. Schirmann, 257, lines 261–62.

39. For an instance of the hand kiss, see Samuel ha-Nagid's poem that concludes with the following hemistich: "I salute her and kiss my hand" (eqod ve-eshaq le-yadi). In Schirmann, *Ha-shira ha-'ivrit bi-Sfarad uvi-Provans*, book 1, 1:156.

40. Mark Cohen, "On the Interplay of Arabic and Hebrew in the Cairo Geniza Letters," 25.

41. "Va-yalinu shenehem medabrim mi-kol-ṭuv mila / ve-lo-qarav ze el-ze kol-ha-layela." Ben El'azar, "Sipure ha-ahava shel Ya'aqov ben El'azar," ed. Schirmann, 258.

42. "Bo teḥeze 'ofra / ve-'akh el-sod heye ne'man." Ben El'azar, 255, line 208. "ve-sorat-hod be-shir nisman." Ben El'azar, "Sipure ha-ahava shel Ya'aqov ben El'azar," 256, line 221b.

43. al-Hamadhānī, *Maqāmāt of Badi' al-Zamān al Hamadhānī*, 72. For Arabic, see al-Hamadhānī, *Maqāmāt Abī al-Faḍl Badī' al-Zamān al-Hamadhānī*, 77.

44. al-Ḥarīrī, *Assemblies of al-Ḥarīrī*, trans. Chenery, 178. For the Arabic, see al-Ḥarīrī, *Assemblies of al Ḥarīrī*, ed. Steingass, 97–98.

45. al-Hamadhānī, *Maqāmāt of Badi' al-Zamān al-Hamadhānī*, 37. For Arabic, see al-Hamadhānī, *Maqāmāt Abī al-Faḍl Badī' al-Zamān al-Hamadhānī*, 27.

46. al-Hamadhānī, *Maqāmāt of Badi' al-Zamān al-Hamadhānī*, 56–57. For Arabic, see al-Hamadhānī, *Maqāmāt Abī al-Faḍl Badī' al-Zamān al-Hamadhānī*, 57.

47. "Lé levretes vremelletes plus que n'est cerisse ne rose el tans d'esté, et les dens blans et menus; et avoit les mameletes dures qui li souslevoient sa vesteure ausi con ce fuissent deus nois gauges." *Aucassin et Nicolette*, 14; *Aucassin and Nicolette*, 26.

48. "Saciés bien que, se je en muir, faide vous en sera demandee; et ce sera bien drois, que vos m'arés ocis a vos deus mains, car vos m'avés tolu la riens en cest mont que je plus amoie." *Aucassin et Nicolette*, 5; *Aucassin and Nicolette*, 10.

49. See, among others, Harden, "*Aucassin et Nicolette* as Parody"; Sargent, "Parody in *Aucassin et Nicolette*"; June Hall Martin, *Love's Fools*; Tattersall, "Social Observation and Comment in 'Aucassin et Nicolette.'"

50. *Aucassin et Nicolette*, 13.

51. "Ani mitbonen alehen / u-ma'azin le-qolehen, / ve-hine khokhav mashgiaḥ min ha-ḥalonot / u-meṣiṣ min ha-pinot." Ibn Ṣaqbel, in Schirmann, *Ha-shira ha-'ivrit bi-Sfarad uvi-Provans*, book 1, 2:557, lines 21–22.

52. "Va-yar ve-hine fanim noṣaṣim / ve-'enayim mitloṣaṣim / ve-sham shene vene khushim ḥaluṣim / va-yemararuhu va-robu va-yisṭemuhu ba'ale ḥiṣim / va-yiṭmenu lo rashet / va-yimṣa'uhu ha-morim ba-qashet." Ben El'azar, "Sipure ha-ahava shel Ya'aqov ben El'azar," ed. Schirmann, 249, lines 59–60. The story again refers to arrows in the prose passages that follow poems 8 and 25.

53. See Schippers for a discussion and examples of the motif of the beloved's shooting arrows from his or her eyes to ensnare the lover. *Spanish Hebrew Poetry and the Arabic Literary Tradition*, 173–76.

54. "Hine ha-ḥiṣim mimekha ve-hale'a / va-ya'anu lo libo ve-nafsho me-ḥiṣim meḥuṣim." Ben El'azar, "Sipure ha-ahava shel Ya'aqov ben El'azar," ed. Schirmann, 253, lines 158–59.

55. "Raʾata ʿeni bi-yme naʿaruti / uvi-zman yalduti / shene anashim ʿivrim niṣim / be-fihem poṣim / milim neḥraṣim / ve-ʿinyanim nimraṣim / uvi-lshonam ḥanit ve-ḥiṣim." al-Ḥarizi, *Taḥkemoni*, ed. Yahalom and Katsumata, 141, lines 2–4; al-Ḥarizi, *Taḥkemoni of Judah al-Ḥarizi*, trans. Reichert, 1:83.

56. "Ve-ʾekh taʿarokh elai / ve-tasig bi-mruṣatkhaʾavaq meshalai / uvi-lshoni meqor ha-sekhel veha-moʿeṣa / uve-libi maʿyan ha-meliṣa." al-Ḥarizi, *Taḥkemoni*, ed. Yahalom and Katsumata, 142, lines 32–33; al-Ḥarizi, *Taḥkemoni of Judah al-Ḥarizi*, 1.84.

57. "Yom yivʿar be-gaḥale esh shevivo." al-Ḥarizi, *Taḥkemoni*, ed. Yahalom and Katsumata, 96, line 71; al-Ḥarizi, *Taḥkemoni of Judah al-Ḥarizi*, 1.62.

58. "Ani Ḥever ve-ze piryi ve-ʾulam / ani va-hu kefire ha-meliṣot / ani evne netivot bin netuṣot / ve-hu yaqim harisot shir peruṣot." al-Ḥarizi, *Taḥkemoni*, ed. Yahalom and Katsumata, 151, lines 259–62; al-Ḥarizi, *Taḥkemoni of Judah al-Ḥarizi*, 1.95.

59. "Ve-khaʾasher qeratim / va-havinotim, / nikar elai mehem tokhaḥat / ve-ʾesh be-qirbi mitlaqaḥat / ve-nehpakh ʿalai libi ve-raḥamai / yaḥad nikhmeru niḥumai." Ibn Ṣaqbel, in Schirmann, *Ha-shira ha-ʿivrit bi-Sfarad uvi-Provans*, book 1, 2:561, lines 107–8.

60. "ʿAd asher ʿavarti ha-delet / u-vati va-ʾesh uva-mayim." Ibn Ṣaqbel, in Schirmann, *Ha-shira ha-ʿivrit bi-Sfarad uvi-Provans*, book 1, 2:561, line 116.

61. Psalms 66.12.

62. "Ve-nishʾaru ve-ṣalʿotav lehavot ve-khidodim / boʾarim ke-marʾe ha-lapidim." Ben Elʿazar, "Sipure ha-ahava shel Yaʿaqov ben Elʿazar," ed. Schirmann, 250, line 81.

63. "Va-yavo el-ha-armon va-yiqrav ʿel-ha-dalet / va-teṣe mi-kevedo geḥalet / va-teṣe Khima nivhelet vi-yḥefa / lirʿot ʿet-ha-serefa / va-tomer le-naʿaroteha: / ma-ha-esh asher ba-delet niseqa / va-yerivun ito be-ḥozqa / va-yaʿan lemor: ʿhalo serefat gaḥelet kevedi / ma-terivun ʿimadi!'" Ben Elʿazar, ed. Schirmann, 261, lines 346–47.

64. This trope recalls the burning flames of love in Song of Songs 8.6. The prose of ben Elʿazar's ninth story is riddled with other such examples. Sahar laments the burning of his heart: Ben Elʿazar, 260, line 312; Sahar is at war with his heart: Ben Elʿazar, 260, line 319; the gazelle (i.e., Sahar) steals Kima's soul: Ben Elʿazar, 260, lines 324–25.

65. Biesterfeldt and Gutas, "Malady of Love," 23n22.

66. "Va-tere Khima ki va hitʾanaf yedidah / va-yefalaḥ ḥeṣ ḥamato kheveda." Ben Elʿazar, "Sipure ha-ahava shel Yaʿaqov ben Elʿazar," ed. Schirmann, 261, line 356.

67. Raʿaya yom le-yom telunot ve-rivot / yaʿaṣor ha-zeman ve-naḥnu merivim
ha-anaḥnu levad meʿunim ke-ele / ohavim o ha-zot teʿudat ahuvim
yaʿaneni yedid beli riv ke-shokhen / ʿim-shekheno ve-e metuqe ahavim
hah ve-im en be-ahava riv u-madon / en neʿim shir o neʿimat ahavim

Ben Elʿazar, 261, lines 340–43. The word used here is *shir*, meaning "poem" or "song."

68. Wacks, "Vernacular Anxiety and the Semitic Imaginary," 168; Kay, *Parrots and Nightingales*, 10–11.

4

THE DEATH OF COURTLY LOVE AND THE POETRY OF PROSE

Immanuel of Rome in Medieval Italy

WHILE *THE DEATH OF COURTLY LOVE* IS CERTAINLY a melodramatic phrase, it is suited both to the context of medieval Italian lyric and, more specifically, to the boisterous and innovative approach to the poetics of love that characterizes Immanuel of Rome's secular Hebrew and Italian compositions: it marks the poet's increasing faith in his individual efforts and his move away from the necessity of obtaining the beloved's affections. The beloved is accordingly no longer merely a beauty, moderately idealized in verse, but rather a muse or deity who enables the persona of the poet to imbue his (or her) poetics indelibly. Inscribing of authorship is, of course, a memorialized practice across literary traditions: poets have long inserted their names to assert their mastery, from Sappho's fragmentary mentions of herself to Ovid's proclamation at the close of *Metamorphoses*, and from paytanim who made acrostics of their names in as early as the sixth century to ibn Ḥazm, who was intent on highlighting his compositional prowess in his eleventh-century *Ṭawq al-hamāma*.[1] Though the poet's persona and stylistic particularities can certainly shine through in courtly lyrics fashioned out of manipulations of conventions (such as those discussed in the second chapter), poems that capture the poet's impassioned yearning for an unattainable beloved tend to focus more overtly on the desirability of the beloved than on the ingenuity of the poet. Immanuel's secular corpus, which is not beholden solely to the theme of love, is less oriented toward defining an *ars poetica* than it is toward emphasizing the achievements of the poet. In this effort, Immanuel is indebted to the Italian Christian poets of his late thirteenth- and early fourteenth-century Italy, in particular to

Cecco Angiolieri (c. 1260–1312) and to Dante Alighieri (1265–1321), whose own compositional corpus is itself an *ars poetica* that renders courtly love obsolete, at least among his fellow poets in Italy.[2]

In this chapter, I address Immanuel's unique drawing on the Italian lyric, which was derived via the Occitan troubadours and Sicilian poets, who were invariably in contact with Jewish and Muslim cultures, as Karla Mallette, María Rosa Menocal, and others have described.[3] I rely on key aspects of Immanuel's writings—the overall structure of the prosimetric *Maḥberot Immanuel*; the poetic trajectory of the third *maḥberet*; and the thematics of two of his Italian compositions—to argue that Immanuel adapts contemporary Italian poetics to craft his own vision of poetry.[4]

Immanuel, a philosopher, biblical exegete, and poet, is known as Immanuel ha-Romi (i.e., Immanuel of Rome) in Hebrew and as Manoello/Manoel/Manuel/Immanuele Romano or Giudeo (i.e., Immanuel of Rome or Immanuel the Jew) in the Italian tradition. While his biblical commentaries might be viewed as derivative—though scholars are working to debunk this—his secular writings are inextricably intertwined with Italian: his Hebrew sonnets were the first sonnets composed in a language outside of Italian and Occitan, and his Italian lyrics are the only Italian lyrics by a Jewish author extant from this period.[5] Further, the placement of his Italian poems in six early modern manuscripts containing medieval Italian lyrics by the most noted poets of the period has led Fabian Alfie to highlight the significance of their including Immanuel, whom they overtly identify as Jewish.[6] According to the manuscript and print tradition, Immanuel is indeed a *sui generis* figure, his compositions constituting the whole of our understanding of vernacular lyric by Jews of fourteenth-century Italy. Still, it is difficult to believe that Immanuel was truly the only of his kind; as Dvora Bregman has noted, in hailing himself as the only author of a *sirventese* in Hebrew, Immanuel (who has no qualm with self-praise) indirectly implies that he was *not* the only author of sonnets in Hebrew.[7] Thus while a close examination of Immanuel's poetics of love might seem to be somewhat limited in scope, it is likely that a cohort of fellow Jewish poets in Italy simply did not enjoy the broad circulation or renown that Immanuel did. We know with certainty, however, that he was not the only author of his time and place who composed philosophical and exegetical texts in Hebrew; while he was clearly an innovator, he was not the sole author of his community.

Even though Immanuel's Italian poems are available today in Italian anthologies of the poets from the thirteenth and fourteenth centuries

(*Duecento*; *Trecento*), few of today's students of Italian are likely to have come across his poems.[8] The same could be said for students of Hebrew: the *Maḥberot Immanuel*—the secular Hebrew text for which he is best known and which was widely disseminated throughout the medieval and early modern Jewish world, from the Mediterranean to Ashkenaz—is not conventionally studied now. Most readers today who have heard of Immanuel likely associate him with anachronistic intrigue rather than poetic prowess, given that the sixteenth-century *Shulḥan ʿarukh* prohibits reading the *Maḥbarot* on Shabbat.[9] Of course, if something is to be banned, it first must have circulated widely, with numerous print editions to bolster its fame.

Biographical data about Immanuel is quite limited and potentially invalid: he was perhaps born in Rome in 1261, is thought to have lived until 1335, and seems to have acted as head of correspondence for the Jewish community of Rome.[10] He might have held a more permanent high post in the Jewish community of Rome until his supposed departure in 1321, perhaps motivated by the possible but unconfirmed 1321 papal order from Avignon to expel Jews from Rome.[11] Unfortunately, the *Maḥbarot* and Immanuel's Italian lyrics (i.e., fiction) have provided historians with the majority of the biographical information that has been accepted and that continues to circulate as fact: scholars believe that he traveled among Perugia, Fabriano, Fermo, Camerino, Ancona, Gubbio, and Verona, a route they traced from Immanuel's fictional writings. Though unconfirmed by historical data, Gubbio is a plausible location: Immanuel exchanged sonnets with poet Bosone da Gubbio and is referred to as "Manuel Giudeo da Gobio" in the Vatican manuscript featuring his Italian lyrics.[12]

Like other polymaths of his time, Immanuel was prolific across disciplines. In addition to the *Maḥberot Immanuel*—his Hebrew-language maqama collection of stories in rhymed prose and poetry—he composed commentaries in Hebrew on nearly the entire Bible and wrote two technical treatises in Hebrew on the Hebrew language—one a study of the symbolism of the Hebrew alphabet (not extant) and the other a hermeneutic work titled *Even boḥan* (Examination of stone). Immanuel also addressed an invective epistle to Hillel ben Samuel of Verona, which scholars have proffered as additional proof that Immanuel visited Verona, the city that serves as setting for his narrative Italian poem that is known in the manuscript tradition as *Bisbio* or *Bisbidis*. Of course, place names in personal titles usually suggest that a person originally hails from that place but does not currently reside there. Further, places named in poems should generally be regarded as fictional details; proof of Immanuel's presence in Verona is simply lacking. In addition to *Bisbidis*, Immanuel also composed four sonnets in Italian, whose chronology with respect to his Hebrew sonnets is unclear.

While his Hispano-Hebraic literary predecessors spoke Arabic in their daily lives, Immanuel's knowledge of Arabic is improbable; rather, Immanuel clearly conversed in a Romance vernacular, likely a variety within the family of Judeo-Italian or Judeo-Romano (*giudeo-romanesco*).[13] This lack of Arabic meant that Immanuel's cohort of Roman Jews absorbed Andalusi intellectualism via Hebrew translations and commentaries of philosophical works from Greek via Arabic, by way of intermediary languages.[14] Still, like the Hispano-Hebraic authors preceding him, Immanuel relied heavily on biblical Hebrew. Indeed, Immanuel's writings further complicate the already intricate language universe of Andalusian Jewry.

Even though the *Maḥberot Immanuel* has the backbone of the classic maqama structure, in which narrator Immanuel encounters his interlocutor, the *sar* (minister, nobleman, or prince), most of the maqamas in his collection depart from the classic scheme, even if they retain its prosimetric structure. The final maqama is the exception to the formal consistency: *Tofet ve-ʿeden* (*Hell and Paradise*) comprises rhymed prose without intercalated rhymed, metered poetry.[15] Immanuel does not hide his familiarity with the Hebrew maqama tradition that originated in Christian Spain: he refers repeatedly to Judah al-Ḥarizi's *Taḥkemoni* throughout the *Maḥbarot*, signaling his awareness of the high stakes for literary Hebrew.[16] Immanuel cleverly chose the introduction to the *Taḥkemoni* as his collection's link to the world of the maqama, referring the reader to a passage in which al-Ḥarizi claims to have composed his maqama collection to show that Hebrew can be as rich and as capable of literary ingenuity as Arabic.

Ordering Poetry, Creating Order: Immanuel Borrows from Dante

Immanuel does not dwell on the necessity of showing Hebrew's superiority to Arabic, as do his fellow Hebrew maqama authors; he was not linguistically capable of such judgment. Rather, he uses the introduction to the *Maḥberot Immanuel* to focus the reader's attention on his own poetic achievement and his own virtuosic way with Hebrew. This is where the reader can first detect Immanuel's indebtedness not only to al-Ḥarizi and to the Hebrew maqama's mission of validating Hebrew's worth but also to Italian—specifically to the poetic project of Dante Alighieri, the most famous author of Italian literature to date and an exact contemporary of Immanuel.

Dante is most famous for the *Divine Comedy*—which Immanuel overtly emulates in *Tofet ve-ʿeden*—but the work to which the *Maḥbarot* is structurally indebted seems to be the *Vita nuova*, which Dante compiled in 1295 and portions of which Immanuel is likely to have seen if he was in fact positioned in Gubbio as the Italian manuscripts have placed him. Arrigo Castellani has proposed that the Martelliano 12, which contains poetry and prose from the *Vita nuova* (alongside other poems by Dante and Dante's friend and fellow poet Guido Cavalcanti), was compiled in Gubbio toward the end of the thirteenth century or beginning of the fourteenth century.[17]

In his famous opening to the *Vita nuova*, Dante indicates the personal nature of his composition, characterizing it as "the book of my memory" (*libro de la mia memoria*), which scholars have termed "a sort of poetic auto-anthology" and an "anthology of his youthful poetry."[18] Further, his anthology "authorizes" the work of love poets, as Martin Eisner explains: "In the *Vita nuova*, Dante already begins to claim this authority [of love lyrics] for himself by joining love to reason through the figure of Beatrice, in a strategy that reaches its climax in the *Commedia*."[19] Dante achieves the effect of an authoritative anthology in choosing and privileging particular compositions, binding them into a form more substantive than singular poems possess, and in the process he creates new meaning by way of contextualizing the verses in prose.[20] Accordingly, Albert Ascoli writes that the *Vita nuova* "may well be the single most innovative text Dante ever composed," its uniqueness "borne of reproducing while also configuring what was already available, of bringing together multiple sources from widely disparate areas of cultural discourse."[21]

While the poetry in Arabic and Hebrew prosimetra has often been ignored or disparaged, the poems of the *Vita nuova* have held utmost interest and importance to Dante's readers. In the *Vita nuova*, Dante traces his developing poetics and acknowledges this effort by dedicating two of the three components of his "little book" (*libello*) to poetry: the poems and their accompanying glosses (*divisioni*).[22] In Dante's time, the treatment of love in Italian vernacular verse was still a developing phenomenon, unlike love poetry of the Arabic and Hebrew literary traditions, which had been tweaked, analyzed, and codified for centuries before ibn Ṣaqbel and ben Elʿazar began writing—hence the need in the Italian tradition to "authorize" "works of vernacular love poets," as Eisner describes in reference to Boccaccio's autograph manuscript of Dante's *Vita nuova*, contained in Chigi L V 176.[23] Unsatisfied with the literary and philosophical worth of vernacular Italian works composed in the century leading up to his own literary endeavors, and equally aware of the need to exhibit his poetic surpassing of Occitan predecessors, Dante was intensely conscious of the newness of his project, as Ascoli explains: the text's "composite form is drawn from an equally composite repertory of sources . . . this eclecticism is the sign of a conscious effort by Dante to locate himself strategically within the range of possibilities available in the cultural field of authorship."[24]

Because of the newness of vernacular Romance composition, the *Vita nuova*, unlike prosimetra such as *Ne'um Asher* and *Sefer ha-meshalim*, did not have to contend with abundant writing on the relative merits of prose and poetry, even if it did have to face criticism from those who considered writing in the vernacular significantly inferior to Latin composition.[25] Nor did it inherit the overarching presence of biblical intertextuality that informed all medieval Hebrew compositions or the complex status of poetry and fiction that permeated the Islamic context. Further, in the classical Arabic literary tradition (from which medieval Hebrew derived many conventions), all prose treatises featured interspersed poetry regardless of subject matter, such that modern scholars have deemed it accurate to consider these texts, all of which are technically prosimetric, simply as prose.[26] Quite the opposite is true for the *Vita nuova*: it seems that early readers considered the *Vita nuova* to be a compilation of lyrics and found the prose of secondary importance to the poetry.[27] Still, Dante's use of prose—of vernacular prose—was radical, as Domenico De Robertis explained: "it is the prose that is the new substance in this book."[28] While the *Vita nuova* is not the first instance of Italian vernacular prose writing, Giulio Bertoni noted that Dante's text provided the first opportunity for prose to fulfill an artistic, rather than didactic, purpose.[29] He further argued that Dante's creation of a vernacular prose style for the *Vita nuova* owes its success to Dante's transfer of elements from love poetry into prose; he asserts that the very prose of the *Vita nuova* is amorous.[30] Charles Singleton defined the prose more rigidly, as the element in the text that "brings in all its high seriousness."[31] De Robertis's characterization of the prose seems to fall somewhere between these two definitions: the prose, which was created on behalf of the poetry, re-presents the poetry in a new mode and with new terms.[32]

Although the *Vita nuova* is not the only Italian vernacular prosimetrum of this period, it seems unlikely—primarily for chronological reasons—that the other prosimetra served as models for Dante's. The anonymous thirteenth-century *Novellino* is the only Italian prosimetrum to have preceded the *Vita nuova*, but it would be somewhat fruitless to compare the two: the *Novellino* contains only one verse passage (in story 64) across its one hundred stories, making it too different from a quantitative standpoint to warrant a comparison.[33] Although Francesco da Barberino was a contemporary of Dante (1264–c. 1348), he composed his prosimetric medical treatise *Reggimento e costume di donna* (*On the Conduct and Manners of a Woman*) roughly half a century after Dante compiled the *Vita nuova*. Other vernacular prosimetra, such as Boccaccio's *Decameron*, Franco Sacchetti's *Libro delle rime* (c. 1335–c. 1400; Book of poems), and Giovanni Sercambi's *Il novelliere* (1348–1424; The collection of novellas), were likewise composed in the second half of the fourteenth century.

Outside the Italian vernacular tradition, contemporary examples of Romance vernacular prosimetra are likewise scarce. The thirteenth-century French romance *Aucassin et Nicolette*, discussed in the previous chapter, is relevant here, since both it and the *Vita nuova* treat the theme of love, but the two are more structurally than thematically kindred. Although the "rigorously distinct" sections of prose and poetry in the *Vita nuova* have been likened to those in *Aucassin et Nicolette*, the characterizations of love in the two do not readily facilitate comparison, since the French chantefable illustrates the principles of courtly love—even if it arguably parodies those principles—while Dante breaks away from this vision of love early on in the *Vita nuova*, creating an alternative to courtly love poetry.[34]

Scholars have pointed to the Occitan *vidas* (lives) and *razos* (commentaries on troubadours' poems) as predecessors to Dante's alternation of poems and self-glossing divisioni in the *Vita nuova*.[35] Indeed, like the *Vita nuova*, the vidas and razos call on love to link prose to poetry: in these prose texts, which were written in the decades after the poems they mention, the authors discuss troubadours' beloveds and weave romantic tales from details that their verses seem to disclose. Although Dante very likely drew on these Occitan compositions, such texts lack a sustained use of mixed forms; they lack, in other words, the very condition that allows the prose and verse of the *Vita nuova* to forge a more complex relationship. It is clear that Dante also drew on medieval Latin prosimetra, particularly Boethius's *Consolation of Philosophy*, to which he refers in his prosimetric *Convivio*

(*The Banquet*) and which introduced him to what Peter Dronke described as "a paradigm of the sublimation of pain and loss, and to the process of attaining an exalted mode of understanding."[36] Still, Dante's revolutionary implementation of vernacular prose as a means to explicate his vernacular love poetics distances the *Vita nuova* from medieval Latin prosimetra and his own vernacular *Convivio* in a profound way.

Outside the context of prosimetra, the tradition of *tenzone* (pl. *tenzoni*), poetic exchanges in Italian vernacular, also might have influenced Dante's construction of the *Vita nuova*. The tenzone seems to be a likely source of inspiration because it is a natural precursor to the ordering and anthologizing of one's own poetry. Indeed, even if the *Vita nuova* does not make any reference to personal anthology, it certainly illustrates the process of Dante's gathering his previously composed verses, as Singleton surmised: "The *Vita Nuova* was, for one thing, a way of using poems probably already written on established themes before it was conceived as a whole made up of poems and prose."[37] He further reminds the reader that Dante's prosimetrum was exceptional in vernacular literature of the period: "nowhere did they [Dante's contemporaries] surround their poems with a prose which in full seriousness reaffirms all that those poems assert."[38]

Like the *Vita nuova*, the *Maḥberot Immanuel* is a prosimetrum, and while Immanuel's use of the mixed form was not an innovation in the medieval Arabic and Hebrew literary traditions, the sentiment he expresses in the introduction to his collection is unprecedented in the world of the Hebrew maqama. He begins by stating that he wishes to protect his poetry from those who might claim it as their own: "There were among us men who in their stupidity sang the praises of others in attendance; some boasted that they had composed verses of my own composition."[39] Once he has established a reason for composing/compiling his prosimetrum, Immanuel positions his interlocutor the sar as the first character to refer to al-Ḥarizi, author of the *Taḥkemoni*: the sar urges Immanuel to gather his poetry and prose together in the style he has seen in the book of "Rabbi Yehuda Ḥarizi." In a manner that recalls the mixture of audacity and self-deprecation of Dante in *Inferno* 2 of the *Divine Comedy*—"For I am not Aeneas, I am not Paul"—Immanuel questions his own ability to undertake such a task, heaps praise on al-Ḥarizi's maqama collection, resolves to compile his own book, and offers a versified prayer to Poesy and thanks to God.[40]

The desire to defend his artistry is Immanuel's sole rationale for having composed a prose structure to encompass all of the text's poetry. Whether or not it is true that Immanuel composed the prose to protect the poetry from impostors is irrelevant; the key is Immanuel's impetus to gather his poetry into one volume, creating an auto-anthology much like the *Vita nuova*.[41] Immanuel was not the only poet concerned with accurate attribution: ibn Gabirol expressed frustration about poetic plagiarism two centuries earlier.[42] There are likewise precedents among medieval Jewish poets for overseeing such anthologies: in al-Andalus, Samuel ha-Nagid supervised as his son compiled his *dīwān*. Late twelfth- and early thirteenth-century Karaite poet Moses Darʿī likewise wrote prose headings in Arabic to accompany his Hebrew poems.[43] The notion of collecting one's own verses gained in popularity in Christian Spain: Todros Abulafia (1247–after 1298) collected his poems into a dīwān titled *Gan ha-meshalim veha-ḥidot* (The garden of stories and riddles), complete with Arabic prose headings.[44] Further, Jonathan Decter illustrates this impetus to collect one's poetry by highlighting early fourteenth-century Yedaʿya ha-Penini, who urged anthologizing as an alternative to becoming "one who harvested an entire field yet holds nothing in his hand."[45] While Immanuel might have been familiar with ha-Penini's work, it is improbable for geographic reasons that he knew of Darʿī's dīwān and also unlikely that Darʿī's or Todros's prose headings influenced Immanuel's own effort to self-anthologize, given that he was unable to access their Arabic.

Even further afield but kindred in form, the *Ṭawq al-hamāma* occasionally offers interpretations of ibn Ḥazm's poems, and unlike treatises by ibn Ḥazm's contemporaries, it features poems primarily of his own composition. Still, even if ibn Ḥazm used this poetry to instruct on poetic composition, he did not treat the poetry of the *Ṭawq* as its prized element as Dante does the poetry of the *Vita nuova*. Thus, even if Immanuel had access to the ideas of the *Ṭawq* if not to the Arabic treatise itself, it seems an unlikely source of inspiration. Similarly inaccessible to Immanuel, the *Tarjumān al-ashwāq* (The translator of desires), by Andalusian mystic poet Muḥyī al-Dīn ibn al-ʿArabī (1165–1240), nevertheless deserves a brief comment, as it could be termed an Arabic counterpart to the *Vita nuova*. An outlier in the Arabic tradition, the *Tarjumān al-ashwāq* comprises sixty-one of the author's love poems alongside his prose commentary on the verses.[46] The prose commentaries figure his poetry as the text's formal and thematic core. Existing outside of Immanuel's linguistic grasp, al-ʿArabī's treatise attests to the self-glossing impetus in Arabic, though it is merely a tempting parallel to the *Maḥbarot*.

Even if Immanuel were aware of all of these precedents, his project is nonetheless singular: he remains the only poet who claims to compile his poetry into a maqama collection, a compositional form whose fictional prose is far more robust and integral to the whole than are prose headings or anthology glosses. Though some kindred Hebrew maqama authors dwell on the art of poetry as a subject within the fictional narrative, such self-conscious self-anthologizing is absent in the narrative frame of maqamas by Immanuel's Jewish predecessors and contemporaries. This self-consciousness has profound implications for the fictional nature of Immanuel's narrative. One such result, as Dan Pagis and Matti Huss have both mentioned, is Immanuel's deep complicating of the authorial *I* and narrative *I*—a phenomenon equally and significantly central to the *Vita nuova* and the *Divine Comedy*.[47]

Immanuel's Hebrew Romances the Sonnet

The contents of Immanuel's collection mirror the hybridity of the framing device in remarkable ways, drawing on Hebrew and Italian poetic forms and themes. The *Maḥberot Immanuel* boasts thirty-eight Hebrew sonnets, in addition to a *sirventese*—likewise an Italian form that he renders in Hebrew. The third maḥberet alone contains ten poems, four of them sonnets—a significant detail, given Immanuel's early adoption of the sonnet for use in Hebrew, long before authors in languages aside from Italian and Occitan adopted the form. The sonnet, invented in the thirteenth century by Giacomo da Lentini, a poet of the *scuola siciliana* (Sicilian School), is a fourteen-verse poem comprising two quatrains and two tercets of eleven- (and sometimes ten-) syllable verses. To compose a sonnet in Hebrew, Immanuel designed what Dvora Bregman has termed a new kind of "quantitative-syllabic" meter, combining elements of both Hebrew (via Arabic) quantitative meter and Italian syllabic meter.[48] Immanuel, who did not know Arabic, nonetheless used its conventional quantitative meter. His rendering of the sonnet in Hebrew while preserving metrics customary to Hispano-Hebraic poetry attests to his astute comprehension of vernacular Italian composition, which his Italian poems corroborate. Beyond formal characteristics, Immanuel's Hebrew sonnets also reveal his deep understanding of the thematic and linguistic components of the late thirteenth- and early fourteenth-century sonnet in Italian.

Umberto Cassuto, Dan Pagis, and Ann Brener have argued that the third maqama, titled *Megilat ha-ḥesheq* (*The Scroll of Love*) in manuscript and print editions of the *Maḥberot Immanuel*, could be viewed as a compact counterpart to the *Vita nuova*.[49] Brener adds to this claim that the *Scroll* is a parody of the *Vita nuova*. While parody is certainly a possibility, it is likewise possible to see Immanuel's individual Hebrew sonnets within the *Scroll of Love* as the opposite: as genuine, remarkable efforts to translate poetic elements that, when plucked from their prose surroundings, follow in the poetic path that Dante and his fellow poets embraced. David Malkiel places the *Scroll* within the context of worldly eros, and in distinguishing Immanuel's conception of Time from the Arabo-Andalusian association of Time with Fate (*al-dahr*), he determines that Immanuel's "eros represents temporal concerns" and "Time represents frivolity."[50] As the following analyses suggest, Immanuel's apparent focus on the physical is anything but worldly; rather, he borrows from contemporaries' meditations on the metaphysical and the universality of eros to profound effect.

In the rhymed prose of the *Scroll of Love*, Immanuel and his patron (the sar) see one beautiful woman and one hideous woman and proceed to offer increasingly hyperbolic descriptions of each. At the end of this rhetorical exercise, Immanuel winds up lovesick for the beautiful one. The sar assures Immanuel that far more perfect than the lady he desires is her sister: a beautiful, devout, chaste, and wise poetess/nun. Immanuel falls in love on hearing the description (a trope in classical Arabic love poetry). He sees her praying and vows to win her affections, even after she rebuffs him in favor of her chastity. Immanuel sends her a letter and sonnet, which she rejects in her letter and sonnet response. He sends her another letter and sonnet and again receives a letter of rebuke. He finally wins her over with a poem so dazzling (though incidentally not a sonnet but an echo poem) that she regrets all of the time she wasted in prayer. When Immanuel informs the sar of his success, the sar is livid: the nun, it turns out, is his half sister, and while he goaded Immanuel, he never expected him to succeed. He demands that Immanuel back down or else he will refuse to patronize Immanuel further. When Immanuel rejects the nun via epistle, scorning her for capitulating so easily, she is so distraught and heartbroken that she stops eating and dies. The maqama closes with a sonnet lamenting her death.

Midway through the narrative, Immanuel rejoices in giddy optimism at the prospect of seducing a nun, a moment he memorializes by showcasing his perceptive spin on an Italian poetic preoccupation: lyrics in praise of the beloved. The poem follows a rhymed prose passage in which Immanuel employs tropes typical of the Hebrew-via-Arabic poetic tradition to express longing for the beloved, focusing his frustration on the beloved's unattainable body parts. The sonnet that follows shifts away from the physical attainment of the beloved to focus on how the beauty of the beloved puts the heavens to shame:

> The heavens say to you, pleasant woman:
> A great welcome, gazelle, from all of us!
> The stars may be ours, but within you are your eyes—
> Against them, we're like a mere display.
>
> And starting today that is the stars' desire:
> To be affixed in your eyes, gazelle.
> No one would say: the work of your Maker was in vain,
> For all have heard of your great renown.
>
> I hear Orion, Ursa Major, and the Pleiades all saying:
> If only we could set ourselves
> In the face of the graceful gazelle—how great for us!
>
> Of what power do the Heavens boast over your eyes?
> By day their powers rise, and by night they fall—
> Exiling us every day![51]

Immanuel's poem strives to capture the sentiment of Dante's canzone of praise that appears in the *Vita nuova—Donne ch'avete intelletto d'amore* (Ladies who have understanding of love)—in which Dante describes the lady as a miracle from heaven: "Heaven, which has no other defect / but to have her" (Lo cielo, che non have altro difetto / che d'aver lei).[52] That Dante's poem *Donne ch'avete* is in the form of a canzone and not a sonnet does not diminish the relevance of Immanuel's borrowing from Dante. In fact, in *De Vulgari Eloquentia*, Dante defines the canzone (a word related to the Occitan canso) as the noblest form of poetry, though it is unclear, given its late textual transmission, whether Immanuel was familiar with the treatise.[53] Even though the Occitan canso is precisely what Immanuel criticizes both in his Genesis commentary and in the sixth maḥberet of his Hebrew collection, it is nevertheless impossible to disregard his feat of translating Dante's expression in *Donne ch'avete* into the metrical constraints of a Hebrew sonnet.

When Immanuel describes the lady as something heavenly, he introduces new content to the medieval Hebrew poetic tradition. In the first tercet, Immanuel figures the constellations as envious of his lady's beauty. Although poets in the golden age of Hebrew poetry in al-Andalus exaggerate the qualities of the beloved, Immanuel's terms here are considerably more extreme. Judah Halevi (1057–1141), for instance, compares the beloved to the sun in a number of his secular love poems, but the effect is to aggrandize the beauty of the beloved by comparison, rather than to demonstrate that her (or his) uncommon beauty has given her (or him) unearthly attributes.[54]

This is also a relatively new trope in Dante's time, used first by the Occitan troubadours and embellished by Guido Guinizelli in his canzone *Al cor gentil rempaira sempre amore* (briefly mentioned in chap. 2), in which the poet dares to have God speak about the beauty of his lady. Guinizelli's lady is so full of *gentilzza*, *vertute*, and *degnità* (gentleness, virtue, and dignity) that God exclaims to his angels that he wants her near him and sends angels to collect her. She dies because she is too perfect to exist on earth.[55] This is one example among many instances of Immanuel's translating not only the form of the sonnet from Italian but also the contents that characterize the dolce stil novo into his Hebrew sonnet—a Hebrew sonnet that is a secular poem but that necessarily carries with it numerous biblical allusions and, accordingly, an accrued complexity of meanings.

In addition to implementing thematic ideals from the stilnovisti, Immanuel borrows language directly from Dante in the final sonnet of the third maḥberet, as Umberto Cassuto first observed: he directly translates into Hebrew verses from the canzone *Donna pietosa e di novella etate* (A lady compassionate and young), which appears in chapter 23 of the *Vita nuova*.[56] In his sonnet, Immanuel places the death of his beloved into a cosmic context: in the quartets, he claims that her death has affected the very course of nature, afflicting both the earth and the heavens with darkness and sighs. In the tercets, the poet discusses the effect of her death on him: like Dante, he is jealous of anthropomorphized Death, figuring it as his lady's new lover. His lady not only possesses control over all the heavens and the earth but also rules over darkness and death; once so cruel, Death has been softened and tamed in her presence:

> O Stars! Because of you I am in love with death
> From today, how sweet is death, because you are in it,
> How wonderful is death, because it clings to you.[57]

Indeed, these verses are a close replica—considering the linguistic and metrical alterations required in moving from Dante's Italian:

> that I said:—Death, in great sweetness I hold you;
> you must hereafter be a noble thing,
> because you have been in my lady[58]

It is conceivable that Immanuel saw the *Vita nuova* in manuscript, which could explain this seemingly close translation of Italian to Hebrew.[59] However, these verses from *Donna pietosa* are just a small part of Dante's whole canzone, which Teodolinda Barolini notes for its highly narrative structure, a seamless fit with the prose of the *Vita nuova*. Barolini further comments on the particular significance of the placement of *Donna pietosa*, which occupies the literal center of the *Vita nuova*, a positioning that underscores the text's "continual meditation on the relationship between narrative and poetry."[60] It is tempting to think that Immanuel considered the significance of the position of *Donna pietosa* within the *Vita nuova*, but whether or not he made this connection, it is still relevant that he would have drawn on both an Italian poetic form and a stilnovist spirit for the genuinely remorseful conclusion of the *Scroll*, especially when one considers that his most grandiloquent and self-aggrandizing poems of this story—including the echo poem that ultimately wins over the nun—follow traditional Hebrew metrical forms.[61] In this rare moment of soul-searching, Immanuel offers a sincere gesture toward the *Vita nuova*, not as an *in bono* counterpart to the *Scroll* but as a text worthy of emulation. If the reader momentarily puts aside the prose of the *Scroll*—which, as we will see, readers of the *Vita nuova* systematically and consciously did with the prose of Dante's text—the sonnets indicate Immanuel's careful study of the stilnovist poetry of his time.

If Immanuel's concluding sonnet and *Donna pietosa* represent analogous positions in their respective texts, then the *Scroll* concludes at the theoretical midpoint of the *Vita nuova*. At the moment when Immanuel laments the death of the nun, Dante has only just envisioned Beatrice's death, in what he terms a "vana imaginazione" (empty imagining). Dante's canzone is thus not a eulogy but rather a kind of morbid dream sequence. When Beatrice does die, as Dante conveys in chapter 28 (a prose passage), he deems it inappropriate to elaborate on the details of her death for three reasons: the subject does not fit into the "presente proposito" (present purpose) of the book; "my language would still be inadequate to deal with it properly"; and "it is not becoming for me to treat of it, for the reason that, by treating it, I would be obliged to be a praiser of myself, which thing is at all times reprehensible to whoever does it."[62] After a lengthy prose passage on the numerological significance surrounding Beatrice's death, Dante presents a canzone of lament, *Li occhi dolenti per pietà del core* (The eyes grieving for the heart's pity), in which he intensifies the sense of sorrow in *Donna pietosa*.[63] He also further develops the theologically precarious notion of

Beatrice's ability to "make the eternal Lord marvel / so that sweet desire / came upon him to summon so much perfection."[64] While Immanuel's final sonnet in the *Scroll* focuses on the moment of his lady's death, *Li occhi dolenti* has a broader scope, as it imagines the effect of Beatrice's death on both the human and divine spheres. This does not necessarily imply that Immanuel's sentiment at the end of the *Scroll* is insincere but rather that his prosimetrum does not (and cannot) explore this particular trajectory of love poetry as fully as Dante does in the *Vita nuova*. Nor is this his goal: while Dante spends the remainder of the *Vita nuova* devising how to praise his beloved beyond her death, the *Scroll* and the love affair end with the nun's death, and Immanuel gamely moves on to the next story to show his competence in yet another area of inquiry. Rather than using the prosimetric form to work toward a theory of love poetry as Dante does, Immanuel uses it to insist on poetry—especially the sonnet that treats love—as a form of power, enlisting Dante's tools of versification to achieve a variety of registers, depending on the storyline he wishes to pursue.

Indeed, both Dante and Immanuel rely on prose to steer the reader's comprehension of love poetry. Dante's perceived humility in the context of the *Vita nuova*, evident in his introspective prose passages, draws the reader's attention away from what one might otherwise interpret as the poet's desire to draw attention to himself. In *Li occhi dolenti*, Dante refers to the act of writing and addresses the canzone directly, but the prose that precedes it diverts the reader from considering these metapoetic elements as overt indications of the poet's dexterity and instead directs the reader toward hearing the poignant cry of a bereaved lover. In a similar way, Immanuel's two sonnets for the nun function as hyperbolic complements to the text's overwrought epistles. If, however, they were separated from the *Scroll* and translated into Italian, these same sonnets would resemble stilnovist verses in praise of the lady.

The key aspects of the *Vita nuova* that Immanuel imports and tweaks in his text are related to poetry rather than to prose, from the impulse to gather his lyrics to his reliance on the sonnet and on the dolce stil novo. In an age when Hebrew poetry was losing its footing to prose, Immanuel's turn toward poetry—and specifically love poetry—reveals a concerted effort to focus on the power of poetry in the text and the power he possessed as its poet. Immanuel's veering from long-standing forms of Hebrew poetry reflects both his awareness of his Italian Christian cultural surroundings and his seeming inclination to incorporate these findings into his composition.

In fact, Immanuel's use of not just any sonnet but the love sonnet is unprecedented; his dependence on the sonnet in the third story of his collection suggests that he viewed this form as particularly fitting for the subject of love.[65] Although Italian poets of this period most certainly did not limit the sonnet to musings on love, here Immanuel does so to great effect: the linking of the sonnet to love in this story allowed him to carve out a special niche for love poetry that the Hebrew forms did not facilitate, since none was historically associated solely with love. I see this narrowing of the sonnet to suit his textual purpose as an instance of great intuition: it indicates Immanuel's broader tendency to flout formal boundaries to suit his own poetic purposes; he translates the idea from Italian and then promptly makes it into his own. If the purpose of the *Maḥbarot* is, as its author informs the reader, to preserve poetry, then the third maḥberet is exemplary: a thematically cohesive auto-anthology whose love poems accrue meaning in their prose surroundings but possess additional significance when considered on their own.[66]

Interestingly, Immanuel was far from alone in his urge to refashion Dante's poetry: Giovanni Boccaccio (1313–75) relegated Dante's glosses to the margins in his autograph transcription of the *Vita nuova*, significantly and profoundly altering the nature and reception history of the composition.[67] Just as the *Maḥbarot* facilitated the spread of Immanuel's interpretation of Dantean poetics to many Hebrew readers, Boccaccio's transcription informed the reading and interpretation of Dante's text for centuries of readers of the *Vita nuova*. In a further striking parallel to the Hebrew maqama's grappling with Hebrew's worth with respect to Arabic, Boccaccio's autograph manuscript corroborated his agenda of showing, as Eisner explains, "that Italian can be as sophisticated and meaningful a literary language as Latin."[68]

Testing the Limits of Love's Form in Jewish-Italian Expression

How does Immanuel render his poetic voice, inevitably inflected with his interpretation of Arabo-Andalusian culture, into the highly codified, post–courtly love world of the stilnovisti? The reader might wonder why Immanuel even bothered or dared to compose in Italian. We do not know the chronology of Immanuel's compositions; one could accordingly surmise he wrote the Italian lyrics to practice the forms in Italian before moving them into Hebrew, but it seems, on closer examination of his Italian lyrics—which address a variety of themes, from Italian politics and theology to love and metapoetics—that Immanuel wrote them for a specifically Italian Christian audience and not merely as a rehearsal for the debut of the first non-Italian or non-Occitan sonnet.[69]

Complicating the interpretation of Immanuel's Italian corpus is the following evidence from the *Maḥbarot* and Immanuel's Bible commentaries, though one should of course be careful not to read all of his writings as a singular trajectory: although Immanuel clearly adopted and adapted key aspects of Italian poetry for use in Hebrew, he harshly criticizes the corpus of Christian lyrics as a whole. As Amnon Shiloah noted, Immanuel writes about music's biblical origins in his commentary on Genesis.[70] He contrasts Yuval (Gen. 4.21), "the father of those who play instruments," with contemporary music practices: "Nowadays, this art is being crushed by the [impure ones] who corrupted its magnificence by using it in taverns and for singing lust songs."[71]

Immanuel's critique of contemporary music is perhaps at odds with his composition of secular lyrics in Italian and in Hebrew: his Hebrew poetry, when imbued with Italian poetics, alters the conventions, in the same way that, three centuries earlier, Hispano-Hebraic poetry embraced innovations. Even so, Immanuel justifies his use of Romance poetics in the sixth maḥberet of his *Maḥbarot* by reasoning, as Shiloah further explains, that music itself had been "stolen": "What says the science of music to the Christians? / The answer was: I was stolen from the land of the Hebrews."[72] Still, there seems to be a distance between the Italian lyrics of Immanuel and those of his contemporary Italian Christian poets. Even without Immanuel's Genesis commentary, the reader of his Italian lyrics immediately senses a subtle but forceful critique of Italian lyric from within the world of Italian poetry and an insistence on his Jewishness—or at least his otherness, as Fabian Alfie has noted: "he is neither fully within nor fully alien to both cultures, and his vernacular poetry often reflects this outlook."[73] Perhaps Immanuel's critique of Italian is akin to the way in which the overarching context of the third maḥberet pokes fun at Italian lyric as Brener has proposed, even if the individual poems emulate Italian poetics in Hebrew. Of Immanuel's four Italian sonnets, the one that most specifically treats love also, as I argue, most readily reveals his critical and innovative approach to Italian composition. *Bisbidis*, also an exploration of love, even more overtly challenges the compositional practices of Immanuel's contemporaries, with its unprecedented homage to apparently unrefined linguistics and unusual prose-like form, which mimics the rhymed prose cadence of a Hebrew maqama.[74]

Immanuel's Hail Mary

Love never read the "Hail Mary."
Love never held to laws or faith.
Love is a heart, which doesn't hear or see:
Love never knows measure or limit.

Love is absolute lordship,
which is determined to get what it wants;
love is like a planet, exerting its influence,
while always becoming more distant.

Love never leaves behind its pride,
ceding neither to "Our Fathers" nor to incantations.
Nor will it uncleave, though in fear I struggle.

Love does that which pains me most:
for without attending to what I say,
It always says, "This is what *I* want!"[75]

The most noticeable aspect of this sonnet is Immanuel's overt use of terms from Christian theology: *avemaria* and *paternostri*. Immanuel could have chosen words or phrases without Christian significance to convey similar meanings. Instead, he lets his reader know that he is familiar enough with Christian customs and vocabulary to incorporate them into his sonnet. Still, his awareness of such vocabulary does not necessitate his using it; in fact, very few Italian poets of the Duecento and Trecento periods employed Christian terminology. Exceptions include Pieraccio Tedaldi (circa 1285–circa 1353), who uses the term *paternostro* in his sonnet to his son Bindo, which forms half of a serious tenzone between father and son; and Cecco Angiolieri (c. 1260–c. 1312), who refers to *Ave Dominus* (Hail the Lord) in a comic sonnet about his beloved Bettina's infidelity.[76] To my knowledge, no other poet of the period uses the term *avemaria*, let alone in this profane manner, in which the poet applies a theological term to a matter of worldly love. In Immanuel's defense, however, he does claim that love *never* reads the Hail Mary, though the mere conflation of two terms, even in a negative sense, nonetheless forges an association; even when the sonnet acknowledges the distinction between the profane and sacred realms in stating that reading the Hail Mary is something love never does, Immanuel subtly suggests that love, rather than being too base for religion, possesses its own power, something on par with, but untouched by, theology. Accordingly,

Alfie remarks that in this poem Immanuel "overturns the Christianization of Love" and simultaneously casts himself as a member of this poetic circle.[77] The *Amor* of Immanuel's sonnet provides a purely courtly definition of love—something that was a given, if passé, among his contemporaries—but positioning it so clearly with respect to religion prods the reader into a genuine assessment of the relationship.

Furthermore, the repetition of *amor* continues to challenge the negative presence of theological terms: it is unrelenting in its repetition, much like the triad of amor in Francesca's famous lament to Paolo in *Inferno* 5:

> Love, that can quickly seize the gentle heart,
> took hold of him because of the fair body
> taken from me—how that was done still wounds me.
>
> Love, that releases no beloved from loving,
> took hold of me so strongly through his beauty
> that, as you see, it has not left me yet.
>
> Love led the two of us unto one death.[78]

Immanuel grasps Dante's purposefully *in malo* use of a Trinitarian-driven reference to love—negative because it exemplifies lustful sinners in hell—and undercuts its anti-sanctity, both by conflating love with philosophy and theology outside the inverted context of Hell and by putting this anaphora to use seven, rather than three, times. Seven could have a range of numerological significances, perhaps the most overt for a Christian reader as the Jewish observance of the Sabbath on the seventh day of the week according to the Jewish calendar (and an obvious calque in Italian, *sabato*, of the Hebrew *shabbat*). To add further meaning to Immanuel's invocation of love from *Inferno* 5, Paolo and Francesca fell into adulterous love while reading, the very activity to which Immanuel refers in the opening verse of the sonnet: "Love never read the 'Hail Mary.'"

Immanuel sprinkles terminology of the stilnovisti throughout this sonnet, signaling to the reader that he is well aware of the importance of using these terms and knowledgeable about their accrued underlying meanings. In the final verse—voiced by personified love, a favorite trope of stilnovisti—Love says to Immanuel, "Ma sempre mi sa dir:—Pur così voglio." Love's words to Immanuel recall the figure of personified love from the *Vita nuova*: "There appeared to me a marvelous vision: I seemed to see in my room a cloud the color of fire, within which I discerned a figure of a master, of an aspect frightening to whoever might behold him."[79] Immanuel again invokes personified love in *Bisbidis*, though not via a direct address:

"For Love is in the hall of Cangrande della Scala: here without wings, seemingly I fly."[80] Other vocabulary likewise places this text firmly within the world of the stilnovisti, such as "pura signoria," which, in capturing the divine-like nature of love, recalls the blasphemous impulse in Guinizelli's canzone *Al cor gentil rempaira sempre amore*. The pride associated with the beloved (*orgoglio*) similarly positions the poem within the rubric of these Italian poets, who held a deified notion of love as capable of maintaining the beloved's well-being. Immanuel draws on the opposition of pain and love favored most notably by Guido Cavalcanti in the Italian tradition, though it is likewise an important trope in secular Hispano-Hebraic lyric.[81] In the Italian tradition, this often plays out in the dichotomy between love and bitterness (*amor/amar*), a blend that is of particular linguistic convenience for Immanuel, given the Hebrew root *m-r* (bitter).

Though Italianists have traditionally classified Immanuel among the *poeti giocosi* (the jocular poets), the entire category of the poeti giocosi has rightfully come under scrutiny in Alfie's innovative and important study of Cecco Angiolieri: "[Cecco] does not remain fixed within the comic style as he receives it, but neither does he excogitate the alterations from his own creative genius. Instead, he learns from all the different types of literature he targets and uses those lessons in his comic compositions. Indeed, the ability to hybridize language, stylemes and traits from other literary traditions might represent Angiolieri's greatest strength as a poet."[82]

It likewise seems shortsighted to limit a poet to one category when not all of his compositions fit a given rubric and especially given that Dante scholars suspend these carefully curated categories for Dante's own corpus, much of which overtly defies classification. It follows that the reader of Immanuel need not envision his sonnet as a satirical poem, for though it does seek to flout some stilnovist conventions, it does not necessarily poke fun at love; love is still a serious matter, but the poet treats it on his own terms. Perhaps in this way it is akin to the sonnets from the *Maḥbarot*, particularly those in the third maḥberet, that seem more genuine than their surrounding prose contexts suggest. Though Immanuel's sonnet *Amor non lesse mai l'avemaria* is unusual and illusive, what remains clear is his thorough comprehension of the prosody, language, and themes of the Duecento Italian sonnet.

Hybridity Capsule: A Jewish Italian Prose Poem of Love

With its complex manipulations of genre and form, Immanuel's strophic Italian poem, known as *Bisbidis*, even more overtly illustrates his mastery of Italian lyric. Scholars have identified this poem as a *frottola*, a kind of early madrigal popularized in the late fifteenth century.[83] I have argued that this poem should not be termed a frottola: Immanuel's familiarity with the frottola is, from a chronological standpoint, dubious, and while calling it a frottola may account for its formal, thematic, and stylistic creativity, it does not aptly characterize *Bisbidis*, a formal cross between poetry and prose replete with unprecedented onomatopoeia.[84] Indeed, *Bisbidis* flummoxed early modern copyists, who, when faced with a text that did not have the characteristics of a sonnet, canzone, or *ballata*, did not know whether to display the poem as rhymed verses or as a prose-like form that just so happened to have rhyme. The copyist of the Casanatense 433 opted for the prose approach, without regard to the poem's rhyme. Thus, the element that draws the reader's eye is the onomatopoeia, since the onomatopoeic words are utterly new to Italian language and lyric and since they are repeated, at times occupying what amounts to one or more lines of text (e.g., *dufduf dufduf, dufduf dufduf, dufduf dufduf*).[85]

In a manuscript that features canzoni and sonnets by the most notable poets of the period, including Dante, Cino da Pistoia, Guittone d'Arezzo, Guido Guinizelli, and Guido Cavalcanti, the appearance of Immanuel's *Bisbidis* is something of a shock: it occupies four pages (two front and back: 132r–133v) that completely disregard the poem's constant *-are* rhyme.[86] In this way, it is strangely akin to the treatment of rhymed prose in the manuscripts and print editions featuring the *Maḥberot Immanuel*, whose rhymed prose appears as prose, without regard to the constant rhyme (as was the custom for the rhymed prose of classical Arabic and medieval Hebrew compositions), but whose rhymed and metered poems, including its thirty-eight sonnets, appear separate from the rhymed prose and are rendered line by line. I have argued that *Bisbidis* itself is like a maqama, both in form and theme, and the stichometry of *Bisbidis* in the Casanatense 433 upholds this assertion: it reveals, as much as do the poem's contents, that the poem is an outsider with respect to form.[87]

In his study on Immanuel published posthumously in 1904, Leonello Modona commented on the stichometric features of *Bisbidis* as it appears in the two manuscripts: "The Casanatense manuscript shows the verses continuously while the Bologna is in imperfect strophes—which is undoubtedly incompetence on the part of the scribe, who was perhaps viewing older manuscripts in which the poetry was spread out in the manner of prose and lacking the signs of punctuation or divisions of strophes, and who also perhaps relied on memory—resulting in tetrastic strophes, in the manner of the *sirventese*, with three verses that rhyme among them along with the last of the previous strophe."[88]

Perhaps the copyist's rendering was a sign not of incompetence but rather of intuition: the language, prosody, and narrative qualities of *Bisbidis* are all indeed more prose-like than one usually finds in Italian lyrics of Immanuel's period. One could perhaps look to the *Divine Comedy* as Immanuel's inspiration, particularly since *Bisbidis* vacillates between high and low registers—from its invocation of personified Love to its verbose animals. Yet all of the variation in Immanuel's poem occurs within the space of roughly half of the words found in one canto of Dante's *Commedia* and without the immensely complex, immutable poetic structure of the *Commedia*. Or perhaps the copyist was simply trying to save space.

In so far as panegyric can be a kind of love poem, *Bisbidis* could fit that rubric: Immanuel praises Cangrande della Scala—who is highly unlikely to have been Immanuel's patron, though he certainly was Dante's—for his championing of arms and letters ("del dire et del fare"); for his generosity to all in need ("here's a large band of the old, the half-blind: / the generosity [of Cangrande] keeps them going"); for the way in which his wealth has facilitated his relaxed attitude toward life's fineries ("But the most costly things—to Cangrande they're nothing"); and for his appreciation of humanity amid differences ("And here fools and pilgrims to Rome and elsewhere, / Jews and Muslims, see how they all arrive").[89] Of course, the narrator has defined the parameters and is thus the arbiter of Cangrande's appreciation of difference, and in this way the poem reflects the onlooker's values and aspirations rather than the reality of Verona. Indeed, especially given how little historians know about Cangrande's Verona, *Bisbidis* is the poet's wish: it is the poet who prefers Verona to all other places he has visited ("the only place that holds the crown is Verona"); who praises Verona for its many languages ("Here Germans, Italians and French, / Flemish and English, speaking together"); and who notes Verona's mingling of philosophy, astrology, and theology.

As for objects of affection, the Verona of the poem seems to have a chastening effect on the poet: he passes by the ladies in town (matrons, maidens, and widows), instead setting his sights on Love herself—a personification of Philosophy intimately connected to the wisdom of Cangrande: "My dear lady causes virtue to reign, for Love is in the hall of Cangrande della Scala: here without wings, seemingly I fly."[90] Even the woman whose words in the manuscript tradition gave her titular status serves not to seduce the poet but rather to give him advice: "Bis bis bis bisbidis bisbidis bis bisbidis you'll hear her advise." Of course, the reader does not know exactly what she advises. Far from the flesh-and-blood nun of the third maḥberet or the personified love from Immanuel's Italian sonnet, *Amor non lesse mai l'avemaria*, whose failure to read the Hail Mary and unfamiliarity with laws and faith torment the poet, the lady of *Bisbidis* is the idealized lady of virtue. Despite the poem's unusually vocal peoples, animals, and instruments, whose sound words animate the poem, she lacks both voice and form, much like Cangrande himself.

Though the poet seems to be onlooker and observer, he is undoubtedly in control, from his imaginative onomatopoeic vocabulary, which lays bare that which he has found lacking in the Italian language, to his invocation of those age-old stars of the mimetic stage—the singers, minstrels, and troubadours who facilitate his staggering lyric experiment. In a final effort to impress on the reader the veracity of his words, Immanuel turns to the strategy of the "truth claim"—a device frequently found in both the *Divine Comedy* and the *Maḥberot Immanuel*: "I could barely believe what I was seeing."[91] Indeed, a murky formal region that exists somewhere between the poetry and prose of love—of self and others—has expertly swept the reader into the intoxicating world of the poem without garnering a moment's consideration that its poet likely never even visited Verona.

Outsiders in Outsider Art, or Women as Teachers of Poetry

The unusually powerful poetic voices of the female protagonists who lead discourses on metaphor, poetics, and love in the prosimetra by Immanuel, ibn Ṣaqbel, and ben Elʿazar require further attention here, as they deepen the hybrid notions of courtly love underlying prosimetra by Jewish authors.[92] Across literary traditions of the medieval Mediterranean, there were very few women poets; exceptions include mystic poet Rābiʿa, the wife of Dunash ben Labrat who wrote one poem in Hebrew, and the female Occitan troubadours, known as *trobairitz*. The other female poetic voices that exist across traditions much more frequently come from within the fictional constructs of prose and poetry, having been granted their voices by male authors. In some cases, women's voices fall somewhere between these real and imaginary lines, since we do not know precisely how certain poems were performed. For instance, a female can voice the refrain, known as the *kharja*, in the Arabic or Hebrew Andalusian strophic muwashshaḥ, allowing for the possibility that a female could have sung, depending on performance practices. This scenario is less likely in the Galician-Portuguese cantigas d'amigo, in which male poets present lyrics voiced by females longing for their lovers' safe returns, since the names of male authors are generally attached to these lyrics.[93] Dante likewise grants poetic power to females within his compositions, notably via Beatrice in the *Commedia*, in the *in malo* Francesca of *Inferno* 5, and in his pronouncement in the twenty-fifth chapter of the *Vita nuova* that vernacular love lyric owes to its existence the inability of women to read Latin.

The female voice in some prosimetra by Jewish authors, though, is remarkable for reasons beyond the fact of her gender: she is the teacher of poetry. This characterization is different from a female muse who inspires poetic composition. We can now look back at the woman in al-Washshāʾ's Arabic treatise who tries to instruct her beloved in matters of love via her use of the lyric. Indeed, the reader knows she is a poet because al-Washshāʾ has the lover in the vignette refer specifically to her elegant poetry. Despite select references to women as versifiers, women in Arabic and in Hebrew maqamas, such as al-Ḥarizi's *Taḥkemoni* and ibn Shabbetai's *Minḥat Yehuda sone ha-nashim*, tend to be the objects of misogynist narratives rather than the purveyors of versification.[94] This is precisely why the presence of women who play active roles in metapoetic instruction in prosimetra by ibn Ṣaqbel, ben Elʿazar, and Immanuel is noteworthy and warrants further thought.

Schirmann associated *Sefer ha-meshalim* with the thirteenth-century French prosimetrum *Aucassin et Nicolette*: he notes that the lovers in *Sefer ha-meshalim* are notably young, as are Aucassin and Nicolette.[95] This preoccupation with youth is likewise at home in the Occitan troubadour lyric (which originated in the region to the south of *Aucassin et Nicolette*), and such youth serves as one of the foundational notions of courtliness, alongside joy and love.[96] Schirmann later suggests, although not in relation to *Aucassin et Nicolette*, that while the lady depicted in Hispano-Hebraic poetry is often distant and cruel, the female characters in *Sefer ha-meshalim* are young, present, and crucial to the plot.[97] This also fits the profile of Nicolette, who plays an active role in the *chantefable* and is responsible for its satisfying ending.[98] Even more compelling than the fact that these females sway the plot is the medium they use to enact their power—through poetry itself. The lady of the apple in *Ne'um Asher*, a few of the women in *Sefer ha-meshalim*, and Nicolette all enlist poetry in attempts to achieve what they desire. The lady of the apple in *Ne'um Asher*, Yemima and Yefefiya (from the seventh story of *Sefer ha-meshalim*), and Kima (from the ninth) all use love poetry to teach others how to be ideal poet lovers; Nicolette disguises herself as a minstrel and sings to Aucassin about their relationship, using poetry in an effort to reunite with her lover.[99]

Ben Elʿazar takes this role of the female a step further than ibn Ṣaqbel and the author of *Aucassin et Nicolette*. While the lady of the apple lures Asher with poetry, her instruction in the metaphysical rewards of love poetry is potent but not entirely successful, though Asher might have succeeded in the probable but nonextant companion stories. In an even less overtly metapoetic fashion, Nicolette's poem drives the plot toward a positive outcome but without didactic intent. Kima, however, who speaks in praise of her lover as a trobairitz, additionally uses her poetic voice to instruct Sahar on how to engage in spiritual love.[100] Spiritual betterment through proper adoration of the lady is a key ingredient of Occitan courtly love, but although female voices in the Romance vernacular lyric traditions certainly learn and engage in poetry, they do not go out of their way to peddle poetic instruction, even if they refer self-consciously to the act of composition.[101]

Immanuel's object of affection in the third maḥberet represents an inversion of this, in accordance with the obsolescence of courtly love: the nun, fluent in the forms, meters, and topics of love lyric, is unable to channel the power of lyric to her advantage. Though Immanuel certainly plays into the misogynist nature of the narrative, his focus seems to be on the ridiculousness of the endeavor; he grants love poetry control of the narrative, only to have it be the cause of the nun's death. How preposterous, his narrative shows, for love poetry to induce someone to alter her moral compass and destroy her physical well-being: indeed, his is a literal and metaliterary death of courtly love.

It seems that ibn Ṣaqbel, ben Elʿazar, and Immanuel have harnessed elements of these poetic practices to construct females not only skilled in composing love poetry but also fully capable of judging others' poetic compositions. In this way, they are poised to be instructors of the lyric, as in al-Washshā''s early example. Ibn Ṣaqbel and ben Elʿazar were both masters of Arabic poetics and experimented with Romance themes, and Immanuel, removed from the Andalusian sphere, adapted Hebrew-via-Arabic forms and tropes to suit his Italian Christian setting. These three, shifting among languages—though in essence existing somewhere within the "minor language" category that Deleuze and Guattari defined—endow females with unusual powers as proxies for themselves: outsiders with the potential to innovate from within the parameters of love lyric.[102]

Notes

1. Sappho, fragment 1, lines 19–20: "Who, O Sappho, is wronging you?" *If Not, Winter*, trans. Carson, 2–3.

2. Dante Alighieri was born in politically turbulent Florence, where he received a thorough education in Latin grammar. He first saw Beatrice, who became his inspiration for both the *Vita nuova* and the *Commedia*, when he was nine years old, and by the time he was eleven, he was betrothed to Gemma Donati, whom he likely married at the age of twenty. He began to write poetry at this time and fostered friendships with Guido Cavalcanti (1250–1300) and Brunetto Latini (1220–95), who informed his own literary development. In 1287, he traveled to Bologna to supplement his literary studies. There, he became familiar with the latest poetic trends put forth by the Bolognese poet Guido Guinizelli (1230–76). Beatrice died in 1290, and Dante subsequently composed/compiled the *Vita nuova*, sometime between 1292 and 1295. During this time, he also pursued studies in theology and philosophy. Dante also led an active life in politics, first as a Guelph (at odds with rival Ghibellines) and then as a White Guelph when the Guelphs split into two in 1300. While Dante was on a political mission to Rome in 1301, the Black Guelphs seized power of Florence and exiled him. A year later, they threatened him with execution if he attempted to return. As an exile, Dante lived in parts of Tuscany and in northern Italy. He wrote the *De Vulgari Eloquentia*, an unfinished treatise in Latin on vernacular language, sometime between 1303 and 1304 and the *Convivio*, a prosimetric philosophical work in the vernacular, sometime between 1304 and 1307. He composed *Inferno*, the first canticle of the *Divine Comedy*, between 1304 and 1309, *Purgatorio* between 1310 and 1316, and *Paradiso* between 1316 and 1321. He wrote his Latin treatise *De Monarchia* and his Latin eclogues sometime during the period in which he composed *Paradiso*.

3. See Ziolkowski, *Dante and Islam*; Mallette, *Kingdom of Sicily, 1100–1250*; Menocal, *Shards of Love*.

4. *Maḥbarot* (singular *maḥberet*) is the Hebrew equivalent of the Arabic *maqāmā*, pl. *maqāmāt*. Brener cleverly translated the title as *The Cantos of Immanuel*; see Brener, "*Scroll of Love*."

5. James Robinson has identified innovation in Immanuel's biblical commentaries, noting that his pastiche in Ecclesiastes is deliberate and meaningful. "Allegorical Interpretation in Immanuel of Rome's Commentary on Qohelet."

6. Alfie, "Immanuel of Rome, Alias Manoello Giudeo," 313.

7. Bregman, *Golden Way*, 16.

8. Immanuel's Italian lyrics are found in Cipolla and Pellegrini ("Poesie minori riguardanti gli Scaglieri"); Marti (*Poeti giocosi del tempo di Dante*); and Vitale (*Rimatori comico-realistici del Due e Trecento*).

9. Known in English as the Code of Jewish Law, the *Shulḥan ʿarukh*, by Joseph Karo, literally means *Prepared Table*. The particular passage that mentions Immanuel's poetry is SA ʾOraḥ ḥayim 307.16.

10. For recent archival research that debunks Immanuel's dating, see Fishkin, "Lifetime in Letters."

11. For general background on Immanuel, see Cassuto and Sáenz-Badillos, "Immanuel (ben Solomon) of Rome"; Levy, "Immanuel of Rome and Dante"; Fishkin, "Situating Hell & Heaven"; Alfie, "Immanuel of Rome, Alias Manoello Giudeo." For historical background on the Jews of Rome and the fourteenth-century papacy, see Schatzmiller, "The Papal Monarchy as Viewed by Medieval Jews."

12. Barb. Lat. 3953, folio 128v. Levy, "Immanuel of Rome's *Bisbidis*," 81.

13. Dante, a contemporary of Immanuel, had a profound role in shaping Italian literature and, eventually, Italy's national language: his beloved Tuscan became the foundation of the formalized and standardized Italian language during the nineteenth century's political and social movement to unite Italy, known as the *Risorgimento.*

14. Jews were established in Rome as early as 139 BCE; see Stern, "Roman Literature."

15. For a translation into English, see Gollancz's 1921 text of Immanuel ben Solomon, *Tophet and Eden (Hell and Paradise).* For a thorough discussion of contents, see Fishkin, "Situating Hell & Heaven."

16. For Immanuel's references to al-Ḥarizi, see Huss, "Status of Fiction in the Hebrew Maqama," 352.

17. Castellani, "Sul codice Laurenziano Martelliano 12."

18. Alighieri, *Vita nuova*, sec. 1, trans. Cervigni and Vasta, 47; Carrai, "Prefazione," 8; De Robertis, *Il libro della Vita nuova*, 11.

19. Eisner, *Boccaccio and the Invention of Italian Literature*, 8.

20. See Barolini, *Dante's Poets*; Barolini's commentary in Alighieri, *Rime giovanili e della "Vita Nuova"*; McLain, "Prose and Poetry and the Making of Beatrice"; Dronke, *Verse with Prose from Petronius to Dante*, 111–12.

21. Ascoli, *Dante and the Making of a Modern Author*, 181.

22. Dante "divides" each poem into parts and explains the contents of each part (*divisioni*). He makes these divisions after the poems for the first twenty poems and before the poems for the final eleven. The remaining third of the text, prose segments called *ragioni* (reasons; i.e., reasons for the poems), is Dante's prose storyline that provides a context for his having composed each poem. For further explanation of *ragioni*, see Singleton, *Essay on the "Vita Nuova,"* 50. Dante denies that he is a glossator, stating after Beatrice's death that he will not treat the matter of her death in greater detail or in poetry but will leave it "to some other glossator" (*ad altro chiosatore*). *Vita nuova*, 28.3, trans. Cervigni and Vasta, 117. Singleton argues, however, that although Dante has proclaimed himself a scribe, he becomes a glossator at points in the prose. *Essay on the "Vita Nuova,"* 34.

23. Eisner, *Boccaccio and the Invention of Italian Literature*, 8.

24. Ascoli, *Dante and the Making of a Modern Author*, 181. Dante refers to the poets who preceded him in writing in the vernacular as "alquanti grossi," translated by Cervigni and Vasta as "unschooled individuals." *Vita nuova* 25.6, 109. Philosophical worth is a natural consideration here, given the intimate connections between poetry and philosophy; see Curtius, *European Literature and the Latin Middle Ages*, 207. Eisner, *Boccaccio and the Invention of Italian Literature*, 7.

25. Curtius, *European Literature and the Latin Middle Ages*, 214.

26. Leder and Kilpatrick, "Classical Arabic Prose Literature," 2.

27. Holmes, "*Vita Nuova* in the Context of Vatican MS Chigiano L. VIII.305," 195.

28. "È la prosa il fatto nuovo di questo libro." De Robertis, *Il libro della Vita Nuova*, 6.

29. Bertoni, *La prosa della "Vita nuova" di Dante*, 12.

30. Bertoni, 26–27, 44.

31. Singleton, *Essay on the "Vita Nuova,"* 100.
32. De Robertis, *Il libro della Vita Nuova*, 5.
33. Ricci, "Tendenze prosimetriche nella letteratura del Trecento," 64.
34. Dronke, *Medieval Latin and the Rise of European Love-Lyric*, 96. Some scholars argue that the author of *Aucassin et Nicolette* presents a parody of courtly love; for instance, see Harden, "*Aucassin et Nicolette* as Parody." But even if the text does, in fact, intend parody, it does not propound a new concept of love or love poetry as the *Vita nuova* does.
35. Ricci, "Tendenze prosimetriche nella letteratura del Trecento," 61. Dronke, *Medieval Latin and the Rise of European Love-Lyric*, 107.
36. Dronke, *Medieval Latin and the Rise of European Love-Lyric*, 108. Dante refers to both Boethius and the *Consolation of Philosophy* a number of times in the *Convivio*, and in *Convivio* 2.12, he describes having read the *Consolation* shortly after Beatrice's death. Other medieval Latin prosimetra include Martianus Capella's *De nuptiis Philologiae et Mercurii* (*On the Marriage of Philology and Mercury*), Bernard Silvestris's *Cosmographia*, and Alan of Lille's *De planctu naturae* (*Complaint of Nature*).
37. Singleton, *An Essay on the "Vita Nuova,"* 83.
38. Singleton, 9.
39. "Va-yiheyu vanu ʾanashim ʾasher higiʿa mi-sikhlutam lehitpaʾer be-shirim ḥiberam zulatam u-qeṣatam hitpaʾaru ve-shirim ḥibartim ve-heʿlamti ʿenai mehem." Immanuel ben Solomon, *Maḥberot Immanuel*, 1:3, lines 11–12.
40. "Io non Enëa, io non Paulo sono." Alighieri, *Inferno* 2.32, trans. Mandelbaum, 15.
41. Bregman mentions the anthology-like quality of Immanuel's collection and notes the similar format of the *Vita nuova*. *Golden Way*, 15–17. See also Decter, "Belles-Lettres," 796.
42. Ibn Gabirol, *Shire Shelomo ben Yehuda ibn Gabirol*, 158. For context, see Schirmann, "Function of the Hebrew Poet in Medieval Spain," 242.
43. Darʿī, who was born in Alexandria and spent most of his adult life in Egypt aside from supposed trips to Damascus and Jerusalem, compiled his 544 poems into a *dīwān*. See Schirmann, "Darʿī, Moses ben Abraham"; Yeshaya, *Medieval Hebrew Poetry in Muslim Egypt*.
44. Solomon Bonafed, who lived in Christian Spain a few generations following Immanuel's lifetime (end of the fourteenth century to middle of the fifteenth century), also anthologized his own poetry. See Decter, "Belles-Lettres," 796; Suler and Sáenz-Badillos, "Bonafed, Solomon ben Reuben."
45. Decter, "Belles-Lettres," 796. For Hebrew: Bedersi, *Sefer ha-pardes*, 22; editor Leopold Dukes has suggested adding a negative (*lo*) because without this negative the phrase does not make sense and with it, it clearly does.
46. Ateş, "Ibn al-ʿArabī." For edition and partial translation, see al-ʿArabī, *Tarjumān al-ashwāq*.
47. Pagis, *Ḥidush u-masoret be-shirat ha-ḥol*, 262; Huss, "The Status of Fiction in the Hebrew Maqama." For a thorough and illuminating discussion of authority in Dante, see Ascoli, *Dante and the Making of a Modern Author*.
48. Bregman, *Golden Way*, 32.
49. See Cassuto, *Dante e Manoello*, 63; Pagis, *Ḥidush u-masoret be-shirat ha-ḥol*, 263; and Brener, *Golden Way*, 151.
50. Malkiel, "Eros as Medium," 58, 51.
51. Yomeru sheḥaqim lakh, ayuma naʾava:
rav lakh, ṣeviya, rav shelom banayikh!

banu—ṣeva marom, u-vakh—ʿenayikh
ki nihye negdam keha-yom ra'ava.

ule-khokheve shaḥaq keha-yom ta'ava,
ha-yaʿala, limshol be-mikhmanayikh.
lo yomeru: shav ʿamelu vonayikh
kol shomeʿe shimʿekh, emunat ga'ava.

eshmaʿ kesil va-ʿash ve-khima yomeru:
mi yitena khayom ve-nihye shoqedim
bifne ṣeviyat ḥen—azai ṭov lanu!

ma el sheḥaqim ki veʿoz yitpa'aru,
bo yaʿalu yomam ve-layla yoredim—
ʿoz ha-sheḥaqim yom le-yom higlanu!

Immanuel, *Maḥberot Immanuel*, 50–51, lines 124–37. Many thanks to Dana Fishkin for her thoughtful comments on my translations of Immanuel's Hebrew poetry. For a rhyming translation of this sonnet, see Brener, "*Scroll of Love*," 157.

52. Alighieri, *Vita nuova*, 19.7, lines 19–20, trans. Cervigni and Vasta, 83.

53. Alighieri, *De Vulgari Eloquentia*, 2.3

54. See Halevi's poems *Lel gileta alai ṣeviya naʿara* and *ʿOfra tekhabes begadeha beme*, in Schirmann, *Ha-shira ha-ʿivrit bi-Sfarad uvi-Provans*, book 1, 2:438–39. For a translation into English, see Scheindlin, *Wine Women, and Death*, 119, 126.

55. De Robertis, in Alighieri, *Vita nuova*, 121n.

56. Cassuto, *Dante e Manoello*, 65–66. The English first verse of the poem was translated by Cervigni and Vasta: Alighieri, *Vita nuova*, 23.17, line 1, 99.

57. "ʿAsh! baʿavurekh ohava hamaveta, / ma mateqa miyom asher bakh daveqa, / ma nifle'a mavet beʿash hitḥabera." Immanuel, *Maḥberot Immanuel*, 70, lines 558–60. I thank Dana Fishkin for pointing out that *daveqa* and *hitḥabera* are synonymous technical philosophical terms meaning conjoining—i.e., the joining of the human potential intellect with the agent intellect. Immanuel's use of this terminology adds layers of meaning to his rhapsody about death.

58. "Ch'io dicea:—Morte, assai dolce ti tegno; / tu dei omai esser cosa gentile, / poi che tu se' ne la mia donna stata." Alighieri, *Vita nuova*, 23.27, lines 73–75, trans. Cervigni and Vasta, 103.

59. A copy of the *Vita nuova* was circulating as early as 1308, and an antegraph of the Martelli 12 copy—which was likely also the antegraph to the Tordi and Trespiano fragments—circulated, probably in northeastern Tuscany or the northwestern part of the Marche. Many thanks to Teodolinda Barolini, Wayne Storey, and Martin Eisner for their input on this circumstance, which I first mention in *Digital Dante*: "Immanuel of Rome and Dante." Castellani proposes that VN Martelli 12 was transcribed in Gubbio in the first decade or two of the thirteenth century. "Sul codice Laurenziano Martelliano 12." Further, Roth surmises that Immanuel was likely in Gubbio in 1321 and probably saw the *Commedia* there, since he composed his final maqama, *Tofet ve-ʿeden* (Heaven and Hell), in 1321. "New Light on Dante's Circle," 28. Roth's historical method is decidedly imperfect—he consistently draws on Immanuel's fictional writings to glean historical truths and geographic locations. Still, it is fairly safe to say that, given Immanuel's correspondence with Bosone da Gubbio and given that Immanuel is referred to as Manoel Guideo da Gobbio in the manuscript tradition, Immanuel is likely to have been in Gubbio, where he could have seen the *Commedia* and the *Vita nuova*. In addition, Immanuel's *Maḥbarot* provides numerous textual parallels to

both the *Commedia* and the *Vita nuova* that strongly suggest his familiarity with them. For additional analysis of these parallels, see Cassuto, *Dante e Manoello*, 64–67.

60. Barolini, commentary in *Rime giovanili e della "Vita Nuova,"* 360.

61. Although *Donna pietosa* is a canzone and not a sonnet, it is still significant that Immanuel took his inspiration from an Italian poetic form for his composition of a Hebrew sonnet. For further reading on the Hebrew echo poem, see Bregman, *Bi-shne qolot*.

62. "Ancora non sarebbe sufficiente la mia lingua a trattare come si converrebbe di ciò"; "non è convenevole a me trattare di ciò, per quello che, trattando, converrebbe essere me laudatore di me medesimo, la quale cosa è al postutto biasimevole a chi lo fae." Alighieri, *Vita nuova*, 28.2, trans. Cervigni and Vasta, 115–17.

63. The English first verse of the poem was translated by Cervigni and Vasta: Alighieri, *Vita nuova*, 31.8, line 1, 119.

64. "Fé maravigliar l'etterno sire, / sì che dolce disire / lo giunse di chiamar tanta salute." Alighieri, *Vita nuova*, 31.10, lines 23–25, trans. Cervigni and Vasta, 121.

65. The eleventh maḥberet of Immanuel's collection seems to corroborate this intuition: the majority of the story comprises a series of digressions on poetic competition and Immanuel's poetic talent. The story showcases Immanuel's ability to compose poems with particularly complex and impressive formal requirements but does not include any poem on the theme of love, nor does it incorporate a sonnet, facts that seem to indicate Immanuel's association of the sonnet with the theme of love. Although Immanuel does compose sonnets on other topics, the evidence from the third and eleventh maḥbarot further suggests his linking of the sonnet with love.

66. Pagis notes that in the sixteenth maḥberet, the poems play a key role in the plot: "The story provides an effective framework for the bawdy poems, but also includes some which directly impinge on the plot." *Hebrew Poetry*, 59.

67. Eisner, *Boccaccio and the Invention of Italian Literature*, 11, and especially chap. 2, "Dante's Shame and Boccaccio's Paratextual Praise," 50–73.

68. Eisner, 15. Boccaccio's transcription of the *Vita nuova* appears in Chigi L V 176, which also contains Boccaccio's *Vita di Dante* (*Life of Dante*); an Italian poem by Guido Cavalcanti; a Latin poem by Boccaccio; fifteen of Dante's canzoni; and Petrarch's *Fragmentorum liber*, "an early version of the Rerum vulgarium fragmenta," i.e., Petrarch's ordered collection of his lyrics. Eisner, *Boccaccio and the Invention of Italian Literature*, 2.

69. For background on and translations of Immanuel's Italian compositions, see Alfie, "Immanuel of Rome, Alias Manoello Giudeo"; Levy, "Immanuel of Rome and Dante."

70. Shiloah, "Passage by Immanuel ha-Romi on the Science of Music."

71. Trans. in Shiloah, 14. For clarity, I substitute "impure ones" for Shiloah's "impures."

72. From the sixth maḥberet: "ma omeret ḥokhmat ha-nigun el ha-noṣerim? / gunov gunavti me-ʾeretz ha-ʿivrim." Immanuel, *Maḥberot Imanuʾel ha-Romi*, 1:120, line 341; trans. in Shiloah, 9. This is a reference to the Joseph story: Gen. 40.15.

73. Alfie, "Immanuel of Rome, Alias Manoello Giudeo," 311.

74. See Levy, "Immanuel of Rome and Dante"; Levy, "Immanuel of Rome's *Bisbidis*," 99.

75. Amor non lesse mai l'avemaria;
Amor non tenne mai legge né fede;
Amor è un cor, che non ode né vede
e non sa mai che misura si sia.

Amor è una pura signoria,
che sol si ferma in voler ciò che chiede;

Amor fa com' pianeto, che provvede,
e sempre retra sé per ogni via.

Amor non lassò mai, per paternostri
né per incanti, suo gentil orgoglio;
né per téma digiunt'è per ch' i' giostri.

Amor fa quello di che più mi doglio:
ché non s'attène a cosa ch'io li mostri,
ma sempre mi sa dir:—Pur così voglio.

Immanuel, in Marti, *Poeti giocosi del tempo di Dante*, 317. My translation first appeared in *Digital Dante*, Columbia University. Many thanks to Teodolinda Barolini for her thoughtful translation advice.

76. For the text of *I' m'ho onde dar pace e debbo e voglio*, see Vitale, *Rimatori comico-realistici del Due e Trecento*, 358.

77. Alfie, "Immanuel of Rome, Alias Manoello Giudeo," 315.

78. Amor, ch'al cor gentil ratto s'apprende,
prese costui de la bella persona
che mi fu tolta; e 'l modo ancor m'offende.

Amor, ch'a nullo amato amar perdona,
mi prese del costui piacer sì forte,
che, come vedi, ancor non m'abbandona.

Amor condusse noi ad una morte

Alighieri, *Inferno* 5, lines 100–106, trans. Mandelbaum, 45.

79. "M'apparve una maravigliosa visione: che me parea vedere ne la mia camera una nebula di colore di fuoco, dentro a la quale io discernea una figura d'uno segnore di pauroso aspetto a chi la guardasse." Alighieri, *Vita nuova*, 3.3, trans. Cervigni and Vasta, 49.

80. "Ch'Amor e'n la sala del Sir de la scala / Quivi senza ala mi parea volare" In Cipolla and Pellegrini, "Poesie minori riguardanti gli Scaligeri," 52.

81. For the opposition of pleasure and pain, see, for instance, the poem by Samuel ha-Nagid, *im te'aveh*, in Schirmann, *Ha-shira ha-'ivrit bi-Sfarad uvi-Provans*, book 1, 1:164.

82. Alfie, *Comedy and Culture*, 192.

83. "Frottola [It.]."

84. Levy, "Immanuel of Rome's *Bisbidis*." For a reading of *Bisbidis* as humorous, see Alfie, "Nonsense and Noise."

85. For discussion of onomatopoeia in *Bisbidis*, see Levy, "Immanuel of Rome's *Bisbidis*."

86. In the later Bologna 1289 manuscript, *Bisbidis* appears line by line and in couplets, according to the *-are* rhyme.

87. Levy, "Immanuel of Rome's *Bisbidis*."

88. "Il Cod. Casantense ne dia i versi di seguito e quello di Bologna in imperfette strofe: e ciò indubbiamente per imperizia degli amanuensi che ebbero forse sottocchio mss. più antichi, nei quali le poesie erano distese a mo' di prosa e prive di segni d'interpunzione o divisione di strofe ed anche, per avventura, si fidavano della memoria—essa resulta di strofe tetrastiche, a mo' di serventese, con tre versi che rimano fra loro, e l'ultimo, coll'ultimo della strofa precedente." Modona, *Vita e opere di Immnuele Romano*, 222–23.

89. For a thorough and illuminating discussion of medieval Hebrew panegyric, see Decter, *Dominion Built of Praise*, especially chap. 6, 160–75.

90. "La mia donna cara Vertu fa regnare / Ch'Amor e'n la sala del Sir de la scala / Quivi senza ala mi parea volare" In Cipolla and Pellegrini, "Poesie minori riguardanti gli

Scaligeri," 52. Fortis notes that although "la donna cara" of *Bisbidis* is likely Immanuel's wife, the reference to Amor exists "in the higher sense of the term." *Manoello Volgare*, 91. Cassuto first characterized the lady in Immanuel's Hebrew sonnets in the third maqama of the *Maḥberot Immanuel* as a lofty, divinely inspired creature, derived from the dolce stil novo. *Dante e Manoello*, 64.

91. Barolini, *Undivine Comedy*, 20. See the discussion of Immanuel's use of "truth claims" in Levy, "Immanuel of Rome's *Bisbidis*," 107. The introduction to the *Maḥbarot* begins with Immanuel's need to create a prose structure to protect his poetry from thieves, itself a vain spin on building reality into his narrative framework. Immanuel, *Maḥberot Imanu'el ha-Romi*, 1:3–7. For further comment on convincing the reader of a truthful reality, see Huss, "Status of Fiction in the Hebrew Maqama."

92. For a thorough treatment of women in medieval Hebrew, see Rosen, *Unveiling Eve*. For remarks on the voicing of poetry by women and others in maqamas, see Pagis, *Hebrew Poetry*, 56–58.

93. Gaylord, "Grammar of Femininity in the Traditional Lyric," 115. Rip Cohen dates the corpus of *cantigas d'amigo* from roughly 1220–1300. *500 Cantigas*, 30n1.

94. For mention of a woman's poetry, see al-Ḥarīrī, *Assemblies of al-Ḥarīrī*, trans. Chenery, 178.

95. Schirmann, "Les Contes rimés de Jacob ben Eléazar de Tolède," 295. To be fair, parallels between *Sefer ha-meshalim* and *Aucassin et Nicolette* might reflect the controversial origins of *Aucassin et Nicolette*, not the hybridity of *Sefer ha-meshalim*: some scholars of medieval French romances have suggested that the French prosimetrum might owe to Arabic influences its structure of prose and verse (unusual in a French romance) and the name Aucassin, possibly derived from Arabic. Bourdillon, Introduction to *Aucassin et Nicolette*, lxix–lxx.

96. Shapiro, "Provençal Trobairitz and the Limits of Courtly Love," 568; Dronke, *Medieval Latin and the Rise of European Love-Lyric*, 7.

97. Schirmann, "Les Contes rimés de Jacob ben Eléazar de Tolède," 295.

98. Scheindlin compares Nicolette's prominence in the story to that of Yemima and Yefefiya in the seventh story of *Sefer ha-meshalim*. "Sipure ha-ahava shel Yaʿaqov ben Elʿazar," 19.

99. For more on the seventh story and poetic instruction, see Levy, "Hybridity through Poetry," 135–36.

100. To describe the proper, nonphysical manner of kissing, Kima tells Sahar in verse, "This is the doctrine of gentle lovers" (*torat yedidim ha-ʿadinim*). Ben Elʿazar, "Sipure ha-ahava shel Yaʿaqov ben Elʿazar," ed. Schirmann, 257, line 262b.

101. For further discussion of the female voice in *Sefer ha-meshalim*, see Schirmann, "Les Contes rimés de Jacob ben Eléazar de Tolède"; Scheindlin, "Sipure ha-ahava shel Yaʿaqov ben Elʿazar." For comments on the correlation between women's virtue and poetic ability in the Romance context (but without any implication of their being teachers of poetry), see Jaeger, *Ennobling Love*, 77, 88.

102. Deleuze and Guattari, *Kafka*.

CONCLUSION

A Prosimetric Inheritance

In these final pages, I consider why subsequent compositions by Jewish authors from around the Mediterranean abandoned the mixed form. Rather than viewing such early modern texts as linguistically, formally, and intellectually distinct from a medieval past, I reflect on potential continuities that seemingly evoke their prosimetric predecessors.[1] To find these links and to intuit their ramifications, I look to thinkers from outside the medieval and early modern world who have contemplated the mixed form. Indeed, Virginia Woolf's recommendation in *A Room of One's Own* is a strikingly apt assessment not only of the medieval authors discussed in the last chapter who placed women in unexpected positions of poetic power but also of maternally linked performers of Judeo-Spanish ballads whose songs blended forms, languages, and cultural settings: "What one must do to bring her to life was to think poetically and prosaically at the same time."[2] In the same period of worldly turmoil, Woolf's contemporary Walter Benjamin wrote that "prose may be called the idea of poetry," a statement that helps shift our expectations away from perfectly constructed poetic jewels and toward a focus on compositions whose ideas convey something akin to the profundity of poetry.[3] Perhaps these ideas can help us acknowledge the beauty inherent in the inevitable disorder of forms, or what Agamben has termed "the essential prosimetry of every human discourse."[4]

Judeo-Spanish Balladry: Waning Prosimetra, Waxing Performativity

Following an unparalleled moment for metapoetic erotic prosimetra, poetry and prose across the Mediterranean continued to jostle for importance, even if their official positions became increasingly standardized across traditions: though poetry continued to maintain its position of intellectual and artistic preeminence, prose was simpler and faster to write and to read. The opinion of the Spanish Marqués de Santillana (1398–1458) in his 1449 *Prohemio y Carta* (Preface and letter)—a near replica of some classical

Arabic treatises—is telling: "How much greater the excellence and prerogative of rhymes and meters than that of free prose. . . . It is with great effort that I say that meter is older, of greater perfection and of more authority than free prose."[5] The marqués further supports his claim of poetry's superiority, citing biblical use of verse, highlighting the greatness of the classical Greek and Latin poets, and referring to kings who have honored poets (such as Petrarch and Boccaccio) for their excellent compositions.[6] Naturally, he composed this statement in prose.

Still, prose was not always the most expedient or burgeoning mode of composition for Jewish authors writing about love, especially at a time when Jewish speakers of Romance engaged not only in spoken communication but also in the composition and recitation of oral poetry.[7] In the shift toward Romance for literary purposes, narrative prose in the Judeo-Spanish world seems to fall by the wayside, even if proverbs (*refranes*, like those for which *Don Quixote*'s Sancho Panza is famous) proliferated, though these phrases might be more aptly characterized as poetic epigrams. Many Judeo-Spanish oral compositions draw on the Galician-Portuguese troubadour lyrics and historically focused Castilian epic balladry—and potentially also on the multilingual and multiregister *muwashshaḥ*—but they do not, like Immanuel's Italian lyrics, seem to communicate self-consciously with the other. They are poems in Romance vernacular, over time imbued with Hebraisms and Judaisms (and, due to forced migration, with elements of other languages and cultures), marking a more enduring shift in secular Jewish Iberian composition toward Romance vernacular thematics and form.[8] But what Sephardic balladry lacks in prosimetric variation—to be expected, given the preference for verse in early vernacular Romance composition—it possesses in its mingling of oral performativity of the popular lyric with Jewish literary themes.[9] Performance adds a degree of variation to a poem that stand-alone written texts do not possess; the voice of the performer lends the song a degree of contrast that is in a way analogous to the mixed form of the texts addressed in this book.

This blend of orality, popular lyric, and Jewish topics simultaneously embraces newness and loss—loss of complex metrical forms and meters, and loss, in part, of the Hebrew language, though not necessarily of biblical content, nor of the Andalusi cultural sphere. What is left in place is an enduring—yet ever shifting, depending on the performer—oral repertoire of culturally sustaining lyrics. The persisting ballad "La bella en misa" ("The Beauty in Church"), which in a 1957 recording maintains its complex blend of biblical, Christian, and courtly love elements in the Salonikan rendering of Judeo-Spanish, attests to this phenomenon:

> Three ladies are going to mass
> to say their prayers.
> With them goes my bride,
> the one I love most of all.
> She wears many pleated skirts
> and a waistcoat of fine cloth.
> Her head is round like a grapefruit;
> her hair is golden thread
> and when she combs it,
> it glistens in the sun.
> Her red cheeks
> are apples from Skopje;
> her small teeth
> are all like ivory.
> In her tiny mouth
> a rosebud would not fit;
> her arched eyebrows
> are like taut bows.
> The priest, reading his prayers,
> stopped in his reading.
> "Read on, little priest;
> I've not come here for you.
> I have come for the king's son,
> for I am dying of love."[10]

After reading (and listening to, if possible) this lyric poem, replete with precise images and metaphors and bound in a neat narrative, one finds it hard to imagine that such so-called popular lyric has been relegated to a position of inferiority with respect to the relatively more formally complex so-called cultured lyric. Though the poem lacks a metapoetic gaze and philosophical undertones, its descriptions of the lady's beauty recall many of the motifs that cultured lyrics across the literary traditions of the medieval Mediterranean possess, from the comparison of the lady's cheeks to apples (stemming from Biblical Hebrew and ancient Greek) to the likening of her arched eyebrows to bows (a common image in classical Arabic). The teeth like ivory recall the classical Arabic and medieval Hebrew comparison of the lady's teeth to pearls, traditions in which the stringing of pearls corresponds to the word *naẓm*, meaning verse, and they likewise recall the necklace and teeth of Song of Songs.[11] The female voice adds additional complexities, recalling both the appropriated female voice of the *cantigas d'amigo* and the embedded historical voice of the Jewess of Toledo, that mythical temptress who allegedly seduced King Alfonso VIII of Castile. Perhaps this poem is not, after all, as far from the metapoetic as it seems, its images tracing a continuum of lyric self-consciousness and alienation. It captures an ethos in verse, just as did the prosimetra in Christian Spain and the martyrological verse in Ashkenaz; indeed, Einbinder's statement also holds true for this tradition: "in Jewish communities under increasing pressure, poetry thus offered a medium for interpreting persecution while striving to shape the behavior of the persecuted under stress."[12]

The disconnect between prose and poetry indicates a new compositional landscape, one that departed from the Hebrew golden age and its decadent period and migrated toward anonymous oral compositions that aptly characterize the impermanence yet universality of love, life, and literature for Jews living amid moments of religious persecution, unrest, and forced migration. Indeed, these poems are not explicitly fictional as are the maqamas but rather are mimetic approaches to lyrics, made even more realistic by the presence of a performer. They move beyond the golden age of Hebrew letters, in which languages were compartmentalized for various purposes, as Drory delineated: "Hebrew served primarily the literary-aesthetic function" while Arabic served the "communicative" function.[13] The Hebrew maqama (and arguably Immanuel's *Bisbidis*) shifts between poetry and prose in one language to achieve this same spread, stretching the capabilities of that language from the aesthetic to the communicative. In the case of Judeo-Spanish balladry, the aesthetic and communicative have coalesced in Romance, leaving Hebrew (for those capable) as the language of prayer, and the unabashedly secular Romance as the language of love and everything else. The robust flourishing of mixed-form compositions by Jewish authors who were trying to define love via poetic inquiry bound up in something particularly Jewish was, it seems, more of an anomaly than a convention. Soon to be supplanted by the novel (which intersperses verse citations from time to time and whose expression becomes inevitably intertwined with the Iberian anxiety of pure blood that proliferated across the Mediterranean) on the one hand and overwrought sonnets on the other, the mixed form no longer reflected the literary mindset of a Jewish expression of secular eros. Somewhere in a parallel plane to these two formal categories of fiction, the indefinite sphere of performative balladry simplified the form and intensified the need for a lyric of longing.

Otherness and Togetherness in Early Modern Italy

This worked out differently in Italy, where compositions by Jewish authors addressing topics related to love fanned out into varying genres, forms, and registers as an influx of Jews fled the Iberian Peninsula. Only a couple of generations after Immanuel, we encounter Moses da Rieti's (1388–1460) response to Dante's *Divine Comedy*, known as *Miqdash meʿat* (The little temple) and composed in Hebrew *terza rima*.[14] This text offers a different kind of complication than we see in the Judeo-Spanish ballad: a formally intricate lyric text engaging complex philosophical and literary concepts. At the same time, it is a poetic composition communicating in a language different from the one to which it is responding, a discordance that—as in the case of the *Maḥberot Immanuel*—calls into question its readership and purpose. Yet despite its complex structure, the *Miqdash meʿat*, like the nascent tradition of Ladino ballads, fulfills a kind of longing, using a form new to Hebrew to make meaning for readers anxious to continue testing the generic and formal limits of their languages.

Deeper into fifteenth-century Italy, Judah Abravanel (c. 1465–after 1521; known in Italian as Leone Ebreo), who was forced to escape Lisbon for Naples, sought to frame love in philosophical terms in his vernacular Italian prose treatise, the *Dialoghi d'amore* (*Dialogues of Love*).[15] In a completely different way, this text's makeup is as novel as is Moses da Rieti's *terza rima* in Hebrew: as one of the earliest Romance vernacular prose treatises to treat love via philosophical inquiry, it would have been an anomaly even without the Jewish identity of its author on display. Despite decades of sparring among scholars who hoped to prove the Hebrew or Judeo-Spanish provenance of the treatise, its Italian is what made waves: the language used in a new way, in a new form—and, indeed, by an outsider.

Romance allowed for Jews and Christians alike to dissolve the distinctions between functional categories of particular languages—even though the language in which an author composed still conveyed the utmost significance, and even if the text existed apart from the language(s) of prayer. This is also the case for *La lozana andaluza* (The lusty Andalusian woman; 1528), whose vernacular prose could not be further in tone and purpose from Abravanel's *Dialoghi*, though it was likewise a text intended for a wide audience spanning religions and languages. Composed in Castilian by Francisco Delicado (c. 1480–c. 1535), a converso residing in Venice, *La lozana andaluza* is one of a handful of picaresque texts that harnesses the maqama's episodic impetus toward the novelesque but without its impassioned obsession with literary dexterity. It provides a snapshot of the multiplicities inherent in such a literary environment: in his focus on love and companionship amid the marvels of quotidian survival, Delicado enlists prose to maneuver among languages and identities of Rome, searching for significance by stretching the social parameters of language.

These texts—some undoubtedly more difficult than others to pin down formally and generically—embody the kind of enjambment that Agamben detects in the amorphous region between poetry and prose:

> Enjambment thus brings to light the original stride, neither poetic nor prosaic, but, in a manner of speaking, the bustrophedon of poetry, the essential prosimetry of every human discourse, which in a precocious attestation in the Gathas of Avesta or in Latin satire confirms the non-episodic character of the *Vita nuova*'s proposition at the threshold of modernity. This turning, which, despite remaining nameless in the metrical treatises, constitutes the kernel of verse (displayed as enjambment) and is an ambiguous gesture, which turns at once in two opposite directions, backward (verse) and forward (prose). This slope, this sublime hesitation between sense and sound, is poetic legacy, through which thought must come. To garner this legacy, Plato, rejecting standard forms of writing, fixed his gaze on the idea of language, which, according to the testimony of Aristotle, was not, for him, either poetry or prose, but their midpoint.[16]

For these Jewish authors (or, in some cases, no longer Jewish—itself a highly questionable and potentially bigoted category) in the Mediterranean in the generations following the Hebrew maqama authors, all writing on love was a kind of enjambment, a re-forming of forms to suit the topic and the language with some creative combination of dignity, honesty, and whimsy. It is in this period of disorder that Jewish authors were able to imagine love as capable of surviving and existing as the essential point of translation amid forms.

Notes

1. I draw on Miron's notion of Jewish literary continuity here to frame my consideration of shifting trends in literary form: "Perhaps the new one, while being truly and totally divorced from some of the older literatures, was not as dramatically different from others. . . . Perhaps the new literature formed more new links or chapters within the chain or narrative, which connected it with much or some of what had preceded it." Miron, *From Continuity to Contiguity*, 6.
2. Woolf, *A Room of One's Own*, 33.
3. Benjamin, *Selected Writings*, vol. 1, 174.

4. "L'esenziale prosimetricità di ogni discorso umano." Agamben, *Idea della prosa*, 20.

5. "Quánta más sea la exçelencia e prerrogatiua de los rimos e metros que de la soluta prosa. . . . Me esfuerço a dezir el metro ser antes en tienpo e de mayor perfecçión e más auctoridad que la soluta prosa." Santillana, *Prohemio e carta*, 53.

6. Santillana, 53–55. For further comment on the historical notion of the relatively older status of poetry with respect to prose, a notion spread by Isidore of Seville, see Weiss, *Poet's Art*, 76, 204–5.

7. The same period experienced a shift toward vernacular Romance for liturgy: the earliest Judeo-Spanish Bibles date to the thirteenth through fifteenth centuries and were written in Romance script. These were likely used for less educated Jewish men and for women. Judeo-Spanish Bibles of the Sephardi Diaspora were written in Hebrew script. See Cassuto, "Bible: Ladino (Judeo-Spanish)."

8. For further reading on balladry, see Armistead, Silverman, and Katz, *Judeo-Spanish Ballads from Oral Tradition*; for Judeo-Spanish linguistics, see Bunis, "Judezmo (Ladino/Judeo-Spanish)"; for a historical perspective, see Ray, *After Expulsion*.

9. This is perhaps not the right moment to redeem the study of Judeo-Spanish ballads as far more compositionally relevant than as a politically motivated means through which to glimpse the linguistic character of medieval Castilian (which has in part motivated the preservation and study of Judeo-Spanish). Still, the sheer volume of Judeo-Spanish lyrics recorded beginning in the 1950s (a tremendously fruitful and important project spearheaded by Armistead, Silverman, and Katz in the style of Albert Lord, of the *Singer of Tales*) attests to the persistence of this poetry for Spanish Jewry living in the Sephardi Diaspora following persecution, forced migration, and the trauma of the Inquisition.

10. Tres damas van a la misa
por hazer la orasión.
Entre'n medio va mi spoza,
la que más quería yo.
Sayo yeva sovre sayo;
un xiboy de altornasión.
Su cavesa, una torongǎ
sus caveyos briles son.
Cuando los tomó a peinare,
en eyos despuntó el sol.
Las sus caras coreladas
mansanas d'Escopia son.
Los dientes tan chiquiticos
dientes de marfil ya son.
Su boquita tan chequetica
y que no le cave'n peñón.
La su seja enarkada
árcol de tirar ya son.
Melda, melda, papazico,
de meldar ya se quedó.
—Melda, melda, papazico,
y que por ti no vengo yo.
Vine por el hijo del reyes,
que de amor v'a muerir yo.

Translation and transcription, Armistead, Silverman, and Katz, *Folk Literature of the Sephardic Jews*. Many thanks to Bruce Rosenstock and the library of the University of Illinois at

Urbana-Champaign, which hosts the Multimedia Archive of Ballads and Other Oral literature in Judeo-Spanish (https://sephardifolklit.illinois.edu) for permission to include this ballad. The informant, Esther Varsano Hassid, was recorded by Armistead and Silverman in 1957.

11. Song of Songs 1.10, 4.2, and 6.6. See chap. 1, note 74, for further discussion.

12. Einbinder, *Beautiful Death*, 21.

13. Drory, "'Words Beautifully Put,'" 54, 58.

14. Guetta, "Moses da Rieti and His *Miqdash meʿat*," 4; Bregman, "Note on the Style and Prosody of *Miqdash meat*."

15. Hughes, *Hebrew Bible in Fifteenth-Century Spain*, 252. Hughes contrasts Abravanel to fifteenth-century scholar Judah Messer Leon, who "sought to translate the Bible, and thus Judaism, using the intellectual categories of the fifteenth century" in his Hebrew-language *Nofet Ṣufim* (*The Honeycomb's Flow*). Hughes, 254.

16.

> L'*enjambement* porta così alla luce l'originaria andatura, né poetica né prosastica, ma, per così dire, bustrofedica della poesia, l'esenziale prosimetricità di ogni discorso umano, la cui precoce attestazione nelle *Gatha* dell'Avesta o nella *satura* latina certifica il carattere non episodico della proposta della *Vita nuova* alle soglie dell'età moderna. La versura, che, pur restando innominata nei trattati di metrica, costituisce il nocciolo del verso (e la cui esposizione è l'*enjambement*), è un gesto ambiguo, che si volge a un tempo in due direzioni opposte, all'indietro (verso) e in avanti (prosa). Questa pendenza, questa sublime esitazione fra il senso e il suono è l'eredità poetica, di cui il pensiero deve venire a capo. Per raccoglierne il lascito, Platone, rifiutando le forme tràdite della scrittura, tenne fisso lo sguardo su quell'idea del linguaggio che, secondo la testimonianza di Aristotele, non era, per lui, né poesia né prosa, ma il loro medio.

Agamben, *Idea della prosa*, 20–21.

APPENDIX A: IMMANUEL'S *BISBIDIS*[1]

Bisbidis di Manoello Giudeo	Bisbidis by Immanuel the Jew
a Mignificentia di Messer Cane de la Scala[1]	to his Magnificence Cangrande della Scala
Del mondo ho cercato Per lungo et per lato	I've searched the world long and wide
Con un caro mercato Per terra et per mare	by land and by sea with little reward.
Vedut'ho Soria Infin Herminia,	I saw Syria all the way to Armenia
et di Romania gran parte mi pare,	and Romania, a large part of it, it seems to me.
Vedut'ho 'l soldano Per monte et per piano	I saw the Sultanate, from the mountains to the valleys,
Et si del gran Cano Poria novellare,	and I can tell you about the Great Khan:
Di quel c'haggio inteso Veduto et compreso	of all I heard and saw and understood,
Mi sono hora acceso À volerlo contare,	now I am inflamed to want to recount:
Che pur la corona ne porta Verona	the only place that holds the crown is Verona,
Per quel che si suona Del dire et del fare,	renowned for its words and deeds:
Destrier' et corsiere Masnate et Bandiere	You'll see knights in armor and cavaliers
Coracce et lamiere Vedrai rimutare	Switching their steeds and flags, coats of arms and weaponry.
sentirai poi li giach che fan quei pedach,	You'll hear the giach of their armored feet:
giach giach giach [giach giach] Quando gli odi andare,	pedach giach giach giach [giach giach] as you hear them go by.
Ma pur li tormenti Mi fan li strumenti,	And their instruments become weapons,
Che mille ne senti in un punto sonare,	thousands of weapons, sounding off at once:
Duduf Duduf, Duduf Duduf	Duduf duduf, Duduf duduf,
Duduf Duduf, Bandiere sventare,	Duduf, duduf, the flapping of flags.
Qui vengon le feste con le bionde teste	Here we have parties, with all the blond ladies,
Qui son le tempeste D'amore et d'amare	here come the storms of love and of loving:
Le donne muz muz, Le donzelle usu usu	The matrons go muz muz, the maidens usu usu
Le vedove sciuvi vu, Che ti possa annegare.	and the widows sciuvi vu—their chatter drowns out everything else!

Trovan fantesche Tutt'hora piu fresche	Here you find maidens, ever fresh,
À menar le tresche Trottare ed ambiare,	Feverishly skipping, trotting and walking along.
L'una fa cosi, et l'altra pur si,	One says, "Like this?" and the other, "Like that"
et l'altra sta qui Ch'io vo per tornare.	and the other "Stay here, since I'm coming back."
In quell'acqua chiara che'l bel fiume schiara,	In that clear water, which makes the beautiful river shine,
La mia donna cara Vertu fa regnare	my dear lady causes virtue to reign.
Ch'Amor e'n la sala del Sir de la scala	For Love is in the hall of Cangrande della Scala:
Quivi senza ala mi parea volare	here without wings, seemingly I fly;
Ch'io non mi credea Di quel ch'i vedea	I could barely believe what I was seeing, but indeed
Ma pur mi parea in un gran mare stare.	it seemed to me to be in a great sea.
Baroni et marchesi De tutti i paesi,	Barons and marquises from every land,
Gentili et cortesi Qui vedi arrivare.	noble and courtly: see them arrive here.
Quivi Astrologia con Philosofia	Here astrology mingles with philosophy
Et di Theologia Udrai disputare.	and theology—you'll hear it debated;
Quivi Tedeschi Latini et Franceschi,	Here Germans, Italians and French,
Fiamenghi e ingheleschi Insieme parlare,	Flemish and English, speaking together:
Fanno un trombombe che par ché rimbombe	They make echoes that reverberate
À guisa di trobe chi pian vol sonare	like a drum that slowly builds momentum.
Chitarre et Liuti, Viole et flauti	Guitars and lutes, violas and flutes:
Voci alte agute Qui s'odon cantare.	loud, shrill voices—here you hear them sing.
Stu tutu ifiu ifiu ifiu Stututu ifiu ifiu ifiu	Stututu ifiu ifiu ifiu Stututu ifiu ifiu ifiu
Stututu ifiu ifiu ifiu Tamburar zuffolare	Stututu ifiu ifiu ifiu drumming, whistling.
Qui bon cantori Con intonatori	And here good singers and minstrels,
Et qui trovatori udrai concordare.	and here troubadours: hear how they complement each other.
Quivi si ritrova mangiatori a prova	Here you'll find eaters contesting: it's a rare treat
che par cosa nova À vederli golare.	to watch them indulge:
Intarlatim Intarlatim	Intarlatim intarlatim
Intarlatim Ghiribare et Danzare.	intarlatim, Playing and dancing.
Li falconi cui cui Li Bracchetti gu gu,	The falcons with their cui cui, the mastiffs go gu gu;

Li Levrieri guuu uu Per volersi sfugare.	the greyhounds guuu uu—to make an escape.
Qui Falconieri Maestri et Scudieri,	And the falconers, masters and squires,
Ragazzi et Corrieri Ciascun per se andare,	boys and messengers, each one goes his own way.
Et quanto et quanto Et quanto	How much and how many, and how much and how many
et quanto Li vedi spazzare,	And how much and how many: you see them rush by:
l'uno va su, et l'altro ven giu,	one goes up and the other comes down;
Tal Donna ven giu che non lassa passare	that lady comes down—she won't let you pass:
Bis bis bis Bisbidis Bisbidis	Bis bis bis bisbidis bisbidis
Bis bisbidis Udrai consigliare.	bis bisbidis, you'll hear her advise.
Qui babbuini Romei et Pellegrini,	Here fools, pilgrims to Rome and elsewhere,
Giudei et Sarracini Vedrai capitare,	Jews and Muslims, see how they all arrive.
Tatim Tatim, Tatim Tatim,	Tatim tatim, tatim tatim,
Tatim Tatim senti trombettare,	tatim tatim, hear the drumming!
Baluf Balauf, Balauf balauf,	Baluf balauf, balauf balauf,
Balauf balauf. Udrai tringuigliare,	balauf balauf, you hear it trill.
Di giu li cavalli Di su i Pappagalli	Below are the horses, above the parrots,
In su la sala i balli Insieme operare,	in the room they dance, moving together.
Dududu Dududu, Dududu Dududu,	Dududu dududu, dududu dududu
Dududu dududu Sentirai naccherare.	dududu dududu, reverberating around you.
Ma quel che piu vale, E al Sir non ne cale,	But the most costly things—to Cangrande they're nothing:
Veder per le scale Taglier trasfugare,	see across the stairs how they steal the precious plates
Con quel Portinaro che sta tanto chiaro	with that doorkeeper, who is so sure of his position,
che quel tien piu caro che me ne'sa fare.	what he holds most dear, he knows best what to do.
Qui de ragazzi vedut'ho solazzi,	Here the young men: I have seen such entertainment,
che mai cotai pazzi non vidi muffare.	you won't see such crazy youths growing mold anytime soon.
Qui non son minazze Ma pugna et mostazze	Here they're not shy, throwing punches and slaps,
Et visi con strazze Et occhi ambugliare.	some with black eyes, some bruises.

Gegegi Gegegi Gegegi Gegegi	Gegegi gegegi gegegi gegegi
Gegegi gegegi Li uccelli sbernare	gegegi gegegi the birds twitter in springtime.
Istruzzi e buovi Selvaggi ritrovi	Cranes and cows, wild animals you will find,
Et animali novi Quant'huó po contare.	and strange exotic beasts—more than one can count.
Qui son Leoni Et gatti mamoni	Here are lions, and monster cats
Et grossi montoni Vedut'ho cozzare	and enormous rams: I saw them butting heads.
Bobobo Bobobo Bottombo Bobobo	Bobobo bobobo bottombo bobobo
Bobobottombo, Bobobottombo Le trombe trombare.	bobobottombo, bobobottombo, the trumpets sound.
Quivi è un vecchiume Che non vede lume,	Here's a large band of the old, the half-blind:
che largo costume Gli fa governare,	the generosity [of Cangrande] keeps them going.
Qui ven poverame con si fatte brame	Here comes the band of the indigent, so full of hunger,
Che'l brodo col rame si vol tranguggiare,	they would gulp down the copper bowl with the broth.
Quivi è una schiera Di Bordon di cera	Here is such an assembly of wax candlesticks
che l'aere la sera si crede abbruciare,	that they seem to burn the evening air.
Tatam Tatam, Tatam Tatam,	Tatam tatam, tatam tatam,
Tatam tatam e Liuti tubare.	tatam tatam, lutes twitter along.
Qui son gran giochi De molti et di pochi	Here are great games, some for many, some for few,
Con brandon di fochi Vedut'ho giostrare	with huge firebrands I've seen them joust.
Qui vengon villani con si fatte mani	Here come the lowly peasants whose hands are such
che paiono Alani Di Ispagna abbaiare.	that they seem to be huge guard-dogs, barking from Spain.
Quivi son le simie Con molte Alchimie	Here are the monkeys with their humanlike smirks
A grattarsi le Timie et voler digrignare	beating each other up, gnashing their teeth.
Et di un risi che ce che ce che ce	And a laugh. What is it? What happened? What is it?
heee heee heee heee ognihuó vuol crepare,	heee heee heee heee each man howls with laughter.
Qui son'altri stati si ben divisati	Here, too, are others so elegantly turned out

Che tra li beati Sen puo ragionare,	their beauty is a topic for the blessed in paradise.
Et questo è'l signore Di tanto valore Che'l	And here is the lord of such great valor that
suo grande honore Va per terra et mare.	his great honor spreads by land and by sea.

1. My translation first appeared in *Digital Dante*, Columbia University. Many thanks to Teodolinda Barolini for her translation suggestions. My transcription is based on Casanatense 433 132r–133v. Though I believe that the Casantense beautifully captures the unclassifiable, prose-like nature of the poem, I have made line breaks according to the *-are* rhyme, akin to the stichometry in Bologna 1289, to facilitate ease of reading and comparing with the English translation. For editions, all of which have modernized the orthography in various ways, see Cipolla and Pellegrini, "Poesie minori riguardanti gli Scaligeri," 51–55; Marti, *Poeti giocosi del tempo di Dante*, 322–27; and Vitale, *Rimatori comico-realistici del Due e Trecento*, 551–60.

APPENDIX B: TIMELINE

Greek	Hebrew	Arabic	Latin	Romance	Ashkenazi / Northern French Hebrew
Homer c. BCE	Hebrew Bible beginning c. 1000 BCE				
Sappho c. 620–570 BCE					
Gorgias 483–375 BCE					
Plato 428/427 or 424/ 423–348/347 BCE					
Aristotle 384–322 BCE					
			Cicero 106–43 BCE		
			Rhetorica ad Herennium c. 86–82 BCE		
			Horace, 65–8 BCE		
			Ovid 43 BCE–17/18 CE		
Galen 129–c. 202/c. 216 CE					

	Early Paytanim c. 300–600 CE	Muḥammad 570–632 CE			
		Rābiʿa al-ʿAdawīya al-Qaysīya 714/18–801			
		Abū Nuwās 747–62 to 813–15			
		al-Jāḥiẓ c. 776–868/69			
		Ibn Qutayba 828–89			
		Ibn Dāwūd al-Ẓāhirī d. 909–10			
		al-Washshāʾ ca. 869–937			
		al-Mubarrad 826–899/900			
		Ibn al-Muʿtazz 861–908			
		al-Hamadhānī 968–1008			
		al-ʿAskarī d. c. 1010			
		al-Marzūqī d. 1030			
	Samuel ha-Nagid 993–1055/56	al-Ṣābī 969–1056			
	Solomon ibn Gabirol c. 1021–c. 1057	Ibn Ḥazm 994–1064			

Greek	Hebrew	Arabic	Latin	Romance	Ashkenazi / Northern French Hebrew
	Baḥya ibn Paquda second half 11th century	Ibn Rashīq 1000–1063/64 /1070/71			
		al-Jurjānī d. 1078			
	Moses ibn Ezra c. 1055–after 1135	al-Ḥarīrī of Baṣra 1054–1122		William IX "The Troubadour," Duke of Aquitaine, 1071–1127	
	Judah Halevi 1057–1141	al-Saraqustī d. 1143			
	Solomon ibn Ṣaqbel 12th century		Andreas Capellanus 12th century	Chrétien de Troyes c. 1135–c. 1185	Judah ben Samuel he-Ḥasid c. 1150–1217
	Judah ibn Tibbon c. 1120–90		Matthew of Vendôme's *Ars versificatoria* c. 1170	Bernart de Ventadorn 1135–94	
	Moses Maimonides 1135–1204			Ramon Vidal de Besalú's *Razos de trobar* c. 1210	
	Samuel ibn Tibbon 1150–1230		John of Garland's *De arte prosayca, metrica, et rithmica* after 1229	Giraut de Bornelh c. 1138–1215	
	Judah al-Ḥarizi 1165–1225			Castelloza early 13th century	
	Jacob ben Elʿazar 12th–13th centuries			King Alfonso X "The Wise" 1221–84	

	Jacob Anatoli 13th century			*Aucassin et Nicolette* 13th century	
	Ibn Falaquera 1223/28–after 1290			*Li romanz de la poire* 13th century	*Sefer ha-ma'asim* late 13th century
				Pae Gomez Charinho 1225–95	
				Guido Guinizelli 1235–76	
				Guido Cavalcanti c. 1258–1300	
	Immanuel of Rome 1261–c. 1335			Dante Alighieri 1265–1321	
	Qalonymos ben Qalonymos 1286–after 1328			Cangrande della Scala 1291–1329	
	Yeda'ya ha-Penini 1280s–1340			Cecco Angiolieri c. 1260–c. 1312	
				Boccaccio 1313–75	
				Petrarch 1304–74	
	Moses da Rieti 1388–1460			Marqués de Santillana 1398–1458	
	Judah Abravanel c. 1465–after 1521			Ariosto 1474–1533	
				Francisco Delicado c. 1480–c. 1535	
				Cervantes 1547–1616	

BIBLIOGRAPHY

ʿAbbās, Iḥsān. *Taʾrīkh al-naqd al-adabī ʿinda al-ʿArab: Naqd al-shiʿr min al-qarnal-thānī ḥattā al-qarn al-thāmin al-hijrī.* Amman: Dār al-Shurūq, 1993.

ʿAbbās ibn al-Aḥnaf, al-. *Dīwān al-ʿAbbās ibn al-Aḥnaf.* Beirut: Dār Ṣādir lil-ṭibāʿah wa-l-Nashr, 1965.

ʿAbd al-Karīm al-Nashalī. *Ikhtiyār min kitāb al-mumtiʿ fī ʿilm al-shiʿr wa-ʿamalih.* Edited by Munjī al-Kaʿbī. Tunis: al-Dār al-ʿArabīyah lil-Kitāb, 1978.

Abu Deeb, Kamal. *Al-Jurjānī's Theory of Poetic Imagery.* Warminster: Aris and Phillips, 1979.

———. "Literary Criticism." In *Cambridge History of Arabic Literature: ʿAbbasid Belles-Lettres*, edited by Julia Ashtiany, T. M. Johnstone, J. D. Latham, R. B. Serjeant, and G. Rex Smith, 339–87. Cambridge: Cambridge University Press, 1990.

Agamben, Giorgio. *Idea della prosa.* Macerata: Quodlibet, 2002.

Akbari, Suzanne Conklin, and Karla Mallette, eds. *A Sea of Languages: Rethinking the Arabic Role in Medieval Literary History.* Toronto: University of Toronto Press, 2013.

Alba Cecilia, Amparo. "El Debate del cálamo y la espada, de Jacob ben Eleazar de Toledo." *Sefarad* 68, no. 2 (2008): 291–314.

Alfie, Fabian. *Comedy and Culture: Cecco Angiolieri's Poetry and Late Medieval Society.* Leeds: Northern Universities Press, 2001.

———. "Immanuel of Rome, Alias Manoello Giudeo: The Poetics of Jewish Identity in Fourteenth-Century Italy." *Italica* 75 (1998): 307–29.

———. "Nonsense and Noise: The Audial Poetics of Immanuel Romano's *Bisbidis.* An Introduction, and the Text with a Facing Translation." *International Studies in Humour* 5, no. 1 (2016): 127–39.

Alighieri, Dante. *Convivio.* Edited by Piero Cudini. Milan: Garzanti, 1980.

———. *De Vulgari Eloquentia.* Edited and translated by Steven Botterill. Cambridge: Cambridge University Press, 1996.

———. *The Divine Comedy of Dante Alighieri: Inferno: A Verse Translation.* Translated by Allen Mandelbaum. New York: Bantam Books, 2004.

———. *La Commedia secondo l'antica vulgata.* Edited by Giorgio Petrocchi. Milan: Mondadori, 1966–67.

———. *Rime giovanili e della "Vita nuova."* Edited by Teodolinda Barolini, with notes by Manuele Gragnolati. Milan: BUR Rizzoli, 2009.

———. *Vita nuova.* Edited by Domenico de Robertis. Milan: R. Ricciardi, 1980.

———. *Vita nuova.* Translated by Dino S. Cervigni and Edward Vasta. Notre Dame, IN: University of Notre Dame Press, 1995.

Arazi, Albert. "Une Épître d'Ibrāhīm b.Hilāl al-Ṣabī sur les genres littéraires." In *Studies in Islamic History and Civilization in Honor of Professor David Ayalon*, edited by M. Sharon, 473–505. Jerusalem: Cana, 1986.

Arendt, Hannah. "Introduction: Walter Benjamin: 1892–1940." In *Illuminations*, edited by Hannah Arendt, translated by Harry Zohn, 1–55. New York: Schocken Books, 1969.

Aristotle. *The Art of Rhetoric.* Translated by Robin Waterfield. Oxford: Oxford University Press, 2018.

———. *On Poetics*. Translated by Seth Benardete and Michael Davis. South Bend, IN: St. Augustine's, 2002.

Arkoun, M. "ʿIshḳ." In *Encyclopaedia of Islam*, 2nd ed. Leiden: Brill Academic. First published online 2012.

Armistead, Samuel G., Joseph H. Silverman, and Israel Katz. *Folk Literature of the Sephardic Jews: A Multimedia Archive of Ballads and Other Oral Literature in Judeo-Spanish*. Library of the University of Illinois at Urbana-Champaign. http://sephardifolklit.illinois.edu.

———. *Judeo-Spanish Ballads from Oral Tradition*. Vol. 6 of *Folk Literature of the Sephardic Jews*. Berkeley: University of California Press; Newark, DE: J. de la Cuesta, 1986.

Arnaldez, R. "Ibn Ḥazm, Abū Muḥammad ʿAlī b. Aḥmad b. Saʿīd." In *Encyclopaedia of Islam*, 2nd ed. Leiden: Brill Academic. First published online 2012.

Ascoli, Albert Russell. *Dante and the Making of a Modern Author*. Cambridge: Cambridge University Press, 2008.

Asín Palacios, Miguel. *Abenházam de Córdoba y su historia crítica de las ideas religiosas*. Madrid: Tip. de la "Revista de archivos," 1927–32.

ʿAskari, Abū Hilāl al-Ḥasan ibn ʿAbd Allāh al-. *Kitāb al-ṣināʿatayn, al-kitāba waʾl-shiʿr*. Edited by ʿAlī Muḥammad al-Bajāwī and Muḥammad Abū al-Faḍl Ibrāhīm. Cairo: ʿIsā al-Bābī al-Ḥalabī, 1971.

Ateş. "Ibn al-ʿArabī." In *Encyclopaedia of Islam*, 2nd ed. Leiden: Brill Academic. First published online 2012.

Aucassin and Nicolette. Translated by Eugene Mason. New York: E. P. Dutton, 1910.

Aucassin et Nicolette. Edited by Mario Roques. Paris: Champion, 1977.

Aucassin et Nicolette: An Old-French Love Story. Edited and translated by Francis William Bourdillon. New York: Macmillan, 1897.

Auerbach, Erich. *Literary Language and Its Public in Late Latin Antiquity and in the Middle Ages*. Translated by Ralph Manheim. New York: Pantheon Books, 1965.

———. *Mimesis: The Representation of Reality in Western Literature*. Translated by Willard R. Trask. Princeton, NJ: Princeton University Press, 2003.

Badawī, M. M. *A Critical Introduction to Modern Arabic Poetry*. Cambridge: Cambridge University Press, 1975.

———. "From Primary to Secondary Qaṣīdas: Thoughts on the Development of Classical Arabic Poetry." *Journal of Arabic Literature* 11 (1980): 1–31.

Barolini, Teodolinda. *Dante and the Origins of Italian Literary Culture*. New York: Fordham University Press, 2007.

———. *Dante's Poets: Textuality and Truth in the Comedy*. Princeton, NJ: Princeton University Press, 1984.

———. *The Undivine Comedy: Detheologizing Dante*. Princeton, NJ: Princeton University Press, 1992.

Bedersi, Yedaʿya ben Abraham (ha-Penini). *Sefer ha-pardes*. In *Naḥal qedumim*, edited by Leopold Dukes. Hanover: be-vet ha-adon Telgener, 1853.

Ben Elʿazar, Jacob. *Kitāb al-kāmil*. Edited by Neḥemiah Allony. Jerusalem: Central Press, 1977.

———. *Sipure ahava shel Yaʿakov ben Elʿazar*. Edited by Yonah David. Tel Aviv: Hoṣaʾat Ramot-Universitat Tel-Aviv, 1992.

———. "Sipure ha-ahava shel Yaʿaqov ben Elʿazar." Edited by Jefim Schirmann. In *Studies of the Research Institute for Hebrew Poetry in Jerusalem*, edited by Heinrich Brody, 5:211–66. Berlin: Schocken, 1939.

Ben Elʿazar, Jacob, and R. Jacob. *Deux versions hébraïques du livre de Kalīlah et Dimnāh: la première accompagnée d'une traduction française / pub. d'après les manuscrits de Paris et d'Oxford.* Edited by Joseph Derenbourg. Paris: F. Vieweg, 1881.

Benjamin, Walter. "The Concept of Criticism in German Romanticism." In *Selected Writings: Walter Benjamin*, vol. 1, 1913–1926, edited by Marcus Bullock and Michael W. Jennings, 116–200. Cambridge, MA: Belknap Press of Harvard University Press, 1996.

Ben Solomon, Immanuel. *Maḥberot Imanu'el ha-Romi.* Edited by Dov Yarden. Jerusalem: Bialik Institute, 1957.

Ben Yehuda, Eliezer. *Milon ha-lashon ha-ʿivrit ha-yeshana veha-ḥadasha.* Berlin: Berlin-Schönberg, Langenscheidt, 1908–59.

Bertoni, Giulio. *La prosa della "Vita nuova" di Dante.* Genoa: A. F. Formiggini, 1914.

Bibring, Tovi. "Fairies, Lovers, and Glass Palaces: French Influences on the Thirteenth-Century Hebrew Poetry in Spain—the Case of Yaʿakov ben Elʿazar's Ninth Maḥberet." *Jewish Quarterly Review* 107, no. 3 (2017): 297–322.

Biesterfeldt, Hans Hinrich, and Dimitri Gutas. "The Malady of Love." *Journal of the American Oriental Society* 104, no. 1 (1984): 21–55.

Bing, P. "Between Literature and the Monuments." In *Genre in Hellenistic Poetry, Hellenistica Groningana III*, edited by M. A. Harder, R. F. Regtuit, and G. C. Wakker, 21–43. Groningen: E. Forsten, 1998.

Blachère, R. "al-ʿAbbās b. al-Aḥnaf." In *Encyclopaedia of Islam*, 2nd ed. Leiden: Brill Academic. First published online 2012.

Blachère, R., and A. Bausani. "Ghazal." In *Encyclopaedia of Islam*, 2nd ed. Leiden: Brill Academic. First published online 2012.

Black, Deborah L. *Logic and Aristotle's Rhetoric and Poetics in Medieval Arabic Philosophy.* New York: Brill, 1990.

Boase, Roger. "Arab Influences on European Love-Poetry." In *The Legacy of Muslim Spain*, edited by Salma Khadra Jayyusi, 457–82. New York: Brill, 1992.

———. *The Origin and Meaning of Courtly Love.* Manchester: Manchester University Press, 1977.

Bogin, Meg. *Women Troubadours.* New York: Norton, 1980.

Bonebakker, S. A. "*Adab* and the Concept of *Belles-lettres.*" In *ʿAbbasid Belles-Lettres, Cambridge History of Arabic Literature*, edited by Julia Ashtiany, T. M. Johnstone, J. D. Latham, and R. B. Serjeant, 16–30. Cambridge: Cambridge University Press, 2008.

Brann, Ross. *The Compunctious Poet.* Baltimore, MD: Johns Hopkins University Press, 1991.

———. "The 'Dissembling Poet' in Medieval Hebrew Literature: The Dimensions of a Literary Topos." *Journal of the American Oriental Society* 107, no. 1 (1987): 39–54.

———. "He Said, She Said: Reinscribing the Andalusi Arabic Love Lyric." In *Studies in Arabic and Hebrew Letters in Honor of Raymond P. Scheindlin*, edited by Jonathan P. Decter and Michael Rand, 7–15. Piscataway, NJ: Gorgias, 2007.

Bregman, Dvora. *Bi-shne qolot: shir ha-hed ha-ʿivri le-dorotay.* Tel Aviv: Deḥaq, 2021.

———. *The Golden Way: The Hebrew Sonnet during the Renaissance and the Baroque.* Translated by Ann Brener. Arizona: Arizona Center for Medieval and Renaissance Studies, 2006.

———. "A Note on the Style and Prosody of *Miqdash meat.*" In "Medieval Jewish Literature," special issue, *Prooftexts* 23, no. 1 (2003): 18–24.

Brener, Ann. "The *Scroll of Love* by Immanuel of Rome: A Hebrew Parody of Dante's *Vita Nuova.*" *Prooftexts* 32, no. 2 (2012): 149–175.

Brockelmann, C. "Kalila Wa-Dimna." In *Encyclopaedia of Islam*, 2nd ed. Leiden: Brill Academic. First published online 2012.

Brockelmann, C., and Ch. Pellat. "Makāma." In *Encyclopaedia of Islam*, 2nd ed. Leiden: Brill Academic. First published online 2012.

Brogan, T. V. F. "Prosimetrum." In *The Princeton Encyclopedia of Poetry and Poetics*, 4th ed., edited by Roland Greene, Stephen Cushman, Clare Cavanagh, Jahan Ramazani, Paul Rouzer, Harris Feinsod, David Marno, and Alexandra Slessarev, 1115–16. Princeton, NJ: Princeton University Press, 2012.

Bruckner, Matilda Tomaryn, Laurie Shepard, and Sarah White. *Songs of the Women Troubadours*. New York: Garland, 1995.

Bunis, David. "Judezmo (Ladino/Judeo-Spanish): A Historical and Sociolinguistic Portrait." In *Languages in Jewish Communities, Past and Present*, edited by Benjamin Hary and Sarah Bunin Benor, 185–238. Berlin: De Gruyter, 2019.

Cacho Blecua, Juan Manuel, and María Jesús Lacarra, eds. *Calila e Dimna*. Madrid: Castalia, 1984.

Caird, George B. *The Language and Imagery of the Bible*. Philadelphia: Westminster, 1980.

Capellanus, Andeas. *The Art of Courtly Love*. Translated by John Jay Parry. New York: Columbia University Press, 1960.

Carrai, Stefano. "Prefazione." In *Il prosimetro nella letteratura italiana*, edited by Andrea Comboni and Alessandra Di Ricco, 7–11. Trento: Dipartimento di Scienze Filologiche e Storiche, 2000.

Cassuto, Umberto. "Bible: Ladino (Judeo-Spanish)." In *Encyclopaedia Judaica*, 2nd ed., edited by Michael Berenbaum and Fred Skolnik, 3:610. Detroit: Macmillan Reference USA in association with Keter, 2007.

———. *Dante e Manoello*. Firenze: Società tipografico-editoriale, 1921.

Cassuto, Umberto, and Angel Sáenz-Badillos. "Immanuel (ben Solomon) of Rome." In *Encyclopaedia Judaica*, 2nd ed., edited by Michael Berenbaum and Fred Skolnik, 9:740–41. Detroit: Macmillan Reference USA in association with Keter, 2007.

Castellani, Arrigo. "Sul codice Laurenziano Martelliano 12." In *Sotto il segno di Dante*, edited by Leonella Coglievina and Domenico De Robertis, 307–29. Florence: Le Lettere, 1988.

Castro, Américo. *España en su historia: cristianos, moros y judíos*. Buenos Aires: Losada, 1948.

———. *España en su historia: cristianos, moros y judíos*. 2nd ed. Barcelona: Crítica, 1983.

Cervantes Saavedra, Miguel de. *Don Quijote de la Mancha*. Edited by Martín de Riquer. Barcelona: Juventud, 2003.

———. *Don Quixote*. Translated by Edith Grossman. New York: Ecco, 2003.

Chaumont, E. "al-Shāfiʿī." In *Encyclopaedia of Islam*, 2nd ed. Leiden: Brill Academic. First published online 2012.

Chaytor, H. J. *A History of Aragon and Catalonia*. New York: AMS, 1969.

Chejne, Anwar G. *Ibn Ḥazm: al-ḥaqq ḥaqq wa-al-bāṭil bāṭil*. Chicago: Kazi, 1982.

Cherchi, Paolo. *Andreas and the Ambiguity of Courtly Love*. Toronto: University of Toronto Press, 1994.

Cherniss, Michael D. "The Literary Comedy of Andreas Capellanus." *Modern Philology* 72, no. 3 (1975): 223–37.

Cicero, Marcus Tullius. *De Oratore* [On the Orator: Books 1–2]. Translated by E. W. Sutton and H. Rackham. Loeb Classical Library 348. Cambridge, MA: Harvard University Press, 1942.

[Cicero, Marcus Tullius]. *Rhetorica ad Herennium*. Translated by Harry Caplan. Cambridge, MA: Harvard University Press, 2004.

Cipolla, C., and F. Pellegrini. "Poesie minori riguardanti gli Scaglieri." In *Bullettino dell'Istituto storico italiano*, edited by C. Cipolla and F. Pellegrini, 24:50–55. Rome: L'istituto, 1902.

Cohen, Mark R. "On the Interplay of Arabic and Hebrew in the Cairo Geniza Letters." In *Studies in Arabic and Hebrew Letters in Honor of Raymond P. Scheindlin*, edited by Jonathan P. Decter and Michael Rand, 17–35. Piscataway, NJ: Gorgias, 2007.

Cohen, Mordechai. "Dimyon ve-higayon, emet ve-sheker: gishotehem shel Ramba ve-Rambam le-metafora ha-miqra-it le-or ha-poetiqa ve-ha-filosofia ha-ʿaravit." *Tarbiz* 73 (2004): 417–58.

———. *Three Approaches to Biblical Metaphor: From Abraham Ibn Ezra and Maimonides to David Kimhi*. Leiden: Brill, 2003.

Cohen, Rip. *500 Cantigas*. Porto: Campo das Letras, 2003.

———. *The "Cantigas d'Amigo": An English Translation*. Baltimore, MD: JScholarship, Johns Hopkins University, 2010.

———. *Poetics of the "Cantigas d'Amigo."* Baltimore: JScholarship, Johns Hopkins University, 2003.

Cudini, Piero, ed. *Poesia italiana del Duecento*. Italy: Garzanti, 1984.

Curtius, Ernst Robert. *European Literature and the Latin Middle Ages*. Translated by Willard R. Trask. Princeton, NJ: Princeton University Press, 1990.

Dana, Joseph. "Who Is Moses Ibn Ezra's 'Jewish Poet'?" *Jewish Quarterly Review*, n.s., 73, no. 3 (1983): 281–83.

David, Abraham. "Jacob ben Eleazar." In *Encyclopaedia Judaica*, 2nd ed., edited by Michael Berenbaum and Fred Skolnik, 11:31. Detroit: Macmillan Reference USA in association with Keter, 2007.

Davidson, Israel. "Eccentric Forms of Hebrew Verse." In *Students' Annual of the Jewish Theological Seminary*, 81–94. New York: Seminary, 1914.

———. "Sarid mi-sefer filosofi li-mḥaber bilti nodʿa." *Ha-ṣofe le-ḥokhmat Yisraʾel* 10 (1926): 94–105.

Decter, Jonathan. P. "Belles-Lettres." In *The Cambridge History of Judaism*, vol. 6, *The Middle Ages: The Christian World*, edited by Robert Chazan, 787–812. Cambridge: Cambridge University Press, 2018.

———. *Dominion Built of Praise: Panegyric and Legitimacy among Jews in the Medieval Mediterranean*. Philadelphia: University of Pennsylvania Press, 2018.

———. "A Hebrew 'Sodomite' Tale from Thirteenth-Century Toledo: Jacob Ben Elʿazar's Story of Sapir, Shapir and Birsha." *Journal of Medieval Iberian Studies* 3, no. 2 (2011): 187–202.

———. *Iberian Jewish Literature: Between al-Andalus and Christian Europe*. Bloomington: Indiana University Press, 2007.

Deleuze, Gilles, and Félix Guattari. *Kafka: Toward a Minor Literature*. Translated by Dana Polan. Minneapolis: University of Minnesota Press, 1986.

Denomy, Alexander J. "Courtly Love and Courtliness." *Speculum* 28, no. 1 (1953): 44–63.

De Robertis, Domenico. *Il libro della "Vita Nuova"*. Florence: G. C. Sansoni, 1970.

Deyermond, Alan. "Juan Ruiz's Attitude to Literature." In *Medieval, Renaissance and Folklore Studies: In Honor of John Esten Keller*, edited by Joseph R. Jones, 113–25. Newark, DE: Juan de la Cuesta, 1980.

Dishon, Judith. "Neʾum Asher ben Yehuda li-Shlomo ibn Ṣaqbel veha-maqama ha-ʿesrim be-Taḥkemoni li-Yhuda al-Ḥarizi." *Biqoret u-farshanut* 6 (1974): 57–65.

Donaldson, E. Talbot. "The Myth of Courtly Love." *Ventures* 5 (1965): 16–23.

Dozy, Reinhart. *Spanish Islam: A History of the Moslems in Iberia*. Translated by Francis Giffin Stokes. London: Frank Cass, 1972.

Dronke, Peter. *Medieval Latin and the Rise of European Love-Lyric*. Oxford: Clarendon, 1968.

———. *Verse with Prose from Petronius to Dante: The Art and Scope of Mixed Form*. Cambridge, MA: Harvard University Press, 1994.

Drory, Rina. "The Hidden Context: On Literary Products of Tri-cultural Contacts in the Middle Ages." [In Hebrew.] *Pe'amim, Studies in Oriental Jewry* 46/47 (1991): 9–28.

———. "The Maqāma." In *The Literature of Al-Andalus*, edited by María Rosa Menocal, Michael Sells, and Raymond P. Scheindlin, 190–210. Cambridge: Cambridge University Press, 2000.

———. *Models and Contacts: Arabic Literature and Its Impact on Medieval Jewish Culture*. Leiden: Brill, 2000.

———. "'Words Beautifully Put': Hebrew versus Arabic in Tenth-Century Jewish Literature." In *Genizah Research after Ninety Years: The Case of Judaeo-Arabic*, edited by Joshua Blau and Stefan C. Reif, 53–63. Cambridge: Cambridge University Press, 1992.

Drucker, J. "Carmina Figurata." In *The Princeton Encyclopedia of Poetry and Poetics*, 4th ed., edited by Roland Greene, Stephen Cushman, Clare Cavanagh, Jahan Ramazani, Paul Rouzer, Harris Feinsod, David Marno, and Alexandra Slessarev, 207–8. Princeton, NJ: Princeton University Press, 2012.

———. "Concrete Poetry." In *The Princeton Encyclopedia of Poetry and Poetics*, 4th ed., edited by Roland Greene, Stephen Cushman, Clare Cavanagh, Jahan Ramazani, Paul Rouzer, Harris Feinsod, David Marno, and Alexandra Slessarev, 294–95. Princeton, NJ: Princeton University Press, 2012.

Eckhardt, Caroline D. "The Medieval Prosimetrum Genre (from Boethius to Boece)." *Genre* 16 (1983): 21–38.

Eco, Umberto. "Metaphor, Dictionary, and Encyclopedia." *New Literary History* 15, no. 2 (1984): 255–71.

Eden, Kathy. *Poetic and Legal Fiction in the Aristotelian Tradition*. Princeton, NJ: Princeton University Press, 1986.

Einbinder, Susan. *Beautiful Death: Jewish Poetry and Martyrdom in Medieval France*. Princeton, NJ: Princeton University Press, 2002.

Eisner, Martin. *Boccaccio and the Invention of Italian Literature: Dante, Petrarch, Cavalcanti, and the Authority of the Vernacular*. Cambridge: Cambridge University Press, 2013.

Fahd, T., W. P. Heinrichs, and A. Ben Abdesselem. "Sadjʿ." In *Encyclopaedia of Islam*, 2nd ed. Leiden: Brill Academic. First published online 2012.

Fahd, T., S. Moreh, A. Ben Abdesselem, A. Reynolds, D. F. Bruijn, J. T. P. de Halman, Talat Sait, Rahman, Munibur Kane, Ousmane, M. Hiskett, and Virginia Matheson Hooker. "Shāʿir." In *Encyclopaedia of Islam*, 2nd ed. Leiden: Brill Academic. First published online 2012.

Faulhaber, Charles. *Latin Rhetorical Theory in Thirteenth and Fourteenth Century Castile*. Berkeley: University of California Press, 1972.

Fenton, Paul. "Gleanings from Môseh Ibn 'Ezra's *Maqâlat al-Hadîqa*." *Sefarad* 36 (1976): 285–98.

Ferrante, Joan M. "*Cortes' Amor* in Medieval Texts." *Speculum* 55, no. 4 (1980): 686–95.

Fidalgo, Elvira. *De amor y de burlas: antología de la poesía medieval gallego-portuguesa.* Vigo: NigraTrea, 2009.

Fishkin, Dana W. "A Lifetime in Letters: New Evidence concerning Immanuel of Rome's Timeline." *Jewish Quarterly Review*, forthcoming.

———. "Situating Hell & Heaven: Immanuel of Rome's Mahberet ha-tophet v' ha-eden." PhD diss., New York University, 2011.

Fishman, Talya. "A Medieval Parody of Misogyny: Judah Ibn Shabbetai's *Minḥat Yehudah sone hanashim.*" *Prooftexts* 8, no. 1 (1988): 89–111.

Fleischer, Ezra. *Shirat ha-qodesh ha-ʿivrit bi-ymei ha-beinayim.* Jerusalem: Keter, 1975.

———. "Studies in Liturgical and Secular Poetry." In *Studies in Literature Presented to Shimon Halkin*, 183–204. Jerusalem: Magnes, 1973.

Fortis, Umberto. *Manoello Volgare: i versi italiani di Immanuel Romano (1265–1331?).* Livorno: Salomone Belforte & C. editori librai dal 1805, 2017.

Frenk Alatorre, Margit. *Lírica española de tipo popular: edad media y renacimiento.* Madrid: Cátedra, 1977.

Friedman, N., and A. L. French. "Dead Metaphor." In *The Princeton Encyclopedia of Poetry and Poetics*, 4th ed., edited by Roland Greene, Stephen Cushman, Clare Cavanagh, Jahan Ramazani, Paul Rouzer, Harris Feinsod, David Marno, and Alexandra Slessarev, 337–38. Princeton, NJ: Princeton University Press, 2012.

"Frottola [It.]." In *The Harvard Dictionary of Music*, 4th ed., edited by Don Michael Randel. Cambridge: Belknap Press of Harvard University Press, 2003.

Gabrieli, F. "Adab." In *Encyclopaedia of Islam*, 2nd ed. Leiden: Brill Academic. First published online 2012.

García Gómez, Emilio. "Un precedente y una consecuencia del *Collar de la paloma.*" *Al-andalus* 16, no. 2 (1951): 309–30.

Garland, John of. *The "Parisiana Poetria" of John of Garland.* Edited and translated by Traugott Lawler. New Haven, CT: Yale University Press, 1974.

Gaylord, Mary. "The Grammar of Femininity in the Traditional Lyric." *Revista / Review Interamericana* 12 (1982): 115–24.

Genette, Gérard. "Rhetoric Restrained." *Figures of Literary Discourse.* Translated by Alan Sheridan. New York: Columbia University Press, 1982.

Gerber, Jane. *The Jews of Spain: A History of the Sephardic Experience.* New York: Free Press, 1992.

Giffen, Lois A. "Ibn Ḥazm and the *Ṭawq al-ḥamāma.*" In *The Legacy of Muslim Spain*, 2nd ed., edited by Salma Khadra Jayyusi and Manuela Marín, 12:420–42. Leiden: Brill, 1992.

———. *Theory of Profane Love among the Arabs: The Development of the Genre.* Vol. 3 of *New York University Studies in Near Eastern Civilization.* New York: New York University Press, 1971.

Gilliot, C. "Shawāhid." In *Encyclopaedia of Islam*, 2nd ed. Leiden: Brill Academic. First published online 2012.

Girón-Negrón, Luis M. "How the Go Between Cut Her Nose: Two Ibero-Medieval Translations of a *Kalila wa-Dimna* Story." In *Under the Influence: Questioning the Comparative in Medieval Castile*, edited by Cynthia Robinson and Leyla Rouhi, 231–59. Leiden: Brill, 2005.

Goldziher, Ignace. *A Short History of Classical Arabic Literature.* Revised and translated by Joseph Desomogyi. Hildesheim: Georg Olms, 1966.

Goodman, Lenn E. "Editor's Introduction: Thematizing a Tradition." In *Neoplatonism and Jewish Thought*, edited by Lenn. E. Goodman, 1–19. New York: State University of New York Press, 1992.

Grunebaum, Gustave E. von. "The Aesthetic Foundation of Arabic Literature." *Comparative Literature* 4, no. 4 (1952): 323–40.

———. "Al-Mubarrad's Epistle on Poetry and Prose." *Orientalia* 10 (1941): 372–82.

———. "Arabic Poetics." In *Indiana University Conference on Oriental-Western Literary Relations*, edited by Horst Frenz and G. L. Anderson, 27–46. Chapel Hill: University of North Carolina Press, 1955.

Guetta, Alessandro. "Moses da Rieti and His *Miqdash me'at*." *Prooftexts* 23, no. 1 (2003): 4–17.

Gutas, Dimitri. "Plato's *Symposion* in the Arabic Tradition." *Oriens* 31 (1988): 36–60.

Habermann, Abraham Meir. "The Beginning of Hebrew Poetry in Italy and Northern Europe: Northern Europe and France." In *The World History of the Jewish People, Medieval Period*, vol. 2, *The Dark Ages*, edited by Cecil Roth, 267–73. Tel Aviv: Jewish History Publications, 1966.

———. "Samuel Ha-Nagid." In *Encyclopaedia Judaica*, 2nd ed., edited by Michael Berenbaum and Fred Skolnik, 17:381–97. Detroit: Macmillan Reference USA in association with Keter, 2007.

Halkin, Abraham Solomon, and Angel Sáenz-Badillos. "Translation and Translators." In *Encyclopaedia Judaica*, 2nd ed., edited by Michael Berenbaum and Fred Skolnik, 17:381–97. Detroit: Macmillan Reference USA in association with Keter, 2007.

Hamadhānī, Badīʿ al-Zamān al-. *Maqāmāt Abī al-Faḍl Badīʿ al-Zamān al-Hamadhānī.* Edited by Muḥammad ʿAbduh. Beirut: al-maṭbaʿah al-kāthūlīkīyah, 1889.

———. *The Maqāmāt of Badiʿ al-Zamān al-Hamadhānī.* Translated by William Joseph Prendergast. London: Luzac, 1915.

Hamilton, Michelle. *Representing Others in Medieval Iberian Literature.* New York: Palgrave Macmillan, 2007.

Hammond, Marlé. *A Dictionary of Arabic Literary Terms and Devices.* Oxford: Oxford University Press, 2018.

Hamori, Andras. "Love Poetry (*Ghazal*)." In *Cambridge History of Arabic Literature: ʿAbbasid Belles-Lettres*, edited by Julia Ashtiany, T. M. Johnstone, J. D. Latham, R. B. Serjeant, and G. Rex Smith, 202–18. Cambridge: Cambridge University Press, 2010.

Harb, Lara. *Arabic Poetics: Aesthetic Experience in Classical Arabic Literature.* Cambridge: Cambridge University Press, 2020.

Harden, Robert. "*Aucassin et Nicolette* as Parody." *Studies in Philology* 63, no. 1 (1966): 1–9.

Ḥarīrī, Abū Muḥammad al-Qāsim b. ʿAlī b. Muḥammad b. ʿUthmān al-. *The Assemblies of al-Ḥarīrī.* Translated by Thomas Chenery. London: Williams and Norgate, 1867.

———. *The Assemblies of al-Ḥarīrī; Student's Edition of the Arabic Text.* Edited by Francis Joseph Steingass. London: Crosby Lockwood, 1897.

Ḥarizi, Judah al-. *Taḥkemoni.* Edited by Yosef Yahalom and Naoya Katsumata. Jerusalem: Ben Zvi Institute for the Study of Jewish Communities in the East and the Hebrew University of Jerusalem, 2010.

———. *The Taḥkemoni of Judah al-Ḥarizi: An English Translation.* 2. Vols. Translated by Victor Emanuel Reichert. Jerusalem: R. H. Cohen's Press, 1965–73.

Harris, M. Roy. "The Occitan Translations of John XII and XIII–XVII from a Fourteenth-Century Franciscan Codex (Assisi, Chiesa Nuova MS. 9)." *Transactions of the American Philosophical Society* 75, no. 4 (1985): 1–149.

Haywood, Louise M. "Juan Ruiz and the *Libro de buen amor*: Contexts and Milieu." In *A Companion to the "Libro de Buen Amor,"* edited by Louise M. Haywood and Louise O. Vasvári, 21–38. Rochester: Tamesis, 2004.

Heinrichs, Wolfhart. *The Hand of the Northwind: Opinions on Metaphor and the Early Meaning of "istiʿāra" in Arabic Poetics.* Wiesbaden: Deutsche Morgenlandische Gesellschaft, Kommissions-verlag Franz Steiner, 1977.

———. "Prosimetrical Genres in Classical Arabic Literature." In *Prosimetrum: Crosscultural Perspectives on Narrative in Prose and Verse*, edited by Joseph Harris and Karl Reichl, 249–75. Cambridge: D. S. Brewer, 1997.

Heller-Roazen, Daniel. "The Matter of Language: Guilhem de Peitieus and the Platonic Tradition." French issue, *MLN* 113, no. 4 (September 1998): 851–80.

Hollander, John. "The Shadow of a Lie: Poetry, Lying, and the Truth of Fictions." *Social Research* 63, no. 3 (1996): 643–61.

Holmes, Olivia. "The *Vita Nuova* in the Context of Vatican MS Chigiano L. VIII.305 and Dante's 'Iohannian' Strategy of Authorship." *Exemplaria* 8, no. 1 (1996): 193–229.

Horace. *Satires, Epistles and Ars Poetica*. Translated by H. Rushton Fairclough. New York: G. P. Putnam's Sons, 1932.

Hrushovski-Harshav, Benjamin. "Prosody, Hebrew." In *Encyclopaedia Judaica*, 2nd ed., edited by Michael Berenbaum and Fred Skolnik, 1:595–623. Detroit: Macmillan Reference USA in association with Keter, 2007.

Hughes, Aaron. "Translation and Invention of Renaissance Jewish Culture: The Case of Judah Messer Leon and Judah Abravanel." In *The Hebrew Bible in Fifteenth-Century Spain*, edited by Jonathan Decter and Arturo Prats, 245–66. Leiden: Brill, 2012.

Hunt, Tony. "Precursors and Progenitors of 'Aucassin et Nicolette.'" *Studies in Philology* 74, no. 1 (January 1977): 1–19.

Huss, Matti. "Clarifications regarding the Time and Date of Composition of Sefer HaMeshalim." [In Hebrew.] In *Meir Benayahu Memorial Volume: Studies in Talmud, Halakha, Custom, Jewish History, Kabbala, Jewish Thought, Liturgy, Piyyut, and Poetry in Memory of Professor Meir Benayahu z"l*, edited by Moshe Bar-Asher, Yehuda Libes, Moshe Assis, and Yosef Kaplan, 1021–56. Jerusalem: Karmel; Jerusalem: Goldshtain-Goren; Jerusalem: Yad ha-Rav Nisim; Tel Aviv: University of Tel Aviv Press, 2019.

———. "The Status of Fiction in the Hebrew Maqama: Judah Alḥarizi and Immanuel of Rome." [In Hebrew.] *Tarbiṣ* 67, no. 3 (1998): 351–78.

Ibn al-ʿArabī. *The Tarjumān al-ashwāq, a Collection of Mystical Odes by Muḥyiʿddīn ibn al-ʿArabī.* Edited and translated by Reynold A. Nicholson. London: Royal Asiatic Society, 1911.

Ibn Dāwūd al-Iṣfahānī, Abū Bakr Muḥammad. *Kitāb al-zahra*. Vol. 6 of *Studies in Ancient Oriental Civilization*. Edited by A. R. Nykl. Chicago: University of Chicago Press, 1932.

Ibn Ezra, Moses. *Kitāb al-muḥāḍara wa-l-mudhākara*. Edited by Montserrat Abumalham Mas. Madrid: Consejo superior de investigaciones científicas, Instituto de filologia, 1986.

Ibn Falaquera, Shem Tov ben Joseph. *The Book of the Seeker* (*Sefer ha-mebaqqesh*). Translated by M. Herschel Levine. New York: Yeshiva University Press, 1976.

———. Sefer ha-mevaqesh. Warsaw: Ṭraqlin, 1924.

Ibn Gabirol, Solomon ben Yehuda. *Shire Shelomo ben Yehuda ibn Gabirol.* Edited by Hayim Naḥman Bialik and Yehoshuaʿ Ḥana Rawnitzki. Berlin: Devir, 1924.
Ibn Ḥazm, ʿAlī ibn Aḥmad. *Marātib al-ʿulūm* in *Ibn Ḥazm: al-ḥaqq ḥaqq wa-al-bāṭil bāṭil.* Edited and translated by Anwar G. Chejne. Chicago: Kazi, 1982.
———. *The Ring of the Dove: A Treatise on the Art and Practice of Arab Love* [*Ṭawq al-ḥamāma*]. Translated by A. J. Arberry. London: Luzac, 1953.
———. *Ṭawq al-ḥamāma.* Edited by Al-Ṭāhir Aḥmad Makkī. Cairo: Dar al-Maʾrifa, 1993.
Ibn al-Khaṭīb, Lisān al-Dīn. *The Jaysh al-tawshīḥ of Lisān al-Dīn ibn al-Khaṭīb: An Anthology of Andalusian Arabic Muwashshaḥat.* Edited by Alan Jones. Cambridge: Gibb Memorial Trust, 1997.
Ibn al-Muʿtazz. *Kitāb al-badīʿ.* Edited by ʿIrfān Maṭrajī. Beirut: Muʾassasat al-Kutub al-Thaqāfīya, 2001.
Ibn Paquda, Baḥya. *The Duties of the Heart.* Translated by Yaakov Feldman. Northvale, NJ: Jason Aronson, 1996.
Ibn Rashīq al-Qayrawānī, al-Ḥasan. *Al-ʿUmda fī maḥāsin al-shiʿr wa-ādābihi.* Edited by Muḥammad Qarqazān. Beirut: Dār al-maʾarifa, 1988.
Ibn Sahula, Isaac. *Meshal ha-qadmoni.* Edited and translated by Raphael Loewe. Oxford: Littman Library of Jewish Civilization, 2004.
Ibn Ṭabāṭabā, Muḥammad ibn Aḥmad. *ʿIyār al-shiʿr.* Edited by Ṭāhā al-Ḥājirī and Muḥammad Zaghlūl Salām. Cairo: al-Maktaba al-Tijārīya al-Kubrā, 1956.
Jackson, Sherman. "Al-Jahiz on Translation." *Alif: Journal of Comparative Poetics* 4 (1984): 99–107.
Jacobi, Renate. "ʿUdhrī." In *Encyclopaedia of Islam*, 2nd ed. Leiden: Brill Academic. First published online 2012.
Jaeger, C. Stephen. *Ennobling Love: In Search of a Lost Sensibility.* Philadelphia: University of Pennsylvania Press, 1999.
Jager, Eric. *The Book of the Heart.* Chicago: University of Chicago Press, 2000.
Jāḥiẓ, Abū ʿUthmān ʿAmr ibn Baḥr al-. *Al-Bayān wa-l-tabyīn.* Edited by ʿAbd al-Salām Muḥammad Hārūn. Miṣr: Maktabat al-Khānjī, 1960.
———. *The Epistle on Singing-Girls of Jāḥiẓ.* [Risālat al-qiyān.] Vol. 2 of *Approaches to Arabic Literature.* Translated by A. F. L. Beeston. Warminster, Wiltshire, England: Aris & Phillips, 1980.
Jauss, Hans Robert, and Elizabeth Benzinger. "Literary History as a Challenge to Literary Theory." *New Literary History* 2, no. 1 (1970): 7–37.
Johnston, Mark. "Literary Tradition and the Idea of Language in the *Artes de Trobar.*" *Dispositio* 2, no. 5/6 (1977): 208–18.
Jurjānī, ʿAbd al-Qāhir ibn ʿAbd al-Raḥmān al-. *Kitāb asrār al-balāgha.* Edited by Helmut Ritter. Istanbul: Maṭbaʿat Wizārat al-Maʿārif, 1954.
Kanazi, George. *Studies in the Kitāb aṣ-Ṣināʿatayn of Abū Hilāl al-ʿAskarī.* Leiden: Brill, 1989.
Kay, Sarah. *Parrots and Nightingales: Troubadour Quotations and the Development of European Poetry.* Philadelphia: University of Pennsylvania Press, 2013.
Kelly, Douglas. *The Arts of Poetry and Prose.* Belgium: Brepols, 1991.
Key, Alexander. *Language between God and the Poets: Maʿnā in the Eleventh Century.* Oakland: University of California Press, 2018.
Khafājī, ʿAbd Allāh ibn Muḥammad al-. *Sirr al-faṣāḥa.* Edited by ʿAbd al-Mutaʿāl al-Ṣaʿīdī. Miṣr: Maṭbaʿat Muḥammad ʿAlī Ṣubayḥ, 1953.
Kozodoy, Neal. "Reading Medieval Hebrew Love Poetry." *AJS Review* 2 (1977): 111–29.

Kushelevsky, Rella. "Chastity versus Courtly Love in 'The Poor Bachelor and His Rich Maiden Cousin.'" *Jewish Studies Quarterly* 20, no. 1 (2013): 61–82.
———. *Tales in Context: "Sefer ha-maʿasim" in Medieval Northern France.* Detroit: Wayne State University Press, 2017.
Lang, H. R. "The Relations of the Earliest Portuguese Lyric School with the Troubadours and Trouvères." *Modern Language Notes* 10, no. 4 (1895): 104–16.
Lazar, Moshe. *The Sephardic Tradition: Ladino and Spanish-Jewish Literature.* New York: Norton, 1972.
Lecker, M. "ʿUdhra." In *Encyclopaedia of Islam*, 2nd ed. Leiden: Brill Academic. First published online 2012.
Leder, Stefan, and Hilary Kilpatrick. "Classical Arabic Prose Literature: A Researchers' Sketch Map." *Journal of Arabic Literature* 23, no. 1 (March 1992): 2–26.
Levy, Isabelle. "Hybridity through Poetry: *Sefer ha-meshalim* and the Status of Poetry in Medieval Iberia." In *A Comparative History of Literatures in the Iberian Peninsula*, edited by César Domínguez, Anxo Abuín González, and Ellen Sapega, 2:131–37. Philadelphia: John Benjamins, 2016.
———. "Immanuel of Rome and Dante." *Digital Dante.* New York: Columbia University. 2017. https://digitaldante.columbia.edu/history/immanuel-of-rome-and-dante-levy/.
———. "Immanuel of Rome's *Bisbidis*: An Italian Maqāma?" *Medieval Encounters* 27, no. 1, 78–115.
Levy, Isabelle, and David Torollo. "Romance Literature in Hebrew Language with an Arabic Twist: The First Story of Jacob ben Elʿazar's *Sefer ha-meshalim.*" *La Coronica* 45, no. 2 (2017): 279–304.
Lewis, C. S. *The Allegory of Love.* New York: Oxford University Press, 1958.
Littlewood, A. R. "The Symbolism of the Apple in Greek and Roman Literature." *Harvard Studies in Classical Philology* 72 (1968): 147–81.
Lord, Albert B. *The Singer of Tales.* Edited by Stephen Mitchell and Gregory Nagy. Cambridge, MA: Harvard University Press, 2000.
Maʿarrī, Abū al-ʿAlāʾ al-. *Rasāʾil Abī al-ʿAlāʾ al-Maʿarrī.* Edited by D. S. Margoliouth. Baghdad: Maktabat al-Muthannā, 1968.
Maimonides, Moses. *The Guide of the Perplexed.* Translated by Shlomo Pines. Chicago: University of Chicago, 1963.
———. *Maimonides' Treatise on Logic (Maqāla fī sināʿat al-mantiq).* Edited and translated by Israel Efros. New York: American Academy for Jewish Research, 1938.
———. *Mishna ʿim perush Rabenu Moshe ben Maimon.* Edited and translated by Yosef Qaʿfiḥ. Jerusalem: Mosad ha-Rav Quq, 1964.
Malkiel, David. "Eros as Medium: Rereading Immanuel of Rome's Scroll of Desire." In *Donne nella storia degli ebrei d'Italia—atti del IX Convegno internazionale "Italia Judaica, Lucca, 6–9 giugno 2005.* Edited by Michele Luzzati and Cristina Galasso, 35–59. Florence: Giuntina, 2007.
Mallette, Karla. *The Kingdom of Sicily, 1100–1250: A Literary History.* Philadelphia: University of Pennsylvania Press, 2005.
Marcus, Ivan. "A Jewish-Christian Symbiosis: The Culture of Early Ashkenaz." In *Cultures of the Jews: A New History*, edited by David Biale, 449–516. New York: Schocken Books, 2002.
———. "Why Is This Knight Different? A Jewish Self-Representation in Medieval Europe." In *Tov Elem: Memory, Community and Gender in Medieval and Early Modern Jewish*

Societies; Essays in Honor of Robert Bonfil. Edited by Elisheva Baumgarten, Amnon Raz-Krakotzkin, and Roni Weinstein, 139–52. Jerusalem: Mandel Institute of Jewish Studies, Hebrew University of Jerusalem, and Bialik Institute, 2011.

Marti, Mario, ed. *Poeti giocosi del tempo di Dante*. Milan: Rizzoli, 1956.

Martin, June Hall. *Love's Fools: Aucassin, Troilus, Calisto and the Parody of the Courtly Lover*. London: Tamesis, 1972.

Martin, W. "Metaphor." In *The Princeton Encyclopedia of Poetry and Poetics*, 4th ed., edited by Roland Greene, Stephen Cushman, Clare Cavanagh, Jahan Ramazani, Paul Rouzer, Harris Feinsod, David Marno, and Alexandra Slessarev, 863–870. Princeton, NJ: Princeton University Press, 2012.

———. "Synecdoche." In *The Princeton Encyclopedia of Poetry and Poetics*, 4th ed., edited by Roland Greene, Stephen Cushman, Clare Cavanagh, Jahan Ramazani, Paul Rouzer, Harris Feinsod, David Marno, and Alexandra Slessarev, 1400–1401. Princeton, NJ: Princeton University Press, 2012.

Marzubānī, Muḥammad ibn ʿImrān al-. *al-Muwashshaḥ fī maʾākhidh al-ʿulamāʾ ʿalā al-shuʿarāʾ*. Edited by Muḥammad Ḥusayn Shams al-Dīn. Beirut: Dār al-Kutub al-ʿIlmīya, 1995.

Marzūqī, Aḥmad ibn Muḥammad al-. *Sharḥ dīwān al-ḥamāsa*. Edited by Aḥmad Amīn and ʿAbd al-Salām Hārūn. Cairo: Lajnat al-Taʾlīf wa-l-Tarjama wa-l-Nashr, 1951.

McFadden, K. "Metalepsis or Transumption." In *The Princeton Encyclopedia of Poetry and Poetics*, 4th ed., edited by Roland Greene, Stephen Cushman, Clare Cavanagh, Jahan Ramazani, Paul Rouzer, Harris Feinsod, David Marno, and Alexandra Slessarev, 862–63. Princeton, NJ: Princeton University Press, 2012.

McLain, Carin C. "Prose and Poetry and the Making of Beatrice." PhD diss., Columbia University, 2007.

Menéndez Pidal, Ramón. *Poesía árabe y poesía europea*. Buenos Aires: Espasa-Calpe Argentina, 1943.

———. "Poesía arabe y poesía europea." *Bulletin hispanique* 40, no. 4 (1938): 337–423.

———. *Poesía juglaresca y orígenes de las literaturas románicas: problemas de historia literaria y cultural*. Madrid: Instituto de Estudios Políticos, 1957.

Menocal, María Rosa. *The Arabic Role in Medieval Literary History: A Forgotten Heritage*. Philadelphia: University of Pennsylvania Press, 1987.

———. *Shards of Love: Exile and the Origins of the Lyric*. Durham: Duke University Press, 1994.

Mermier, Guy R. "The Diaspora of the Occitan Troubadours: Influence of Occitan Troubadour Lyrics on the Poetry of Galician-Portuguese Trovadores." *Mediterranean Studies* 7 (1998): 67–91.

Miron, Dan. *From Continuity to Contiguity: Toward a New Jewish Literary Thinking*. Stanford, CA: Stanford University Press, 2010.

Mirsky, Aharon, Avrum Stroll, Angel Sáenz-Badillos, and Hanoch Avenary. "Al-Ḥarizi, Judah ben Solomon." In *Encyclopaedia Judaica*, 2nd ed., edited by Michael Berenbaum and Fred Skolnik, 1:655–57. Detroit: Macmillan Reference USA in association with Keter, 2007.

Modona, Leonello. *Vita e opere di Immnuele Romano. Studio postumo del prof. Leonello Modona*. Florence: R. Bemporad & figlio, 1904.

Molinier, Guillem. *Les leys d'amours; manuscrit de l'Académie des juex floraux*. Edited by Joseph Anglade. Toulouse: E. Privat, 1919.

Monroe, James T. "Maimonides on the Mozarabic Lyric (A Note on the Muwassaḥa)." *La corónica* 17, no. 2 (1989): 18–32.

Montgomery, James. "Speech and Nature: al-Jāḥiẓ, *Kitāb al-bayān wa-l-tabyīn*, 2.175–207, Part 1." *Middle Eastern Literatures* 11, no. 2 (2009): 169–191.

Moore, John C. "'Courtly Love': A Problem of Terminology." *Journal of the History of Ideas* 40, no. 4 (1979): 621–32.

Murphy, James J. *Rhetoric in the Middle Ages: A History of the Rhetorical Theory from Saint Augustine to the Renaissance*. Tempe, AZ: Arizona Center for Medieval and Renaissance Studies, 2001.

Nagid, Samuel ha-. *Divan Shemu'el ha-Nagid*. Edited by Dov Yarden. Jerusalem: Hebrew Union College Press, 1966.

Navarro Peiro, Angeles. "Un cuento de Jacob ben Eleazar de Toledo." *El Olivo* 15 (1962): 49–82.

Nicholson, R. A. *A Literary History of the Arabs*. Cambridge: Cambridge University Press, 1985.

Nirenberg, David, and Leonardo Capezzone. "Religions of Love: Judaism, Christianity, Islam." In *The Oxford Handbook of the Abrahamic Religions*, edited by Adam J. Silverstein and Guy G. Stroumsa, 518–35. Oxford: Oxford University Press, 2015.

Norberg, Dag Ludvig. *An Introduction to the Study of Medieval Latin Versification*. Edited by Jan Ziolkowski. Washington, DC: Catholic University of America Press, 2004.

Omri, Mohamed-Salah. "'There Is a Jāḥiẓ for Every Age': Narrative Construction and Intertextuality in al-Hamadhānī's Maqāmāt." *Arabic and Middle Eastern Literatures* 1, no. 1 (January 1998): 31–46.

Ouyang, Wen-chin. *The Literary Critic in Medieval Arab Society*. PhD diss., Columbia University, 1992.

———. *Literary Criticism in Medieval Arabic-Islamic Culture: The Making of a Tradition*. Edinburgh: Edinburgh University Press, 1997.

Ovid. *The Art of Love and Other Poems*. Translated by J. H. Mozley. Edited by G. P. Goold. Cambridge, MA: Harvard University Press, 1979.

Pabst, Bernhard. *Prosimetrum. Tradition und Wandel einer Literaturform zwischen Spätantike und Spätmittelalter*. Köln: Böhlau, 1994.

Paden, William D. "Occitan Poetry." In *The New Princeton Encyclopedia of Poetry and Poetics*, edited by Alex Preminger, T. V. F. Brogan, Frank J. Warnke, O. B. Hardison Jr., and Earl Miner. Princeton, NJ: Princeton University Press, 1993.

———. "Pastourelle." In *The Princeton Encyclopedia of Poetry and Poetics*, 4th ed., edited by Roland Greene, Stephen Cushman, Clare Cavanagh, Jahan Ramazani, Paul Rouzer, Harris Feinsod, David Marno, and Alexandra Slessarev, 1008–9. Princeton, NJ: Princeton University Press, 2012.

Paden, William D., Jr., Mireille Bardin, Michèle Hall, Patricia Kelly, F. Gregg Ney, Simone Pavlovich, and Alice South. "The Troubadour's Lady: Her Marital Status and Social Rank." *Studies in Philology* 72, no. 1 (1975): 28–50.

Page, D. L., ed. *Further Greek Epigrams*. With R. D. Dawe and J. Diggle. Cambridge: Cambridge University Press, 1981.

Pagis, Dan. *Hebrew Poetry of the Middle Ages and the Renaissance*. Berkeley: University of California Press, 1991.

———. *Ḥidush u-masoret be-shirat ha-ḥol*. Jerusalem: Keter, 1976.

———. "Shire temuna ʿivriyim ve-ʿod ṣurot melakhutiyot." In *Ha-shir davur ʿal ofnav: meḥqarim u-masot ba-shira ha-ʿivrit shel yeme ha-benayim*, 81–108. Jerusalem: Magnes, 1993.

———. "Trends in the Study of Medieval Hebrew Literature." *AJS Review* 4 (1979): 125–41.

———. "Variety in Medieval Rhymed Narratives." *Scripta Hierosolymitana* 27 (1978): 79–98.

Paris, Gaston. "Etudes sur les romans de la Table Ronde. Lancelot du Lac, II: La conte de la Charette." *Romania* 12, no. 48 (1883), 459–534.

Pearce, S. J. *The Andalusi Literary and Intellectual Tradition: The Role of Arabic in Judah Ibn Tibbon's Ethical Will*. Bloomington: Indiana University Press, 2017.

Pérès, Henri. La *poésie andalouse en arabe classique au XIe siècle: ses aspects généraux, ses principaux themes et sa valeur documentaire*. Paris: Adrien-Maisonneuve, 1953.

Pessin, Sarah. *Ibn Gabirol's Theology of Desire: Matter and Method in Jewish Medieval Neoplatonism*. Cambridge: Cambridge University Press, 2013.

Petrocchi, Giorgio. "Il prosimetro nella *Vita Nuova*." In *Prosimetrum et spoudogeloion*, edited by Francisco Della Corte, 101–13. Genova: Università di Genova, Facoltà di lettere, Istituto di filologia classica e medievale, 1982.

Plato. *Republic*. Translated by Chris Emlyn-Jones and William Preddy. Cambridge, MA: Harvard University Press, 2013.

Poe, Elizabeth Wilson. *From Poetry to Prose in Old Provençal: The Emergence of the "Vidas," the "Razos," and the "Razos de trobar."* Birmingham, AL: Summa, 1984.

Qudāma ibn Jaʿfar. *Naqd al-shiʿr*. Edited by Kamāl Muṣṭafā. Miṣr: Maṭbaʿat al-Khānjī, 1963.

Qurʾān. Translated by M. A. Abdel Haleem. New York: Oxford University Press, 2005.

Rābiʿa al-ʿAdawīyah al-Qaysīya. "My Cup, My Wine and the Companion Make Three." Translated by Nancy Coffin. *Princeton Online Arabic Poetry*. http://www.princeton.edu/~arabic/poetry/.

Rabinowitz, Louis Isaac, Jacob I. Dienstag, Arthur Hyman, Suessmann Muntner, and Bernard R. Goldstein. "Maimonides, Moses." In *Encyclopaedia Judaica*, 2nd ed., edited by Michael Berenbaum and Fred Skolnik, 13:381–97. Detroit: Macmillan Reference USA in association with Keter, 2007.

Raven, Wim. "Ibn Dāwūd al-Iṣbahānī and His *Kitāb al-zahra*." PhD diss., University of Leiden, 1989.

———. "al-Washshāʾ, Abu ʾl-jayyib Muḥammad b. Aḥmad b. Isḥāq al-Aʿrābī." In *Encyclopaedia of Islam*, 2nd ed. Leiden: Brill Academic. First published online 2012.

Ray, Jonathan. *After Expulsion: 1492 and the Making of Sephardic Jewry*. New York: New York University Press, 2013.

Ricci, Lucia Battaglia. "Tendenze prosimetriche nella letteratura del Trecento." In *Il prosimetro nella letteratura italiana*, edited by Andrea Comboni and Alessandra Di Ricco, 57–96. Trento: Dipartimento di Scienze Filologiche e Storiche, 2000.

Riquer, Martín de, ed. *Los cantares de gesta franceses*. Madrid: Gredos, 1952.

Roberts-Zauderer, Dianna Lynn. *Metaphor and Imagination in Medieval Jewish Thought: Moses ibn Ezra, Judah Halevi, Moses Maimonides and Shem Tov ibn Falaquera*. Cham: Springer International, Palgrave Macmillan, 2019.

Robinson, Cynthia. *In Praise of Song: The Making of Courtly Culture in al-Andalus*. Boston: Brill, 2002.

———. *Medieval Andalusian Courtly Culture in the Mediterranean: Ḥadīth Bayāḍ wa-Riyāḍ*. London: Routledge Studies in Middle Eastern Literature, 2007.

Robinson, Cynthia, and Leyla Rouhi, eds. *Under the Influence: Questioning the Comparative in Medieval Castile*. Leiden: Brill, 2005.

Robinson, James Theodore. "Allegorical Interpretation in Immanuel of Rome's Commentary on Qohelet." AJS Conference Paper, 2020.

Robson, J. "Ḥadīth." In *Encyclopaedia of Islam*, 2nd ed. Leiden: Brill Academic. First published online 2012.

Rosen, Tova. "The Story of Maskil and Peninah by Jacob Ben Elʿazar: A Thirteenth-Century Romance." *Florilegium* 23, no. 1 (2006): 155–72.

———. *Unveiling Eve: Reading Gender in Medieval Hebrew Literature*. Philadelphia: University of Pennsylvania Press, 2003.

Rosenthal, Franz. "On the Knowledge of Plato's Philosophy in the Islamic World." *Islamic Culture* 14, no. 4 (1940): 387–422.

Rosin, David, ed. *Reime und Gedichte des Abraham Ibn Ezra*. Part 1, no. 3. Breslau: Verlag von Wilhelm Koebner, 1888, 146.

Roth, Cecil. "New Light on Dante's Circle." *Modern Language Review* 48 (1953): 26–32.

Roth, Norman. "Deal Gently with the Young Man: Love of Boys in Medieval Hebrew Poetry of Spain." *Speculum* 57, no. 1 (1982): 20–51.

———. "Maimonides on Hebrew Language and Poetry." *Hebrew Studies* 26, no. 1 (1985): 93–101.

Rotman, David. "At the Limits of Reality: The Marvelous in Medieval Ashkenazi Hebrew Folktales." In "The Hebrew Story in the Middle Ages II," special issue, *Jewish Studies Quarterly* 20, no. 2 (2013): 101–28.

Sadan, Joseph. "Identity and Inimitability: Contexts of Inter-religious Polemics and Solidarity in Medieval Spain in the Light of Two Passages by Moshe Ibn ʿEzra and Yaʿaqov ben Elʿazar." In *Israel Oriental Studies XIV*, edited by Ilai Alon, Ithamar Gruenwald, and Itamar Singer, 325–47. Leiden: Brill, 1994.

Sáenz-Badillos, Angel. "Maimonides y la poesía." In *Sobre la vida y obra de Maimonides*, edited by Jesús Peláez del Rosal, 483–95. Córdoba: El Almendro, 1991.

Salvatierra Osorio, Aurora. "Shem Tov ibn Falaquera: From Logic to Ethics; A Redefinition of Poetry in the Thirteenth Century." *Comparative Literature Studies* 45, no. 2 (2008): 165–81.

Sanni, Amidu. *The Arabic Theory of Prosification and Versification: On Ḥall and Naẓm in Arabic Theoretical Discourse*. Beirut: In Kommission bei Franz Steiner Verlag Stuttgart, 1998.

Santillana, Marqués de. "Prohemio e carta." In *Las poéticas castellanas de la edad media*, edited by Francisco López Estrada, 51–65. Madrid: Taurus, 1984.

Sappho. *If Not, Winter: Fragments of Sappho*. Translated by Anne Carson. New York: Vintage Books, 2002.

Sargent, Barbara Nelson. "Parody in *Aucassin et Nicolette*: Some Further Considerations." *French Review* 43 (1970): 597–605.

Schatzmiller, Joseph. "The Papal Monarchy as Viewed by Medieval Jews." In *Italia Judaica VI: Gli ebrei nello Stato pontifico fino al Ghetto (1555)*, 30–41. Rome: Ministero per i beni culturali e ambientali, Ufficio centrale per i beni archivistici, 1998.

Scheindlin, Raymond P. "Asher in the Harem." In *Rabbinic Fantasies: Imaginative Narratives from Classical Hebrew Literature*, edited by David Stern and Mark Jay Mirsky, 253–67. New Haven, CT: Yale University Press, 1998.

———. "Fawns of the Palace and Fawns of the Field." *Prooftexts* 6, no. 3 (1986): 189–203.
———. *The Gazelle: Medieval Hebrew Poems on God, Israel, and the Soul*. Philadelphia: Jewish Publication Society, 1991.
———. "Rabbi Moshe Ibn Ezra on the Legitimacy of Poetry." *Medievalia et Humanistica* 7 (1976): 101–15. Cambridge: Cambridge University Press.
———. "Sipure ha-ahava shel Yaʿaqov ben Elʿazar." In *The Eleventh World Congress of Jewish Studies*, edited by David Assaf, 16–20. Jerusalem: Magnes, 1994.
———. *Wine, Women, and Death*. Philadelphia: Jewish Publication Society, 1986.
Schippers, Arie. "Hebrew Andalusian and Arabic Poetry: Descriptions of Fruit in the Tradition of the 'Elegants' or ẓurafāʾ." *Journal of Semitic Studies* 33, no. 2 (1988): 219–32.
———. *Spanish Hebrew Poetry and the Arabic Literary Tradition*. Leiden: Brill, 1994.
Schirmann, Jefim. "Darʿī, Moses ben Abraham." In *Encyclopaedia Judaica*, 2nd ed., edited by Michael Berenbaum and Fred Skolnik, 5:434. Detroit: Macmillan Reference USA in association with Keter, 2007.
———. "The Ephebe in Medieval Hebrew Poetry." *Sefarad* 15 (1955): 55–68.
———. "The Function of the Hebrew Poet in Medieval Spain." *Jewish Social Studies* 16, no. 3 (1954): 235–52.
———. "Ha-Rambam ve-ha-shira ha-ʿivrit." *Moznayim* 3 (1935): 433–36.
———. *Ha-shira ha-ʿivrit bi-Sfarad uvi-Provans*. Jerusalem: Mosad Bialik, 1954.
———. "L'Amour spirituel dans la poésie hébrïque du moyen âge." *Les Lettres Romanes* 15 (1961): 315–25.
———. "Les Contes rimés de Jacob ben Eléazar de Tolède." In *Etudes d'orientalisme dediés à la memoire de Lévi-Provencal*, edited by R. Brunschvig, 285–97. Paris: G. P. Maisonneuve & Larose, 1962.
———. *Le-toledot ha-shira veha-drama ha-ʿivrit*. Jerusalem: Mosad Byaliq, 1979.
———. "Poets Contemporaneous with Moses Ibn Ezra and Judah Halevi." *Studies of the Research Institute for Hebrew Poetry* 2 (1936): 62–152.
———. *Toledot ha-shira ha-ʿivrit bi-Sfarad ha-noṣrit uvi-drom Ṣarefat*. Edited by Ezra Fleischer. Jerusalem: Magnes, 1997.
Schrötter, Wilibald. *Ovid und die Troubadours*. Halle a.S.: Max Niemeyer, 1908.
Scodel, Ruth. "Two Epigrammatic Pairs: Callimachus' Epitaphs, Plato's Apples." *Hermes* 131, no. 3 (2003): 257–68.
Sedgwick, Eve Kosofsky. *Between Men: English Literature and Male Homosocial Desire*. New York: Columbia University Press, 1985.
Sellheim, R. "al-Mubarrad, Abu 'l-ʿAbbās Muḥammad b. Yazīd b. ʿAbd al-Akbar al-Thumālī al-Azdī." In *Encyclopaedia of Islam*, 2nd ed. Leiden: Brill Academic. First published online 2012.
Sells, Michael. "Love." In *The Legacy of Muslim Spain. Handbook of Oriental Studies, The Near and Middle East*, 2nd ed., edited by Salma Khadra Jayyusi and Manuela Marín, 12:126–58. Leiden: Brill, 1994.
Shapiro, Marianne. "The Provençal Trobairitz and the Limits of Courtly Love." *Signs* 3, no. 3 (1978): 560–71.
Sharman, Ruth Verity. *Cansos and Sirventes of the Troubadour, Giraut de Borneil: A Critical Edition*. Cambridge: Cambridge University Press, 2006.
Shepkaru, Shmuel. "To Die for God: Martyrs' Heaven in Hebrew and Latin Crusade Narratives." *Speculum* 77, no. 2 (2002): 331–41.

Shiloah, Amnon. "A Passage by Immanuel ha-Romi on the Science of Music." *Italia: studi e ricerche sulla storia, la cultura e la letteratura degli ebrei d'Italia* 36, no. 10 (1993): 9–18.

Singleton, Charles. "Dante: Within Courtly Love and Beyond." In *The Meaning of Courtly Love*, edited by Francis X. Newman, 43–54. Albany: State University of New York Press, 1969.

———. *An Essay on the "Vita Nuova."* Cambridge, MA: Harvard University Press, 1958.

Smith, Margaret, and Ch. Pellat. "Rābiʿa al-ʿAdawiyya al-ḳaysiyya." In *Encyclopaedia of Islam*, 2nd ed. Leiden: Brill Academic. First published online 2012.

———. *Tophet and Eden (Hell and Paradise): In Imitation of Dante's Inferno and Paradiso, From the Hebrew.* Translated by Hermann Gollancz. London: University of London Press, 1921.

Stern, Menahem. "Roman Literature." In *Encyclopaedia Judaica*, 2nd ed., edited by Michael Berenbaum and Fred Skolnik, 17:403–4. Detroit: Macmillan Reference USA in association with Keter, 2007.

Suler, Bernard, and Angel Sáenz-Badillos. "Bonafed, Solomon ben Reuben." In *Encyclopaedia Judaica*, 2nd ed., edited by Michael Berenbaum and Fred Skolnik, 4:53–54. Detroit: Macmillan Reference USA in association with Keter, 2007.

Ṣūlī, Muḥammad ibn Yaḥyā al-. *Akhbar Abī Tammām.* Edited by Khalīl Maḥmūd ʿAsākir, Muḥammad ʿAbduh ʿAzzām, and Naẓīr al-Islām al-Hindi. Cairo: Lajnat al-Taʾlīf wa-l-Tarjamah wa-l-Nashr, 1937.

Tate, J. "Plato and 'Imitation.'" *Classical Quarterly* 26, no. 3/4 (1932): 161–69.

Tattersall, Jill. "Social Observation and Comment in *Aucassin et Nicolette.*" *Neuphilologische Mitteilungen* 86, no. 4 (1985): 551–65.

Thibaut, Messire. *Le roman de la poire.* Edited by Christiane Marchello-Nizia and Mireille Demaules. Arras: Artois presses université, 2017.

———. *Romanz de la poire.* Edited by Christiane Marchello-Nizia. Paris: Société des anciens textes français, 1984.

Tobi, Yosef. *Between Hebrew and Arabic Poetry: Studies in Spanish Medieval Hebrew Poetry.* Leiden: Brill, 2010.

Turki, Abdel-Magid. "al-ẓāhiriyya." In *Encyclopaedia of Islam*, 2nd ed. Leiden: Brill Academic. First published online 2012.

Vadet, Jean-Claude. "Ibn Dāwūd, Muḥammad b. Dāwūd b. ʿAlī b. Khalaf." In *Encyclopaedia of Islam*, 2nd ed. Leiden: Brill Academic. First published online 2012.

———. *L'Esprit courtois en Orient dans le cinq premiers siècles de l'Hégire.* Paris: G-P Maisonneuve et Larose, 1968.

———. "Littérature courtoise et transmission du *ḥadīṯ*: Un exemple: Muḥammad b. Ǧaʿfar al-Ḫarāʾiṭī." *Arabica* 7, no. 2 (1960): 140–66.

van Gelder, Geert Jan, ed. and trans. *Classical Arabic Literature: A Library of Arabic Literature Anthology.* New York: New York University Press, 2013.

van Gelder, Geert Jan, and Marlé Hammond, eds. *Takhyīl: The Imaginary in Classical Arabic Poetics.* Cambridge: Gibb Memorial Trust, 2008.

Varty, Kenneth. "Medieval Romance." In *The New Princeton Encyclopedia of Poetry and Poetics*, edited by Alex Preminger, T. V. F. Brogan, Frank J. Warnke, O. B. Hardison Jr., and Earl Miner. Princeton, NJ: Princeton University Press, 1993.

Vidal, Ramon. *The "Razos de trobar" of Raimon Vidal and Associated Texts.* Edited by J. H. Marshall. London: Oxford University Press, 1972.

Vinsauf, Geoffrey of. *Poetria nova*. Translated by Jane Baltzell Kopp. In *Three Medieval Rhetorical Arts*, edited by James J. Murphy, 32–108. Berkeley: University of California Press, 1971.

Vitale, Maurizio, ed. *Rimatori comico-realistici del Due e Trecento*. Torino: Unione Tipgrafico-Editrice Torinese, 1989.

Wacks, David. *Double Diaspora in Sephardic Literature: Jewish Cultural Production before and after 1492*. Bloomington: Indiana University Press, 2015.

———. *Framing Iberia: Maqāmāt and Frametale Narratives in Medieval Spain*. Leiden: Brill, 2007.

———. "Vernacular Anxiety and the Semitic Imaginary: Shem Tov Issac Ibn Arduitiel de Carrión and his Critics." *Journal of Medieval Iberian Studies* 4, no. 2 (2012): 167–84.

al-Washshā', Muḥammad ibn Isḥāq ibn Yaḥyā. *El libro del brocado*. [Kitāb al-muwashshā]. Introduction by Teresa Garulo. Madrid: Alfaguara, 1990.

———. *Kitāb al-muwashshā*. Beirut: Dār Ṣādir, 1965.

Weiss, Andrea L., Dan Pagis, Abraham Meir Habermann, Yonah David, and Angel Sáenz-Badillos. "Poetry." In *Encyclopaedia Judaica*, 2nd ed., edited by Michael Berenbaum and Fred Skolnik, 16:254–78. Detroit: Macmillan Reference USA in association with Keter, 2007.

Weiss, Julian. *The Poet's Art: Literary Theory in Castile c. 1400–60*. Oxford: Society for Mediaeval Languages and Literature, 1990.

Woolf, Virginia. *A Room of One's Own*. Malden, MA: John Wiley/Blackwell, 2015.

Wright, Jerry W., and Everett K. Rowson, eds. *Homoeroticism in Classical Arabic Literature*. New York: Columbia University Press, 1997.

Yassif, Eli. *The Hebrew Folktale: History, Genre, Meaning*. Bloomington: Indiana University Press, 1999.

Yeshaya, Joachim. *Medieval Hebrew Poetry in Muslim Egypt: The Secular Poetry of the Karaite Poet Moses ben Abraham Dar'ī*. Leiden: Brill, 2011.

Zeeman, Nicolette. "The Lover-Poet and Love as the Most Pleasing 'Matere' in Medieval French Love Poetry." *Modern Language Review* 83, no. 4 (1988): 820–42.

Ziolkowski, Jan, ed. *Dante and Islam*. New York: Fordham University Press, 2015.

———. "The Prosimetrum in the Classical Tradition." In *Prosimetrum: Crosscultural Perspectives on Narrative in Prose and Verse*, edited by Joseph Harris and Karl Reichl, 45–65. Cambridge: D. S. Brewer, 1997.

INDEX

ISABELLE LEVY (BA Columbia; PhD Harvard) is Academic Program Director and Lecturer at the Institute for Israel and Jewish Studies, Columbia University. She has held positions as fellow at the Italian Academy for Advanced Studies and Rabin Postdoctoral Research Fellow at the Institute for Israel and Jewish Studies, both at Columbia, and was a Fulbright Fellow in Spain.

www.ingramcontent.com/pod-product-compliance
Lightning Source LLC
Chambersburg PA
CBHW030306100426
42812CB00002B/586
9780253060150